Where Paths Cross

A History of the Newman Center at St. Cloud State University

Linda Wall

All photos of Newman Club and officers in the first chapter are from *Talahi*, except for the photo on page 20.

Cover design and photo: Don Bruno.

Pre-press assistance provided by North Star Press of St. Cloud, Inc., St Cloud, Minnesota.

Printing by Versa Press, Inc., East Peoria, Illinois.

Published by Christ Church Newman Center

To my father,

Charles Walter Wall
1931 to 1999

*who traveled through many crossroads in his lifetime,
and listened with openness, compassion, and respect
to all he encountered along the way.
He tried to teach me to do the same.*

*He was a man of great courage and tenderness
who loved me into being.
My love for him will never die.*

Acknowledgements

This chronicle could never have been completed without the gracious and generous assistance of individuals too numerous to name. There are a few, however, who must be singled out. My heartfelt gratitude and deepest thanks go:

to the members of the Newman History/Archives Committee, who were my research assistants, constant encouragers and patient advisors. Mil and Fran Voelker, who spent many long hours videotaping and editing interviews and perusing old newspapers and yearbooks, deserve special thanks. So do Barb and Art Grachek, Chuck and Pat Ernst, Ed Pluth, Mary Jo Bot, Rita Dwyer, Lee Fitzharris, and the committee's chair, Vern Bartos, whose dedication to the cause, broad smile and mischievous meeting minutes kept us all going;

to Chuck Ernst, who authored the appendix on John Henry Newman's life with care and sensitivity, and to Mary Jo Bot, who sorted through countless files and read endless pages of old minutes with great patience in order to compile the appendix recording all past and present Newman officers and staff members;

to Don Bruno, whose photographic skill, artistic acumen, discerning eye, and gracious spirit produced the book's cover;

to Corinne and Rita Dwyer at North Star Press, who guided me through the book's production with unfailing patience and kindness, and whose talents produced what I think is a book with an extraordinarily fine "look";

to Nic Dressen, whose friendship, care, and unconditional support kept me going through dark hours and looming deadlines; and

to Wil Illies, whose vision, commitment, and love gave birth to the St. Cloud Newman community as we know it today, and whose wisdom, wit, compassion, insight, and laughter have touched and taught many, many people through the years, including myself. His belief in me, and in this project, sustained my determination, and my inspiration, more than he will ever know.

St. Cloud, Minnesota
Summer 1999

Contents

Introduction

When the Spanish explorer Alvarez de Pineda first encountered the great river that native peoples called "Mississippi," or "Father of Waters," he was so moved by its majesty and mystery that he christened it, "The River of the Holy Spirit." Perhaps, even now, the Spirit still lurks in the flowing

A view of Christ Church Newman Center today, from across the Mississippi River.

depths of the Mighty Mississippi and lures those brave enough to dwell on her banks into life-transforming adventures. The Newman movement affiliated with what is today St. Cloud State University in St. Cloud, Minnesota, has made its home on the west bank of the Mississippi River since 1923. The people, the events, and the adventures that have been a part of its story since then show definite signs of having been touched and transformed by the Spirit.

From the dawn of the twentieth century, the Newman movement in the United States has worked to support the faith of young women and men attending public, "non-Catholic" institutions of higher learning. That such institutions were viewed with suspicion and mistrust by people of faith for more than half of the twentieth century is ironic, for the very land which gave birth to our Judeo-Christian faith—the land which summoned and sustained our ancestors in their journey toward God—has much in common with the secular university campus.

Israel is located on a land-bridge between two continents. Within an area approximately 150 miles long and fifty miles wide, enormous varieties of elevation, climate, vegetation, animal life, and geology exist. In biblical times, this narrow strip of settled land along the seacoast served as a natural, intercontinental highway for merchants, visitors, pilgrims, and invaders, connecting Mesopotamia and Babylon in the east with Egypt in the west.[1] Numerous travelers and countless caravans passed along the northwestern shore of the Sea of Galilee and then down along the Mediterranean coast, bringing with them the influences of their diverse ideas, lifestyles, religious beliefs, political systems, and commercial goods.[2] To be situated in the middle of a highway like this one was to experience the crossing over, and, at times, the colliding of many and varied mind sets, motives, and missions.

And so it has always been on the university campus. John Henry Newman called the university a "Middle Station," and more than a century later in 1988, Francis Nosbisch and Nic Dressen, who served the Christ Church Newman community in St. Cloud for eleven and twelve years respectively, together reflected that:

> Campus Ministry is much like living in the middle of a highway: a campus is a place where many people, many ideas, and many values intersect (with or without harm) or pass by each other on the way to some goal. Into this world steps the campus minister as a prophet, a poet, a preacher, a social critic, a patriot, a moralist, a reconciler, a counselor, a witness.[3]

Despite the fact that a highway experience every bit as bustling and bohemian as that encountered on a university campus shaped the land that first cradled our faith, church officials from the earliest days of the Newman movement were adamant in their warnings about the dangers of taking up residence in a secular "crossroads" environment. That environment was, after all, often openly hostile to religious influences and had been known to try and drive faith off the road all together. Those who were willing to acknowledge the needs of Catholic students enrolled in state universities encouraged them to band together in order to study their heritage, reinforce their commitment, and hold fast to one another as they would to a lifeboat being tossed about by a dangerously raging storm at sea. Even as recently as 1985, the U.S. Catholic bishops felt compelled to warn that in an environment like the university, where the crossing over and colliding of many different ideas, values, and perspectives occurs, questions and confusions are bound to arise, and the danger ever lurks that moral relativism will creep in, reducing freedom to license and open-minded tolerance to mindlessness.[4] In light of that danger, Newman Centers and campus ministers have regularly been reminded that they must work tirelessly at assisting in the solid formation of sound Catholic consciences in their college students through meaningful personal encounters, homilies, liturgical celebrations, theology classes, workshops, and seminars.[5]

"Formation" in faith is a hallowed concept in Catholic catechetical circles, but for most people it is not a word in common, every day usage. In their lived experience, however, formation is a concept with which almost all people are familiar. Quite simply, formation is what happens when all the varied aspects of culture—family affection, educational, political and social structures, and scientific and technological know-how—make their influence known as human beings grow up and prepare to take a place in the world. A positive experience of formation provides a sense of direction, a supportive framework and a backdrop for all later experiences. It enables individuals to understand themselves and the world they share with others, to adjust themselves to both without either undue aggressiveness or fearful conformity, and to form satisfying and stable emotional relationships.[6]

Much of the general uproar over the disconnected and disquieting state of life in late-twentieth-century North America has at its root a fear-filled sense that the formation process can no longer be relied upon. While they do not always name the predicament as such, those who decry the existence of widespread violence, abuse, disrespect for institutions and offices, rampant individualism, self-centeredness, greed, and a loss of "family values," in essence decry the loss of a formation process at work in our midst that was once self-evident and reliable but obviously is no longer.

From the point of view of the outside world, the church is, and always has been, an integral part of the formation system and has some power, still, to exert a stabilizing and civilizing influence. Providing ample opportunities for individuals of all ages to be instructed, guided, supported and strengthened in the foundations of religious belief and moral conviction is an inescapable responsibility of Church leaders and ministers. But that perception of the church's mission in the world is far from being complete.

Among those of us who dare to call ourselves Christian, there is another belief about what creates whole and ideally developed individuals, capable of building whole and ideally developed communities. Theologian Rosemary Haughton warns that if the influence of formation goes unbroken for long periods of time, it leads not to life but to the death of love through asphyxiation.[7] Formation is important, but it must never overshadow the far-more-important process called "transformation."

Transformation, simply defined, is a change of form. Transformation in the Christian tradition typically refers to a change in moral perspective, both internal and external, and to consequent changes in behaviors. Transformation usually implies a fairly radical shift in the horizons of one's mind and heart, which prompts the embracing of a wholly new self-understanding, a wholly new world view.[8] From a faith perspective, such changed horizons in transformed hearts and transformed communities allow the power of God's Spirit to be released so that breakthroughs of love occur that heal wounds and nudge human life toward greater fullness and freedom for all.[9] We all possess deep within ourselves a tremendous reservoir of untapped spiritual potential and an unused capacity to love that come to be released in our lives through—and only through—the process of transformation.

A primary component of the church's mission, then, is to see to it that transformation occurs. Certainly, the task of the Church is not to destroy indiscriminately the work of formative influences in individuals and communities. But it is also the task of the Church to see to it that encounters happen that lead to new levels of self-discovery, eye-opening shifts in perspective, and changed ways of understanding life and others. As far as Christian discipleship is concerned, the most valuable kind of formation is the kind that will make transformation more likely, and ultimately give way to it.[10] As Haughton aptly describes it, most often transformation can only occur when formation in some way breaks down because it is no longer adequate to embrace the demands of love. On the way to such breakdowns, there are nearly always experiences of conflict, tension, and pain. But moving through them releases the power of the Spirit and sets us free to be transformed. Ironically, such transforming encounters frequently happen in "the wilderness"—in situations that provoke feelings of uncertainty and unsettledness, of being pulled away from reassuring and familiar ways of interacting, and of being discomforted by new sights, sounds, thoughts, and learnings.[11]

Living in the middle of a highway like the university, where many different ideas and values meet, cross over and even collide with one another, can be just such a wilderness experience. The human encounters that occur as a result can be unsettling, frightening, threatening and even dangerous. But they are fraught with as many opportunities as they are dangers. When a Christian community places itself doggedly in the middle of such a volatile highway, as most Newman Centers do, that community has a unique opportunity, and a profound responsibility, to see to it that the interactions and intersections between people happening in its environs become true events of the Spirit—occasions where the life and the power of God are released and work to prod us toward greater holiness, deeper freedom, new insight, and broader love, as individuals and as a human community. As Nic Dressen and Frances Nosbisch put it in 1988:

> We believe not only that everyone comes to our campuses already formed in conscience, but also that everyone is in need of transformation. Each individual on campus contributes to and is influenced by the land from which they come and the traffic patterns of the particular campus. Each faces some type of breakdown and conflict. Can they encounter self-discovery, release of power, reconciliation and transformation? Campus ministers are to provide a voice of vision. . . . Campus ministers challenge and encourage, and travel with people through a never-ending process of transformation. Over tough roads, through construction zones, by way of detours and wrong-turns, people come to grace-filled milestones on their journeys.[12]

The intersection of First Avenue South and Sixth Street at St. Cloud State University.

This book will dare to suggest that the local Newman movement in St. Cloud, which first made its home on the banks of the River of the Holy Spirit in 1923 and exists in our day and age as the Christ Church Newman Center parish, has been a catalyst for some very powerful crossroads encounters. The crossing over of people, values, and ideas that has transpired there has been life-enhancing, growth-producing and transformative for past and present Catholic college students at St. Cloud State University, for past and present members of the Newman Center parish that grew up around them over the years, and for the always imperfect yet remarkably beautiful thing we dare to call the Church—the living presence of Christ in our world.

One purpose of this book, of course, is to provide some historical record of all that has occurred during the past three-quarters of a century as a club-like organization serving the Catholic students of the St. Cloud Teachers College evolved into a vital parish embracing a unique blend of people from St. Cloud State University and many surrounding communities. An equally important aim of this work, however, is to ask pointedly what things, in particular, have intersected in especially meaningful ways throughout the course of Newman's seventy-five year highway-history, leading that unique blend of people to be lured, and at times propelled, toward life, growth, and transformation.

An article that appeared in the St. Cloud State *College Chronicle* in 1967 lamented the fact that the campus turns its back on the Mississippi. Few college buildings were constructed over the years in such a way as to enhance, rather than obstruct, the view of the mighty river. With a little more foresight, insight, or imagination, the article went on to say, the majestic Mississippi might have been made the center of the St. Cloud State campus. As it is, there are but a few well-placed windows around that serve to open eyes to the Mississippi's beauty and grandeur. The Newman Center was gratefully acknowledged as a case in point. Perhaps the willingness of its founders to construct such a well-placed window opening out to the great River of the Holy Spirit is reflective of that remarkable openness to the movement and the call of the Spirit that has guided the Newman community over the course of the past seventy-five years of its life in the middle of the highway. During that time, many seemingly disparate ideas have crossed over and touched one another. Despite the warnings of skeptics and naysayers that such meetings would prove to be disastrous, they have instead proven to be spirit-filled catalysts of growth. They have certainly, at times, produced a temporary wilderness of darkness and confusion, but in the end they have nearly always engendered compelling transformations that have allowed a new dimension of the light of Christ to be proclaimed—to the Catholic Christian community gathered at the Newman Center in St. Cloud, and to the whole church as well.

Notes

1 Lawrence Boadt, *Reading the Old Testament, An Introduction* (New York: Paulist Press, 1984), p. 36.

2 Nic Dressen and Frances Nosbisch, OSF, "Living in the Middle of the Highway," in *Prepare the Way of the Lord 1988: Biblical People as Models for Campus Ministry*, ed. Michael Galligan-Stierle, Barbara Humphrey, John B. Scarario, and Julie Butson (Dayton: Catholic Campus Ministry Association, 1988), p. 182. Highway metaphor further developed by Frances Nosbisch in her thesis submitted to the School of Theology at Boston University in partial fulfillment of the requirements for the degree of Doctor of Ministry: *Living in the Middle of the Highway: Campus Ministry Confronting Racial Bigotry among Undergraduate Students*, 1994.

3 Dressen and Nosbisch, p. 182.

4 National Conference of Catholic Bishops, *Empowered by the Spirit: Campus Ministry Faces the Future* (Washington, D.C.: United States Catholic Conference, Inc., 1985), no. 61.

5 National Conference of Catholic Bishops, nos. 63-69.

6 Haughton, *The Transformation of Man* (Springfield: Templegate Publishers, 1967, 1980), p. 7.

7 Haughton, p. 35.

8 Benjamin Baynham, "Transformation," in *The New Dictionary of Catholic Spirituality*, ed. Michael Downey (Collegeville: The Liturgical Press, 1993), pp. 967-968.

9 Haughton, p. 115.

10 Haughton, pp. 244-246.

11 Haughton, p. 275.

12 Dressen and Nosbisch, p. 184.

Chapter 1

Settling In at the Crossroads:
Faith and Knowledge Begin to Meet

"I want the intellectual layman to be religious,
and the devout ecclesiastic to be intellectual. . . . It will not satisfy me, what satisfies so many, to have
two independent systems, intellectual and religious, going at once side by side,
by a sort of divison of labor, and only accidentally brought together."
— John Henry Newman

It has been a perennial temptation for people of faith to want to separate the things of "the flesh" and the things of "the spirit." From almost the earliest days of Christianity, there were those who believed that achieving detachment and separation from the natural world would advance their attachment to the supernatural world and that minimizing their connections to the ordinary, material trappings of life would maximize their capacity to connect to the spiritual. But as Christians, we boldly profess that the Word took on flesh; holiness unashamedly embraced physical existence, and God became human. In making that profession, replete with all of its confusing elements of paradox, we in effect renounce the right to reject any aspect of the world as irrelevant. Whenever and wherever Christians disparage some aspect of everyday life, we fail miserably as Christians. We place our faith in a transcendent God who keeps on choosing immanence, and the goal of all human action thus becomes for us not escape from bodily existence but rather transformation with it, through it and in it.[1]

In the middle of the highway called the state university campus, the "sacred" and the "secular" have crossed over often, and have sometimes been forced into collision by those who perceive them to be antithetical. Whether benign or malevolent, whether deliberately encouraged or arising as an accidental by-product of other cultural movements, when an artificial separation of the sacred and secular occurs, it almost always produces destructive fragmentation within individuals, within fields of study, and within institutions as a whole.[2] It was for this reason that, more than a century ago, John Henry Newman felt compelled to speak out against that facet of the sacred-secular split that commonly manifested itself on university campuses even in Newman's own age: the separation between faith and knowledge. As the good cardinal observed, it is all too commonly thought that, "because some follow duty, others pleasure, others glory and others intellect, that, therefore, one of these excludes the other so that duty cannot be pleasant, virtue cannot be intellectual, goodness cannot be great and conscientiousness cannot be heroic."[3] Frequently, Newman lamented, virtuous women and men are not as attractive as those who lack virtue. Too often cleverness, or wit, or taste, or keenness of intellect, or depth or knowledge, or pleasantness, or humor, or agreeableness, are all on the side of error and not on the side of virtue. It appeared to Newman, in fact, that the "Evil One" was at work whispering in the world that duty and religion are all very admirable indeed but that religious people are commonly either very dull or very tiresome.

Cardinal John Henry Newman, a nineteenth-century scholar and theologian who became the patron of the Newman movement.

The remedy proposed by Newman for this tragic state of affairs later became famous, especially as it was finally put forth in those great lectures delivered in Dublin, Ireland, which make up a good part of Newman's *Idea of a University*. In essence, Newman believed that individuals and institutions had to work to reunite those things that were in the beginning joined together by God, but which were later put asunder through human sinfulness. Newman's passionate conviction was that theology must be subjected to the same honest inquiry as every other science, even if that investigation brought it into public controversy. He had no desire to "confine, distort or stunt" the intellectual growth of human minds with church supervision. No, Newman insisted, the intellect must range with utmost freedom, and religion must enjoy an equal freedom:

. . . what I am stipulating for is, that they should be found in one and the same place and exemplified in the same persons. I want to destroy that diversity of centers, which puts everything in confusion by creating a contrariety of influences. I wish the same spots and the same individuals to be at once oracles of philosophy and shrines of devotion. It will not satisfy me, what satisfies so many, to have two independent systems, intellectual and religious, going at once side by side, by a sort of division of labor, and only accidentally brought together. It will not satisfy me, if religion is here and science there, and young men [sic] converse with science all day, and lodge with religion in the evening. . . .[4]

When the United States bishops today speak of the importance of educating the "whole person," when they define "wisdom" for college students as "the union of knowledge and love," and when they remind campus ministers that the search for truth must always include the ability to handle ethical issues and achieve a harmonious integration of intellect and will,[5] they betray their indebtedness to the far-reaching insight of the nineteenth-century scholar and theologian named Newman. Given his adamant insistence upon the integration of faith and knowledge, it is hardly surprising that, when Catholic women and men first started to band together on state university campuses, John Henry Newman became their patron.

Newman understood that the transformation of individuals, institutions, and societies can only happen if faith and knowledge are allowed to intersect and interact with each other freely, so that genuine encounters and conversations can emerge that will lead to new discoveries for both, as well as to the release of untapped power and potential in both. From the very beginning, the Newman movement as it took shape on the west bank of the River of the Holy Spirit in St. Cloud was a locus of such transforming encounters. But some essential groundwork had to be laid at other places before the movement in St. Cloud could come to birth.

A Bit of Background

Before World War I, Christianity strongly influenced the atmosphere on all North American college campuses; even those that were not church-related tended to absorb the feel and flavor of liberal Protestantism.[6] Most presidents and administrators in those institutions saw great value in cultivating religious and ethical values in their students, yet found it difficult in an age of growing pluralism, sectarianism, and legal complexity to advance required course work in religion or to retain compulsory religious services. Administrators began to rely more and more on voluntary faculty involvement in the religious formation of students and on the growth of voluntary organizations designed to support and enhance the religious and moral life of the college community. For more evangelical Protestants, campus chapters of the YMCA and the YWCA frequently fulfilled this function, as did the growing movement among mainline Protestant denominations to create campus pastorates designed to serve the spiritual needs of university students.[7] For Catholics, however, the situation was complicated by a different set of factors.

Young Catholics who pursued college educations were expected as a matter of course to attend Catholic universities. As the twentieth century dawned, however, in increasing numbers they did not. In 1906, Denis O'Connell, then rector of the Catholic University of America, tried to explain to authorities in Rome why enrollments of Catholics in public colleges were rising faster than those in church-related colleges by pointing out that the latter were "comparatively fewer in number, often situated in remote localities and generally too expensive for the children of the people."[8] As Newman movement chronicler John Whitney Evans explains it, at non-Catholic universities young Catholics found a wide range of electives, specialized professional and occupational training, top-notch libraries and laboratories, proximity to home, low tuition, and the possibility of forming beneficial business and professional connections. In Catholic colleges, furthermore, what Evans labels "ecclesiasticism" was having deleterious effects. Emphasis on papally-endorsed Scholastic philosophy insulated students from modern scientific and philosophical thought, while "moralism undercut and devotionalism diluted" solid intellectual inquiry.[9] Unfortunately, for making what seemed an eminently reasonable and responsible choice under the circumstances, Catholic women and men at public universities typically found themselves accused of gross disloyalty. In 1875, the Vatican had denounced American public schools as an occasion of sin, and Catholic students entering college decades later could attest to the still-persistent power of that attitude. Pastors lambasted them for giving bad example to the young and for exposing their faith and morals to corruption in the interest of seeking worldly advancement. Some college-town priests refused to permit students to attend their services, and many of those who did admit them to the pews did not hesitate to make a habit of condemning their campuses from the pulpit.[10] St. Cloud was by no means immune from such attitudes. Pauline Penning, a member of the college art department who served as a faculty advisor to the Newman Club in the 1930s and 1940s, recalls that one St. Cloud priest who was asked to come and talk to the club on "What the Catholic Student Is on a Secular Campus," replied tartly that such a talk would consist of only one word: "Nothing."[11]

Life on the secular campus itself, furthermore, was not always easy for the young adult Catholic. There was emerging a kind of "studied indifference" to religion in academia that began to affect all committed Christians in that era, coupled with a Protestant dominance among students, faculty, and administrators that sometimes expressed itself through both explicit and implicit anti-Catholic bigotry. Even as late as 1958, a student publication at the University of Georgia, for example, carried an article denouncing the Catholic Church as more dangerous than Communism and in league with Fascism. The Newman Club of that university delivered an appropriate, tongue-in-cheek counter blast by distributing an official-looking document which read:

CATHOLIC STUDENTS!
ATTENTION!
EMERGENCY ORDERS!

All Catholic students at the University of Georgia, as sworn agents of the Catholic Church's plot to take over the United States, are hereby commanded by the Hierarchy to disregard all previous plans and orders, and proceed immediately to execute:

1. Reread all "bulls" and "encyclicals."
2. Weapons will be issued at the Newman Arsenal, Catholic Students' Center on Lumpkin Street.
3. Take captive only those who can be brainwashed; kill others.
4. Remember that these groups are our allies: a. Communists, b. Fascists, c. Nazis, d. Stoics, e. Purple-People Eaters.
5. There will be a pep rally at the covered bridge over the Oconee River at 1600 to crown the Pope who will be arriving by submarine at 1545. Marching from the river, the Pope's first stop will be the Varsity, where he will dine and sign autographs . . .
6. The official ring is for sale only in the book store.
7. Don't think—act![12]

In short, in both the Catholic arena of home and parish church from which they had come and the non-Catholic arena of the university campus to which they migrated, Catholic students enrolled at public universities in the early twentieth century frequently found they were living as "strangers in a strange land."[13]

Even though they may not have framed the instinct as eloquently as Cardinal Newman did one hundred years earlier, these beleaguered students sensed that things should be different; the sacred and secular dimensions of their lives should not only be able to dwell together in harmony but should also be able to enrich and enlarge one another. In 1883, a Catholic pre-law student at the University of Wisconsin named John McAnaw celebrated Thanksgiving at the home of Mr. and Mrs. John C. Melvin and expressed frustration at the attitudes toward Catholicism that he sometimes encountered on campus. In response to a suggestion Mrs. Melvin offered during that dinner-time conversation, McAnaw established the "Melvin Club"—an independent student society dedicated to the study of Catholic history and literature that flourished for the next fifteen years. While the club explored such topics in its meetings as "The Temporal Power of the Pope" and "The Tendencies in Large Universities Toward Disbelief," its members were generally convinced that their study should not become narrow in any sectarian sense and often reported that the club broadened their minds and spirits greatly. One of the original members of this nascent Melvin Club, Timothy Harrington, transplanted the idea to Catholic students at the University of Pennsylvania where he later attended medical school. Harrington named his Catholic society the "Newman Club," because, after reading the story of John Henry Newman's personal conversion journey in *Apologia Pro Vita Sua* for the second time, he firmly believed that no better name could be found for an organization of young Catholics seeking to improve themselves socially, intellectually and religiously in a university setting.[14] By 1905, students had organized "Newman Clubs" similar to these prototypes on fifteen campuses around the nation as scattered and varied as Cornell, Michigan, Minnesota, Brown, Harvard, Berkeley, Chicago, and Columbia.[15]

Sadly, this unofficial movement to create Catholic societies dedicated to providing support in non-Catholic educational settings encountered rough waters when it began to seek out official sanction. Its growth was slowed and at times stalled by a scarcity of funds, by a shortage of priests willing and capable of investing in the movement, and by the actions and attitudes of religious communities, clerics, and others who insisted that when bishops assigned funds, personnel, or other kinds of support to Newman-type organizations on secular campuses, they betrayed their commitment to Catholic campuses and endangered the future of parochial schools at every other level as well.[16] But students, dedicated lay professionals, and members of the "lower" clergy persevered. By the time the Newman Club at St. Cloud State Teachers College was established in 1923, a national federation of such clubs existed, most of which had at least one faculty advisor, some of which had chaplains assigned to support their work, and a few of which even had "halls" constructed specifically for their use. A survey, conducted just three years after the establishment of the St. Cloud Newman Club, reveals that of the one hundred thirty-four Catholic clubs then in existence, eighty-three belonged to the national "Federation of Catholic College Clubs," twenty-seven had Newman "halls," twenty-three provided some sort of religious education, and more than thirty chaplains were assigned to Newman work, of whom at least six were full-time.[17] The movement to insure that the force of intellect and the forces of faith would find a fruitful meeting ground at the crossroads called the university had taken root and begun to grow.

A Newman Club Settles in on the Banks of the Mississippi

It was apparently the fourth bishop of the St. Cloud diocese, Joseph Francis Busch, who decided that Newman work should go on at the "TC"—the "Teachers College"—on the east side of St. Cloud. The president of the college at the time, Joseph Brown, was also an avid promoter of student groups and associations, and the atmosphere on campus was ripe. Busch was forty-eight years old and in his prime when he came to St. Cloud to assume the bishop's chair in 1915. He had a keen mind, sharpened by twelve years of academic training by the Jesuits, and he had been one of the first students enrolled at the Catholic University of America in Washington, D.C. In the years since his ordination, he had accumulated experiences that were much broader and more varied than those of most priests of his era, and he was among the pioneers who espoused the social teaching of the Catholic Church and sought to apply it to the changing structures of American society during the early decades of the twentieth century.[18] Like many others in these ghetto years in American Catholicism, the fourth Bishop of St. Cloud was deeply committed to providing ample religious instruction for all children, and had a great fondness for establishing Catholic societies and organizations that would protect Catholic laity from undesirable and indifferent influences in the outside world that might weaken their faith.[19] Perhaps most relevant of all to the emergence of Newman ministry in St. Cloud, however, was Busch's well-known devotion to the Holy Spirit. Many believed that it simply was not possible for the bishop to preach without mentioning the works and the indwelling of the Spirit. Providentially, then, it was Busch who took it upon himself to insure that Catholic Christianity would make itself known and felt at the college crossroads that had arisen on the banks of the Holy Spirit's river.

Though the details of the appointment are unclear, Busch charged T. Leo Keaveny with the task of organizing a Newman Club at the small St. Cloud Teachers College in the fall of 1923. Keaveny was a fitting choice; ordained in 1919, he was only twenty-nine years old at the time of his appointment and had already completed a doctorate in education and psychology. He was a man of strong intellect and exceptional ability who would, five years later, be named rector of the pro-cathedral, director of the diocesan high school, and superintendent of all schools in the diocese.[20]

Campus life at the St. Cloud Teachers College in the 1920s was certainly not devoid of religious influences. The school was quite small and close-knit in those years; most students pursued not bachelor's degrees but a two- or three-year course of study which enabled them to teach upon graduation. In 1926 two convocations for the entire student body were held weekly at which all the faculty would sit on a platform surrounding President Brown while he read from the Bible and offered prayers. Miss Stella Root, chair of the music department, would then lead the student body in singing hymns with great enthusiasm and thus taught hundreds of St. Cloud students to love the old music of the Church.[21] Nevertheless,

A young Reverend T. Leo Keaveny, first spiritual advisor to the St. Cloud Newman Club.

Students study in the main reading room of the Teachers College library in the 1920s.

the Newman Club was the first campus organization that sought to gather students together for a specifically religious purpose. As the 1924 edition of the college yearbook, *Talahi*, summed it up, the Newman Club was founded in order to "promote the moral and religious interests of Catholic students at the college, to bring them into closer relationship with one another, and to undertake a study of current social problems." As one of many student groups existing at the Teachers College, the Newman Club organized itself along lines that were standard on campus at the time. The club was required to have elected student officers, an elected student representative to the campus Student Council and at least one faculty advisor. The addition of a "Spiritual Advisor" was unique to Newman as a religious organization. The first three student officers of the Newman Club were women: Delia Tise was the club's first president, Margaret Brennan its vice-president, and Alice McCauley its secretary-treasurer. In the following 1924/1925 school year, the officers were again all female, and the club's two advisors were also women: Agnes H. Kerlin, and Marguerite McBride. These advisors were followed in 1926 by Mrs. A.J. Tschumperlin, and Miss C. Sheehan, and then Pauline Penning in 1927 and John Weismann in 1928. Miss Penning and Mr. Weismann (who later became Dean of Men at the College), would

The first officers of the Newman Club, elected for the 1923-1924 school year: Delia Tise, Margaret Brennan, and Alice McCauley.

remain faithful guiders of the club for many years and can claim no small credit for the fact that the young club survived, and later began to thrive.

Bishop Busch once remarked: "We'll build our castle next to their castle." As the St. Cloud Newman Club took shape, however, it was obvious that neither Busch, his appointee Keaveny, nor the lay members of the college faculty who took a special interest in the project desired to build a castle fortified against the influences of modern university life. The club's mandate to promote the moral and religious interests of Catholic students at the college was never interpreted to mean that active involvement in non-religious aspects of life on and off campus should be avoided. From the start, a healthy engagement with all aspects of the social and intellectual life of the campus was encouraged by the club, and meetings of the sacred and the secular were defended, supported and promoted in a wide variety of ways.

The hand-written minutes of the St. Cloud Newman Club's activities in these early years leave an impressive record of fairly serious intellectual discussion and concern. At its Wednesday night meetings held in various rooms on campus every other week, such topics were discussed as: "Conditions in Europe," "Prison Reform," "Darwinism," "Health Work in the State," "Evolution," and the "Tendencies of Modern Government." Throughout the decade of the 1920s, *Talahi* reported often on the "interesting" programs offered by the club, where members were, at times, "delightfully entertained and enlightened" by the wisdom and expertise of prominent local and out-of-town speakers who appeared regularly at their meetings. It was not uncommon for such speakers to include the president of the Teachers College and the Right Reverend Joseph Busch, Bishop of St. Cloud. At the time of her retirement in 1959, Pauline Penning looked back on her early years with the club and remembered that when Bishop Busch came to speak, his favorite topic, of course, was always the Holy Spirit. "His talks

Pauline Penning, retiring head of the Art Department who served as a faculty advisor to the Newman Club during her first eighteen years on campus. Here, Penning receives a corsage from Peg McIntyre at the First Annual Newman Awards Banquet at which she was honored in 1959. Wil Illies sits at right.

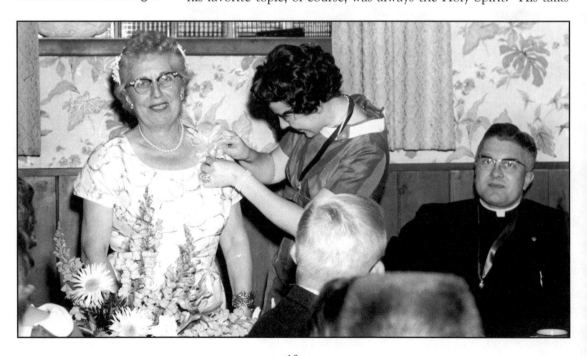

18

were quite deep," Miss Penning mused, and the bishop himself suspected that, more often than not, the students didn't know what he was talking about.[22]

In keeping with the spirit of John Henry Newman, who believed that healthy and holy things could arise out of meetings between the sacred and the secular, as the club's membership grew throughout the 1920s and 1930s, so did its identity as a social, as well as an educational and religious, organization. Teachers College students were active joiners in the 1930s, so much so that a point system had to be established for campus clubs in order to prevent students from taking part in so many activities that their academic studies suffered. Catholic students embraced their Newman Club with enthusiasm. In 1929, the club won the silver loving cup presented by the *Talahi* staff for the best "Whoopie Nite" stunt, and by 1930 the yearbook was reporting that the Newman Club is "prominent in the social life of the campus and is an active organization taking part in every college activity with characteristic enthusiasm." In 1932, as its contribution to the Thursday-night student assemblies held on campus at the time, the Newman Club procured as its speaker Coach Heenan of Cathedral High School. Heenan entertained the whole student body by sketching out the life of the the late Knute Rockne, the famous coach of the very Catholic "Fighting Irish" of Notre Dame. Sponsoring both formal and informal dances, organizing an annual sleigh ride and spring picnic, building floats for the Homecoming parade and putting together a skit each year for the annual *Talahi Revue* were regular activities of the club (the 1938 skit, entitled "A Take-Off on a Faculty Tea," sounds particularly interesting. Records of critical evaluations offered at the time, however, are not available). In 1932, the club had one hundred-fifty members participating in its

Students perform a skit for the *Talahi Revue* in 1934 entitled "There Ain't No Mortgage No More."

19

Members of the 1934 Newman Club. Pauline Penning stands in the center of the second row from the front, ninth from the left. John Weismann is first on the left in the top row. Two hundred thirty-eight students graduated from the Teachers College that year.

discussion sessions, dances, parties, and monthly communion breakfasts. One year later, the club had two hundred-fifty members, had inaugurated the first annual retreat for all Catholic students on campus, and had taken an active role in the formation of the Minnesota Federation of Newman Clubs. By 1939, the Newman Club became a member of the "Youth Council" of the city of St. Cloud, which included representatives of every Catholic organization in the city and had as its purpose the unification of St. Cloud's Catholic Action.

Throughout the years between 1935 and 1946, for a mere twenty-five cents in dues per annum, students were exposed to some marvelous reflections on how the sacred and the secular could intersect and present transforming challenges to all people of faith who lived and worked in the world. Topics presented for discussion in those years included "The History of Catholic Church Music," "Problems Facing the Catholic Teacher in the Public School System," "Religion and the Development of Personality," "The Influence of Educational Movements in China," "Mercy Killing," "The Nature and Dignity of Man [sic]," "Catholic Literature," "Labor Problems," "The Social Message of the New Testament," and "Catholicism in Europe," as well as the ever-popular "Mixed Marriages" and "Catholic Marriage and Divorce." In 1937, a priest-geologist named Henry Retzek traveled to campus to give an "interesting and enlightening illustrated lecture on Prehistoric Man [sic]." Retzek, apparently, was a big hit, for club minutes all the way up to 1955 record him making periodic guest appearances at meetings in order to offer presentations on evolution, archeology, and geology, which were always described as "most entertaining and stimulating." For a brief time, small groups were organized to meet and discuss issues in greater depth at the homes of the club's faculty advisors, at Holy Angel's Rectory, at the home of the club's spiritual advisor, and at the private homes of some of the club's members, an initiative encouraged by the Reverend Ferdinand Falque, secretary of the diocesan Catholic Action Council.

NEWMAN CLUB
Communion Breakfast
Holy Angles Church   9:00 o'clock Mass
November 24, 1946   Admission $.25

Sponsorship of monthly "Communion Breakfasts" was a very popular Newman Club activity throughout the 1930s, 1940s, and 1950s.

While *Talahi* in these early decades never failed to report on the Newman Club's study and discussion of "present day" social and religious problems, it is apparent that at times the club faced the same growing pangs and conflicting pulls that plagued other developing Newman groups throughout the country. There lurked the perennial temptation, not always discouraged by either parents or members of the Church hierarchy, for Newman Clubs to allow themselves to be reduced to safe Catholic havens where good Catholic boys could meet good Catholic girls while participating in some wholesome recreational activity. A perusal of club minutes kept between 1924 and 1941 reveals that at times an inordinate number of meetings were spent planning social events and activities for the year that did not necessarily advance the creative meeting of religion and knowledge, the life of the mind and the life of faith. Many of those activities were, of course, highly worthwhile and included important contributions to campus life as well as to charitable organizations, like the planning of an annual Christmas program for the children of the St. Cloud Orphanage, "adopting" orphans each year for whom club members would purchase Christmas gifts, and making donations from the treasury to various world service and missions groups. But even though an unbalanced emphasis on purely social activity would hold sway for a while, spiritual advisors, faculty advisors, and students themselves would eventually urge a return to more purposeful pursuits. One such pursuit that became an enduring favorite was the "Question and Answer Session," at which students submitted questions on small slips of paper to the club's spiritual advisor who then made his best attempt to answer and explain. The students' questions were many: "Why is the Mass said in Latin?" "Why can a man who has been divorced and remarried a number of times be buried a Catholic?"

and "Why can't a Catholic go to another church?" As Frederick (Fritz) Kampsen, Newman spiritual advisor between 1939 and 1944, put it in an interview fifty years later, students always had many, many questions, and he considered that a good thing, "because when you have questions, it shows that you're thinking." Other kinds of queries students ventured to make in this era indicated that they were thinking deeply, at times, about the political turmoil and tales of human suffering that were becoming a part of their everyday lives as Hitler rose to power in Germany and peace between the nations became tentative and unsettled. Their questions, furthermore, revealed the existence of a reflective instinct in their minds and hearts that somehow the sacred and the secular ought to be intersecting and affecting one another much more powerfully and persuasively than they appeared to be as the world marched doggedly toward the brink of a second world war. "Why doesn't the pope prevent the war?" students asked. "Is Mussolini a practicing Catholic?" they wanted to know, and "How many Catholics are there in Ethiopia?"

In addition to shaping the questions and concerns that students had, the entrance of the United States into World War II also had a more immediate impact on the life of the Newman Club, and of the entire campus. Drawing students away to serve in the armed services or to seek jobs in the booming war industries, World War I had reduced attendance at the school by approximately one-third. World War II, however, left only about one-third of the student body still in attendance. At one time during the war years there were only thirteen male students on the entire campus.[23] The minutes of the March 25, 1943, Newman meeting note rather sadly that President Myron Kennedy called the club to order for the last time: "he left April 3rd for the Army." That very night, a "very interesting discussion" took place on "War Marriages," led by Myron Kennedy, Leon Schertler, Eleanor Porwall, and Rose Vasaly. As did most other campus organizations in those years, the Newman Club took up regular donations for the Red Cross and involved itself in blood drives and other local volunteer efforts. Meanwhile, the St. Cloud State Teachers College was selected as one of one hundred fifty schools nationwide to house an Army Air Force College Training Program. Thus it was that the Catholic "Army Air Corps Boys" became the special guests of the Newman Club on more than one occasion at both educational and social events. When World War II finally came to an end, "Veterans Guidance and Counseling" programs were established throughout the nation to help soldiers adjust to civilian life. The St. Cloud State Teachers College was selected as one of many guidance centers, and the Newman Club's long-time faculty

The Newman Club in 1947.

Officers and advisors of the 1948 Newman Club. First row, seated: Ruth Swedzinski, Harold Kost (spiritual advisor), Paul Porwall, Tina McFarlane; second row: John J. Weismann (faculty advisor), Wendaline Wagner, James Carlin, Richard Meinz (faculty advisor), and Louis Jackson.

advisor, John Weismann, became the director and head counselor of that program. As the resources provided by the G.I. Bill became available to veterans, providing them with assistance in finding jobs and in continuing their schooling, university campuses throughout the country gradually came to life again. In St. Cloud, the 1945 spring enrollment roster listed eighteen men on campus; by fall of that same year, the number had risen to over six hundred. The men out-numbered the women at the St. Cloud Teachers College for the first time in 1947 when over 1,000 men enrolled. Harold Kost, Newman spiritual advisor in those post-war years, remembers how powerfully campus life was affected by those students who were returning G.I.'s. "The war matured them," Kost reflects, and they were determined to build a nation and a world where there were no more wars. They were less ready to accept pat answers without questioning, and there was a depth to their thought and their concern that their peers had not yet managed to achieve.

Through all of these early post-war developments, the Newman Club continued its efforts to encourage the constructive crossing-over of the sacred and the secular and to promote education in faith as an essential component of that total education of the mind and heart meant ideally to take place during the college years. The club commanded increasing respect on campus; with its more than two-hundred members, it was the largest student organization then in existence. In this era, the club experimented with publishing a small paper, or "bulletin," called *The Newman News*, and student Florian Savekoul took on the job of being the paper's first editor. A Newman Club "library" of books, pamphlets, and articles was established in Dean John Weismann's office so that Catholic students would have access to more information regarding faith topics. There the library remained until 1952 when it was moved for a while to the children's literature section of the main campus library, where it kept up residence until it, like the Newman movement it served, acquired a more permanent home. The Daughters of Isabella in St. Cloud, in fact, made several book donations in support of the effort, and during one Lenten season, students were even asked to contribute to a regular "self-denial collection" whose proceeds were used to buy books for the nascent library. St. Cloud's coadjutor bishop, Peter Bartholome, became a frequent guest at club meetings, coming to share his thoughts on such varied topics as secularism, the importance of being broad-minded and tolerant, the association of church and state, how education can be a "dangerous pursuit," and "Women and their Place in the World Today." Unfortunately, the club's minutes give no hint as to what Bartholome actually said about these topics! In 1945, study groups were formed that met in Carol Hall and "information classes" were held at Holy Angels Grade School to which everyone was welcome, "especially non-Catholics." Leonard Gaida, who was the club's spiritual advisor from 1944 to 1946, seems to have been particularly concerned with the personal spiritual development of the Catholic students he had been assigned to shepherd. Under his tutelage, students urged the administration (unsuccessfully) to allow Mass to be celebrated on campus during Lent, and the 1945-1946 school year minutes record some fascinating details of the "Step-of-the-Two-Weeks" strategy that Gaida implemented. At every club meeting, students would be given a new spiritual "step" or exercise to work on during the two weeks that would pass before the next regular meeting:

September 14, 1945:   "To say our morning and
                         evening prayers"

September 27, 1945:	"To take a 'Spiritual Bath' each day; that is, to say an examination of conscience."
October 10, 1945:	"To offer up everything we do during the day for the greater honor and glory of God."
November 15, 1945:	"To stick by our guns, Confession and Communion, against . . . temptation."
December 13, 1945:	"To build a crib for Jesus. We can do this by getting rid of some fault."
Lent, 1946:	"During Lent we should try to do a good house-cleaning job by getting rid of the sin that is leading us on the path to Hell."
April 25, 1946:	"To really act as Catholics; to appreciate the gift of grace and use and practice our pearls of the truth of religion."

Officers of the 1949 Newman Club: Gerald Adamic and Louis Iacarella (both standing). Seated are Betty Saunders, Valjean Tomaseski, President Helen Mayer, and Tecla Karpens.

This relatively new desire to use the forum of the Newman Club to help students foster a commitment to personal spiritual growth beyond that encouraged through participation in the liturgical rites of the Church appears to have been taken one small step farther in early 1949 when one of the club's first "retreats" was planned under the initiative of club president Helen Mayer, an event extending from a Friday evening to a Sunday morning and culminating, of course, with a corporate communion breakfast.

For the most part, however, no major changes occurred in the primary focus the club assumed during the first two and one-half decades following its foundation. Club dues increased a bit over the years, but the increase seemed to cause little or no restlessness among the ranks. As late as 1950, after all, one could still secure a full year's membership for the bargain rate of one dollar. Overall, the Newman Club at the St. Cloud State Teachers College did an admirable job of being faithful to the spirit of John Henry Newman, educating students about their faith, contributing in a positive way to the overall life and health of the college campus, and facilitating a more effective balance of the sacred and the secular in the lives of those Catholic students who chose to affiliate themselves with the organization. A Catholic Christian community at the crossroads had been successfully established.

Page from a publication of the National Newman Club Federation entitled, "A New Look."

A New Decade, A New Direction

A period of increasing organization and more focused activity began for the St. Cloud Newman Club with the arrival of the new decade of the fifties. In the spring of 1948, the club ratified its first set of formal constitutions drawn up by a student subcommittee, and by 1950 the group had voted to connect itself officially with the Newman movement across the country by enrolling in the National Newman Club Federation. It was a timely decision. The St. Cloud club had affiliated itself nominally with the "Federation of Catholic College Clubs" in the 1930s, but the "National Newman Club Federation," established in 1938, was by

1950 becoming increasingly sophisticated and active nationwide, in spite of the struggles it had faced in its nascent years.

The National Catholic Welfare Council (NCWC), of which the Federation of Catholic College Clubs became a part in 1920, initially supported the Newman movement as a valuable asset with the potential to become a powerful aid in efforts to further Catholic education nationally.[24] It was not long, however, before the NCWC backed off of its support for the movement because of pervading pressures not to encourage Catholic educational opportunities outside of private, denominational schools. The bishops in general, and especially the Jesuits, made use of *America* magazine to snipe at the Newman movement. As John Whitney Evans describes it, a kind of educational domino theory controlled the thinking of most Church leaders. The Catholic college system was perceived as providing essential support for the whole fabric of the Catholic school system; if the college failed, real fear existed that parochial schools could not continue to exist. The Newman movement, in other words, was almost done in by the parish school.[25] John Keogh, first "Chaplain General" of the National Newman Club Federation, made a noble effort in the early 1930s to inspire bishops to recognize the critical role of the Newman effort in American Catholic society. Keogh also succeeded in connecting the Newman movement with the "Catholic Action" call to the laity to engage in active, apostolic work that Pius XI was making a central effort of his pontificate. When the Newman Club Federation was given an official place within the Youth Department of the NCWC in 1940, Newman leaders rejoiced; unfortunately, they paid a price for their acceptance into the family for, in the assessment of Evans, being in the harbor also meant being penned.[26] The Youth Department, for example, took responsibility in 1942 for issuing a Manual for Newman Leaders, which published for the first time some important, basic information on the identity, mission, and methods of the Newman movement that could be dispersed nationally. But, the unsigned preface of the book explicitly affirmed the "primacy" of the Catholic college. Newman Clubs, the preface indicated, could in no way be considered equals of the Catholic college and had no right to support until Catholic colleges had all been taken cared of adequately. The power to deal the hand, in essence, still rested with those threatened protectors of Catholic schools who relegated Newman Clubs to the world of boy scouts and parish basketball teams.[27] As the years progressed, however, glimmers of hope and glimpses of deeper insight appeared, and the beginning of the 1950s was actually a very opportune moment for the St. Cloud group to choose to throw in its lot more committedly with the national movement.

It was in 1950 that an official from the University of Notre Dame attended that year's National Newman Club Federation Conference and found himself quite favorably impressed with the "Newmanites" he encountered. Obviously, the clubs that nurtured these students could not be rightfully accused of being little more than excuses for Catholic students to socialize and date, and he mused later in print over how "it was somewhat mortifying to me to find that these Catholic students from non-Catholic schools are so much more apostolic in their zeal than students I encounter on Catholic campuses."[29] What's more, in the summer of 1950, *America* published two articles whose appraisal of the Newman movement was significantly less antagonistic than that taken by the magazine twenty-five years earlier. In one of those articles, Jerome Kerwin, a political scientist from the University of Chicago, pointed out that many future leaders of the Church's lay apostolate would inevitably come from the ranks of the Newman movement. He thus underlined the importance of full-time appointments to chaplaincies and quoted a university president who informed his bishop that he did not want a priest-chaplain for the Newman movement on his campus who would simply "dry the students tears and hold their hands or be a glad-hand artist." Ministers were needed who could be the intellectual equal of any person on the faculty and who had the ability to deal with contemporary students who were "stubborn questioners," asking in ever greater numbers to study liturgy, apologetics, philosophy, social problems, and theology. If such needs go unmet, that university president declared, then students "will go away disgusted, perhaps lost to the faith forever, and the Church will certainly lose the chance to bring forth great, intelligent lay apostles."[30] Kerwin even went so far in that article as to recommend the establishment of "houses of study" with libraries at great secular universities to which "eminent Catholic scholars" could be invited to meet with local scholars. The St. Cloud Newman Club, as we shall soon see, was one group which took the spirit of Kerwin's challenge seriously.

As the warm summer months began to unfold in 1950, the "National Newman Chaplain's Association" was founded, a significant step toward the professionalizing of Newman ministry. By 1954, national leaders had sufficient financial resources at their disposal to bolster Newman Clubs around the nation in concrete ways. The National Newman Federation set up a "Religious Education Committee," adopted criteria governing club libraries and courses, and encouraged the development of local programs such as the "Newman Forum," which took root and flourished at the University of Minnesota. Summer seminars for chaplain enrichment were held and a host of new publications began to come from the national office. Nearly half of these were educational, and students and chaplains received them enthusiastically, often applying them creatively at the local level.[31] Some nationally designed programs came complete with prepackaged class outlines, bibliographies, and action projects and were organized around yearly themes like "The Courageous Catholic," focusing on personal morality, "The Informed Catholic," focusing on history, philosophy, theology, psychology, and the arts, "The Prayerful Catholic," focusing on ascetical theology and liturgy, and "The Apostolic Catholic," centering on papal encyclicals and their applications to social questions. Journalistic efforts also began to blossom among local Newman clubs at this time, reflecting a new seriousness about penetrating the academic milieu on its own terms, facilitating the integration of faith and intellect and walking responsibly and creatively through the middle of the highway called the university.[32] A publication of the National Association of Newman Club Chaplains put it thus: "For the Catholic college student, it is not simply a problem of holding on to his [sic] faith, nor of raising his religious knowledge. Personal and social wholeness must permeate his education."[33]

The official seal of the National Newman Club Federation, designed and patented in 1925 by John W. Keogh, first national chaplain of the federation. The seven-sided emblem circumscribes the shield taken from Cardinal John Henry Newman's coat of arms. Newman's motto, "Cor ad Cor loquitur," or "Heart Speaks to Heart," surrounds the shield.

St. Cloud Connects with the Federation

The newly fused connection to the Newman movement on a broader scale, which began around 1950 for the St. Cloud Newman Club, signaled the emergence of many new phenomena which became a regular part of club life, including setting off on excursions to national conventions, attending and hosting province conventions, peddling official Newman Club pins and other assorted paraphernalia which members were encouraged to wear with pride, and coaching students more deliberately in the goals, the work and the ideals of the Newman philosophy. Members even voted to begin their meetings by singing the Federation "Alma Mater," and often closed by praying the official "Prayer of John Henry Newman." The words of each are forever etched in the memory of many Newman alumni and alumnae:

Newman Club Alma Mater

(*Chorus*)
Let Heart speak to heart
In love and truth.
We're all together
Far across the land—
In every school one Alma Mater.
Hail our Mother Church—
We pledge to Thee undying Faith.
Lead, O Kindly Light—
Your brightness be our guiding star
Through all our life.

(*Verse*):
Dream days for every one,
Hearts stirred by victories won,
Joys of our college days,
Steal back and repay.
Wisdom to fill the mind,
Precious gifts of every kind,
Friendship of Newman Club
Live forever more (*Chorus*)[35]

Prayer of Cardinal Newman

May Christ support us
all the day long,
till the shadows lengthen and
the evening comes,
and the busy world is hushed,
and the fever of life is o'er,
and our work is done.

Then in His mercy may He give us
a safe lodging and a holy rest
and peace at last.

In May 1950, the Newman Club in St. Cloud stepped forward boldly and agreed to host the annual convention of the North Central Province of the National Newman Club Federation, welcoming representatives from Newman Clubs in North and South

Dakota, Wisconsin, and Minnesota. Back in 1936, St. Cloud had hosted a smaller regional gathering of Newman clubs and, since that time, had periodically sent representatives to regional gatherings held in other parts of the state. But the 1950 meeting was a major event and seemed to set the tone for the assumption of a higher-profile for the Newman Club in St. Cloud in the decades ahead. All meetings of the 1950 convention were held in Stewart Hall on campus, and the general theme of the gathering was "Problems of the Catholic Student in a Lay College." St. Cloud State student Harold Riley was the general chairperson of the convention, and St. Cloud's spiritual advisor, Harold Kost, led the opening prayer and gave the opening address. The keynote speech was delivered by Leonard Cowley, University of Minnesota Newman Club chaplain and pastor of St. Olaf's Church in Minneapolis. Additional talks, socials, mixers, elections of officers, an address by St. Cloud Bishop Peter Bartholome, and a corporate communion breakfast at the diocesan Cathedral were also part of the agenda for the weekend.

John Laky, the club's spiritual advisor in the early 1950s, dreamed of securing a building for the Newman Club, a spiritual home that Newman members could call their own. The time was not yet ripe, but Bishop Busch did grant the club full use of a room in the basement of Holy Angels Church as a place to hold socials. More significant, however, were the increasingly sophisticated efforts being made to address the integration of faith, life, and intellect among those young Catholic women and men who came as students to St. Cloud State College once the decade opened. A Philosophy Study Club, first suggested by Newman student Ray Bares, was established within the framework of the Newman organization, and some students lobbied on campus to have a priest-taught philosophy course included in the college curriculum. Fairly formal evening classes began to be offered once a week by the club in areas such as rational psychology, philosophy, and ethics. During the 1950-1951 school year, a number of professors from St. John's University in nearby Collegeville, Minnesota, came to present lectures on timely topics in their respective fields. That such a spirit of cooperation existed between members of the St. John's faculty and their diocesan colleagues guiding the Newman movement at St. Cloud State College is noteworthy; not all faculties at Catholic colleges were willing to offer their support to a movement that was held suspect by some members of the hierarchy, trivialized as a "youth program" by many, and considered a threat to the future of Catholic education by still others. As the decade of the 1950s progressed, Godfrey Diekmann, OSB, who would make a lasting mark

Ray Bares, an active member of the Newman Club during his years as a student who later became a state senator and the director of Catholic Charities in St. Cloud. Bares, his wife and their young daughter were killed in a car accident in 1964. The bust of Cardinal Newman that sits today in the Newman Center lobby is dedicated to his memory.

at the Second Vatican Council in the early 1960s, was invited to speak to the St. Cloud Newmanites on several occasions; others came to orate on topics such as "Church and State in Education," "What a Catholic Scientist thinks of the Book of Genesis," and "The Catholic Church in American History."

Three full decades had passed since the young Newman movement first planted itself on the banks of the River of the Holy Spirit and began to encourage transforming intersections between faith and knowledge in the middle of the highway called the university. In 1954, the St. Patrick's Day edition of the Newman Club newsletter provided a reprint of a reflection written by Minnesota's own Charles Lindbergh in his book, *Of Flight and Life*. Lindbergh's sentiments sum up well the spirit behind those encouraged crossroads encounters. While they had at times been prompted with varying levels of enthusiasm and success, overall they had laid a foundation sturdy and compelling enough to enable many Newman graduates to grasp forever the wisdom of Lindbergh's powerful confession:

> To me in youth, science was more important than either man [sic] or God. I worshipped science. I was awed by its knowledge. Its advances had surpassed man's wildest dreams. In its learning seemed to lie the key to all mysteries of life.
>
> It took many years for me to discover that science, with all its brilliance, lights only a middle chapter of creation. I saw the science I worshipped, and the aircraft I loved, destroying the civilization I expected them to serve, and which I thought as permanent as earth itself. Now I realize that to survive, one must look beyond the speed and power of aircraft—beyond the material strength of science. And, though God cannot be seen as tangibly as I had demanded as a child, His [sic] presence can be sensed in every sight and act and incident. Now I know that when man loses this sense, he misses the true quality of life—the beauty of earth, its seasons and its skies; the brotherhood of men; the joy of wife and children. He loses the infinite strength without which no people can survive— the element which war cannot defeat or peace corrupt.
>
> Now I understand that spiritual truth is more essential to a nation than the mortar in its cities' walls. For when the actions of a people are unguided by these truths, it is only a matter of time before the walls themselves collapse.
>
> The most urgent mission of our time is to understand these truths, and to apply them to our way of life . . . it is our only hope.

Paul VI, before he became pontiff, announced that the mission of the Church is "to relate the secular and the sacred so that the second will not be contaminated but communicated, and the first will not be adulterated but sanctified."[36] Such communication of the sacred and sanctification of the secular so that both are humbled, enriched and transformed, happens in unique and powerful ways in the crossroads environment of the university. Encouraging them to meet under the same roof as Cardinal Newman believed they must, and then facilitating their fruitful interaction, has long been the responsibility and the joy of the women and men who have embraced the Newman vision.

On October 1, 1953, the Newman Club's minutes read as follows:

> Our first Newman Club meeting of the new school term was held in the old library. Our president opened up the meeting by welcoming the members. Father Laky was introduced to the freshmen and transfer students. He gave a short farewell speech and introduced Father Illies, our new Newman Club chaplain.

The young traveler, Wilfred Illies, had arrived on the highway which was St. Cloud State Teachers College and, while few could possibly have predicted it at the time, the new era that had begun to dawn for the St. Cloud Newman Club at the start of the 1950s was about to emerge with full force into the light of day. The Spirit was spilling over the banks of her river, and, some would say, was orchestrating holy magic. A remarkable series of encounters, intersections, collisions, conversations, constructions, and conversions would mark the sixteen years of Illies' tenure as spiritual leader of the Newman movement on campus. Nothing would ever quite be the same again.

Wil Illies walks through the door to a new sixteen-year adventure.

Notes

1 Rosemary Haughton, *The Catholic Thing* (Springfield: Templegate Publishers, 1979), pp. 229, 231-232.
2 John Whitney Evans, *The Newman Movement* (Notre Dame: University of Notre Dame Press, 1980), p. 5.
3 John Henry Newman, from a sermon entitled, "The Union of Knowledge and Religion."
4 John Henry Newman, *John Henry Newman, Sermons on Various Occasions* (London: Longmans, Green & Co., 1904) p. 12.
5 National Conference of Catholic Bishops, nos. 17, 19.
6 Evans, pp. 6-7.
7 Evans, pp. 8-9.
8 Evans, footnote #4, p. 191.

9 Evans, pp. 15, 32-33.

10 Evans, pp. 16, 25.

11 *Newman News*, 24 April 1959, p. 3.

12 *Newman News*, 30 October 1958, p. 3.

13 Evans, pp. 16-17.

14 Evans, pp. 18-23.

15 Evans, pp. 19-20.

16 Evans, p. 54.

17 Evans, pp. 53-55.

18 Vincent Yzermans, *The Spirit in Central Minnesota* (St. Cloud, Sentinel Printing Company, 1989), I, p. 230.

19 Yzermans, I, pp. 232-234.

20 Yzermans, II, pp. 890-891.

21 Edwin Cates, *A Centennial History of St. Cloud State College* (Minneapolis: Dillon Press, 1968), p. 168.

22 *Newman News*, 24 April 1959, p. 3.

23 Cates, pp. 201-202.

24 Evans, p. 73.

25 Evans, pp. 82-83.

26 Evans, p. 96.

27 Evans, pp. 97-98.

28 Evans, pp. 89-90.

29 Evans, p. 101.

30 "Newman Clubs—New Tasks and Opportunities," *America*, 9 September 1950, pp. 582 ff. (referred to in Evens, pp. 108-109).

31 Evans, p. 114.

32 Evans, pp. 103-104.

33 *Second Spring*, May 1955, pp. 48-49.

34 National Association of Newman Club Chaplains, "The Newman Club in American Education," (Huntingdon: *Our Sunday Visitor*, 1953).

35 Newman Club Manual, 1954. Words by Rev. G. Maguire and Rev. J. MacEachin. Music by D'Artega.

36 *The Mission of the Church*, Major Documents on Catholic Action from the Second World Congress of the Lay Apostolate, Rome, October 6-13, 1957. Notre Dame: National Catholic Action Study Bureau, 1958, p. 51. As quoted by Butler.

Chapter 2

Where There's a Wil, There's a Way

"God has created me to do some definite service. He has committed some work to me which He has not committed to another. I have my mission—I may never know it in this life, but I shall be told it in the next. I am a link in a chain, a bond of connection between persons. God has not created me for nought."

—John Henry Newman

Wilfred Illies was born in the small town of Elrosa, Minnesota, also the home town of Frederick (Fritz) Kampsen, who was chaplain of the Newman Club from 1939 to 1944. "Fritz was a sort of hero and a mentor for me when I was growing up," Wil recalls, "because he was a great ball player—a good pitcher—and I thought that was what the seminary was all about." After two years of public high school in Sauk Centre, Minnesota, Wil thus went off to the Pontifical College Josephinum in Worthington, Ohio and, eleven years later, on June 3, 1950, was ordained to the priesthood at the age of twenty-seven.

Wilfred Illies, whose vision and commitment gave birth to Christ Church Newman Center as we now know it.

Illies' first assignment was to serve as one of four assistant pastors at St. Mary's Cathedral in St. Cloud. It was at the cathedral, in 1952, that he met the newly ordained Vincent (Art) Yzermans, a man who would eventually become his dearest friend and closest collaborator in the building up of a vital Newman ministry on the banks of the Mississippi River. Decades later, Yzermans penned a touching description of Illies and of their first encounter, and his words capture well the spirit of the deep and enduring relationship that blossomed between the two of them. Yzermans wrote:

> Little did I realize that from that moment until the present he would be the closest friend and confidant in my life's journey.

35

Wil Illies, right, and Art Yzermans, center, greet their friend Hans Küng at the airport. The young, brilliant and already controversial Swiss theologian delivered an address at St. John's University in 1963 entitled, "Freedom—Unfreedom."

We shared everything together throughout the years—our work, our recreation, our prayers, our families, and friends. By some we were called the "gold dust twins," after a cleansing powder that was popular at that time. He often entered into my life, in good times and bad, always as sturdy and sheltering as an oak in a storm and yet also as gentle and playful as a willow.[1]

Three years after his arrival at St. Mary's, the young, but already sturdy, Illies was approached by John Laky and asked if he might be interested in taking on the chaplaincy of the Newman Club at the St. Cloud Teachers College in addition to his duties at the Cathedral. Though Wil knew very little about Newman or Newman Clubs, a chat or two with his always persuasive friend Art Yzermans, who promised to help, was enough to convince him to plunge in and explore the waters.

Learning the Way

Illies' first official task as chaplain in the fall of 1953 was to attend a Newman convention at the University of Minnesota. All those "high-powered Newman people," remembers Wil, "really stirred my interest in the whole thing." It was an interest that would prove to be long-lived and extraordinarily fruitful. In the early months of Wil's presence with the club, Dean John Weismann and Mr. Richard Meinz continued to provide important support and direction as faculty advisors. By the fall of 1954, *Newman News* reported that at least 350 members were expected to march in procession—led by the Catholic War Veterans Color Guard—into St. Mary's Cathedral for their annual Mass at the start of the school year. A competent and committed slate of student officers who would remain loyal to the spirit of Newman on the banks of the Mississippi for decades to come led the club into that new year; Sanford Banker and Carol Conoryea served as president and vice-president, respectively, Rose Marie Simone was the club's secretary, Charles Ernst took responsibility for the treasury, while Dennis Johnson and Charlene Morse guided the library. In addition, Don Keefler was the club's representative to the Inter-Religion Council and Mary Jo Vashro and Pat Jean Walker took

Wil Illies with some of the 1954-1955 Newman Club officers. Back row, left to right: Wil Illies, Sandy Banker, Dennis Johnson, and Chuck Ernst; front row: Kay Thomas, Carol Conoryea, and Jeannette Rehkamp.

charge of all club publications. Club meetings and discussion sessions continued to be held in classrooms on campus, sleigh rides, hayrides, and dances were held off-campus, and retreats, lunches, communion breakfasts, and other such activities found their home at St. Mary's Grade School or church basement. From the start, "I remember that I liked the students very much," says Wil. "They were still sometimes treated like second-class citizens by the Church because they weren't in Catholic schools, but I often noticed that the most active students were the ones who had come from public, not parochial schools."

Wil Illies and the student leaders of the 1954-1955 Newman Club at work. President Sandy Banker is at the microphone. Mary Jo Vashro, at far left, and Pat Walker, third from the left, were in charge of all club publications for the year. Vice-president Carol Conoryea sits at Illies' right.

"cardinal newman in the 20th century"

CARDINAL NEWMAN WEEK

Illies began to grow quickly in confidence and vision; a real passion emerged within him for the potential of Newman ministry and for the challenges that came with choosing to do commerce and cross paths with other travelers on the university highway. He began to guide the club toward more serious intellectual study of faith-related matters and more ambitious ways of making full, fearless and creative use of the powerful crossroad experiences that are inevitably part of life in a university community. He developed an avid interest in the person and the legacy of John Henry Newman, as well as an avid belief in his fitness as a patron for the movement. The more he read of Newman's work, the more Illies would try to inspire his students to read. In 1958, Illies and Yzermans together implemented an annual event called "Newman Education Day," which sought to introduce new students to the Newman vision of educated women and men as people full of reverence "for the Eternal Light they have been bidden to shed over all of creation." The event required an all-day commitment and consisted of a keynote address and a series of several workshops focused on the person of Newman and on the relevance of the Newman movement. As time went on, Illies would also inaugurate "Cardinal Newman Week" on the St. Cloud State campus, a nationally-promoted effort to publicize and promote understanding of Newman.

The Path Becomes a Road

What Illies began to foster locally as the 1950s progressed was very much in keeping with the spirit sweeping the Newman movement throughout the country at that time. In 1955, the National Newman Club Federation set up a "Religious Education Committee," adopted criteria governing the development of club libraries and the organization of courses, and urged students at every campus to form local boards of education so they could design and implement programs that would win their clubs certification as "superior Catholic centers."[2] The St. Cloud Newman Club responded to that advice with enthusiasm, as did Newman clubs and centers on many other college campuses, investing considerable time and energy in the development of the educational arm of the three-pronged, religious, educational and social mission now articulated by the national Newman movement. Clubs throughout the country benefited from a host of educational materials that the national office could at last afford to publish. They built up libraries, created speaker's series and formal discussion groups, added lectures as part of the "Communion Breakfast" agenda and published their own newsletters and annuals containing some impressively scholarly articles written by students and chap-

Wil Illies gives a pep talk to incoming students about the value of the Newman Club at the new-student orientation meeting, September 20, 1962.

lains alike. By 1958, five "Newman Schools of Catholic Thought" had been established throughout the country that offered attending students a week-long series of lectures and workshops on theology, liturgy, the lay apostolate, and ecumenical relations. There was much interest in making the disciplined development of the religious dimension of life a regular, integrated part of the college experience and of the college curriculum in order to fill up the "hole in the whole" of university education, as Newman Federation literature of the time liked to call it. The University of Iowa, The University of Illinois, and the University of North Dakota were pioneers in this regard and were among the first to arrange for the provision of *accredited* religion courses for which students would register just as they registered for any other class. Some Newman clubs even succeeded in helping to establish bona fide "Departments of Religion" on their state university campuses, while others implemented a wide variety of non-credit opportunities. Louisiana State University, for example, offered a comprehensive, four-year program for Newman students in philosophy and theology designed to "educate and train" students over a period of four years and equip them with leadership skills and a religious formation that could be put to use later in whatever field they might enter upon graduation.

Wil Illies, of course, was ambitious enough to want to establish a Department of Religion on the campus that had nestled in and was continuing to grow on the west bank of the Holy Spirit's river. In the late 1960s, in fact, a committee consisting of Illies, two members of the student senate and representative members of St. Cloud State's history, sociology, psychology, and philosophy departments actually drafted a concrete proposal for the establishment of a religious studies curriculum at the college but, in the end, their efforts failed to bear fruit. The Newman Club persisted, however, in its determination to encourage serious study of the faith among Catholic students because, as *Newman News* put it at the time, the mind must have food, "not the shallow pablum so often passed off as learning, but the real, red meat of sound philosophy and science rooted in the rich soil of the Catholic heritage." A few of Illies' colleagues among the St. Cloud diocesan clergy offered their teaching services, and the abbot at St. John's University in neighboring Collegeville, Minnesota, willingly sent an impressive array of his Benedictine faculty members to St. Cloud in order to conduct weekly classes or present lectures on various theological topics, all gratis, of course, because the $2.00 annual dues that students were paying at the time to maintain their Newman membership did not accommodate the paying out of stipends. Yzermans also was

Illies and Yzermans put together the "Newman School of Religion" at St. Cloud State. Says one Newman alum of the Illies/Yzermans team: "Their spiritual leadership was intertwined with humorous antics and intellectual stimulation. The walls of Newman rang with it."

NEWMAN SCHOOL of RELIGION

FALL QUARTER 1963

"There is a knowledge worth possessing for what it is, and not merely for what it does."
— John Henry Newman

THE NEWMAN CENTER
385 First Avenue South
DIAL BL 1-3260

relentless in pursuing speakers of renown, some of whom would come to lecture at St. John's University in Collegeville or at the University of Minnesota in Minneapolis and then allow themselves to be persuaded to make an additional stop in St. Cloud. Numbered among this early parade of lecturers were such notables as English philosopher Martin D'Arcy, Swiss theologian Hans Küng, and the English

Two students chat with Martin D'Arcy.

author and philosopher Thomas Gilby, who delivered a lecture entitled, "Are Christians Really Neurotic and Proud of It?" Gilby attested that they ought to be, much to the delight of his audience. After presenting his lecture, Gilby agreed to remain in St. Cloud for four days in order to conduct the annual Newman Student Retreat. It was the appearance of stimulating scholars such as these that first began to draw people from the broader St. Cloud community to events sponsored by the St. Cloud Newman Club. As the years progressed, these sporadic visits became more formalized; some were jointly sponsored by the Newman Center and the diocesan paper, which Yzermans eventually edited, while others became part of an organized quarterly lecture series that evolved, offering a regular slate of thought-provoking speakers. Monsignor Luigi Ligutti was one such lecturer of particular note; a leading figure in the American church at the time, one of the founders of the National Catholic Rural Life Conference, the official Vatican representative to the United Nations Food and Agricultural Organization and an outspoken defender of the Church's social teachings, Ligutti both delighted and enlightened listeners with his challenging political and religious perspectives on the United Nations, and on the rights of the world's underdeveloped nations.

Walking a Balanced Path

"All work and no play makes Jack a dull boy" was an old but oft-repeated adage in this era, and the Newman Club took that adage to heart. Despite the concerted efforts being made to foster creative and transforming interactions between intellect and faith in the middle of the highway called the university, the St. Cloud Newman Club also worked to provide social opportunities for its members as well as academic ones. As the *Newman News* explained it, channeled social activity was the means the Newman Club used to form "complete Christian souls" in Catholic students, "not despising the things of this earth while all the time seeking after higher things." The October, 1954 edition of *Newman News* produced the following, rather charming report of the first "Freshman Mixer" held that year, presumably before the celebration of homecoming when first-year students were finally allowed to remove the green "beanies" which marked them off as novices:

A Newman Club volleyball game.

I don't care for hot-dogs, but I ate one anyway to keep from twiddling my thumbs for the first few minutes. I generously handed a hot-dog to the gal with the same ticket number as

All work and no play makes
Jack a dull boy!

mine—they were free, you know. It must have made her sick
for I didn't see her when the music started.

Then someone turned a few lights down, and those crazy
cats just about wore a hole in the dance floor. The music furnished by the slightly used record machine which was donated to us made for good dancing, and then some of the records
allowed us to rest and chat a while. Whenever someone
would stamp too hard on the floor, the needle would jump
back a little, but we all appreciate a gift, so there were few
complaints.

A few students venture on to
the dance floor during a
freshman mixer.

As the evening wears on, the dancing gets better, and so does the mixing.

The party lasted until about a quarter to eleven when most of the girls decided it was time to get back to the security of their house mothers. We all enjoyed ourselves immensely, and most of us are eager to have another mixer just like it. It's things like mixers, hayrides, along with our Communion Breakfasts and prayers that make a club want to work together, and it's a good feeling to know others are enjoying themselves because you're one of them.

Yzermans Helps to Make the Map

As time went on, the evolution of the St. Cloud State Newman Club under the direction of Illies and his "inspirator," Yzermans, was extraordinary, and the small, local club grew steadily into one of the best centers of Newman ministry in the nation. The stars came out and aligned themselves, and the Spirit was afoot. Yzermans became the editor of the St. Cloud diocesan paper, *The Visitor*, in 1958, and was not long after appointed director of the diocese's Bureau of Information. Thus it was that in addition to teaching classes, presiding at masses, giving talks himself and persuading others to come and speak to the Newman students on the St. Cloud State campus, Yzermans also provided the club with an abundance of positive press and positive attention. He submitted articles as well to religious journals like *Crosier*, where in 1958 he penned a glowing description, augmented by photos, of the work of the Newman Club at St. Cloud State College in Minnesota. "Like all other Newman Clubs," wrote Yzermans, "it knows that its work is missionary. Its members must become the apostles who will bring the knowledge of God, the love of Christ and the wisdom of the Church to all enrolled in a secular college." Constantly seeking to enhance and advance the image of Newman ministry among naysayers who still frowned at the thought of expending funds on college students enrolled in non-Catholic institutions, Yzermans displayed typical political savvy and journalistic persuasiveness as he crafted a caption for a photograph of a Newman Club dance which read:

> Soft music, a spacious floor, and dim lights. You have the makings of a dance. Newman Club seeks to provide the setting for a truly Christian dance. It frowns on rock 'n roll, it encourages a stag line, it advises getting home early and closes with prayers in common lead by the Chaplain.

Beyond his skill with the written word, however, Yzermans' own personal interest in the Newman movement and in the potential of campus ministry impelled him to become Wil's unofficial partner and unconditional supporter. One former Newman student, Sandy Banker, reflects today that Yzermans and Illies seemed to serve as one another's "alter egos." Yzermans was more outspoken than Illies, Banker remembers. His lectures and his way of convers-

Students work on *The Newman News*. Ed Pluth, a member of the Christ Church Newman community today, is second from right.

Students work hard preparing articles for *The Newman News*, the club's official newspaper. In the top photo, Sister Loyola provides some valuable lessons in technique. Below, from left to right, are Jan Lucier, Don Klarkowski, Pat Chmielewski, and Gerry Meyer. Seated is Judy Hartman.

ing were stimulating because he "told it the way it was" and "didn't pull any punches." Illies, on the other hand, was soft-spoken and "got you thinking" in more gentle ways. Yzermans was "always pushing," Illies himself remembers with affection, and he had incredibly ambitious ideas. The Newman Club's simple, bulletin-type newsletter, for example, had begun to take on new life in 1953 and 1954 under the leadership of editor-in-chief Mary Jo Vashro, and her associate editors Pat Flynn and Pat Jean Walker, who would later wed the club's treasurer in that era, Charles Ernst. Yzermans' interest in journalism moved him to spearhead the expansion of the newsletter into an authentic newspaper because he was convinced that "a good paper is a necessary medium of Catholic action." He organized a "Press Conference" for club members at which Sister Loyola (Jeannette) Klassen, OSB, from Cathedral High School and Mr. Thomas McKeown, publicity director at St. John's University, conducted instructional workshops. And then Yzermans went even farther: he personally purchased a used printing press that he thought would be of help in advancing the quality of the *Newman News*. It was beleagured and looked, "old enough to have printed *Poor Richard's Almanac*."[3] The press was affectionately named "the Monster" by Newman students who had quite a time moving the two-thousand-pound machine into Yzermans' basement. As the first issue of the

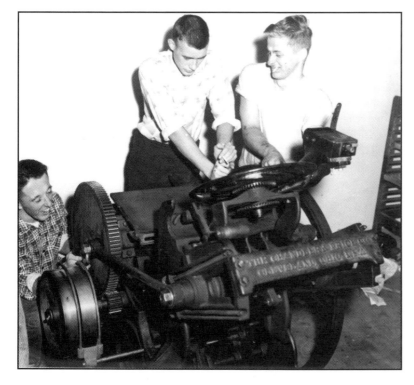

John Fandel, Bill Determan and Tom Herzing with "The Monster."

paper actually printed by the Monster described it, "after several baths in gasoline, lye, and water, the true character of the press was revealed—and it still didn't look very promising." By the winter of 1959, the newly-formatted paper was being sent to every Catholic student and faculty member at St. Cloud State College, and to every priest in the St. Cloud Diocese as well, in order to acquaint them with the work of the Newman movement on campus. Yzermans also pushed for the establishment of credible student publications in longer form, and thus it was that in 1954 student editors Joan Schmid and Sam St. Pierre guided the production of the Newman Club's very first annual which was christened *ERA*. It was an impressive piece of work; the annual's first edition focused on the work and thought of Cardinal John Henry Newman. It contained articles that flowed after much research and thought from the pens of twelve different students, and its editors expressed their heartfelt hope that many future writers would take it upon themselves to interpret Christian thought creatively in relation to the contemporary world. Newman Chaplain Wil Illies wrote in his introduction to the work:

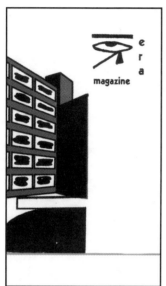

> I would like to make two observations concerning the contents of this annual. It is, to say the least, a striking coincidence that in these pages are delineated two points which both Father Yzermans and myself have been trying to propagate throughout the past year. The first of these is the necessity of religion, of theology, as an essential and radical part of any integral college curriculum. . . . The other point is that there is no contradiction between faith and reason but, rather, the two fit hand in glove; the former enlightening the latter and the latter aiding the former.

A second edition of the annual, entitled *Second Spring*, was published the following year under the editorship of Lynn Johnson. There then appears to have been a hiatus in publication until the annual's rebirth in 1961.

Annuals published by the St. Cloud Newman Club in 1954 and 1955.

The Newman Club's First Home:
A Castle With an Open Drawbridge and No Moat

Though there were obstacles to be faced and overcome, Wil Illies approached the challenge of building up of a credible, creative and vital Newman presence at St. Cloud State with unshakeable faith in the advice of Cardinal Newman himself, who once counseled that nothing would ever be done at all if we all waited until we could do it so well that no one could find fault with it. The atmosphere in both the St. Cloud Diocese and the larger Church at the time was also growing in openness to the dreams of those who believed in the power and the beauty of the Newman cause. Peter Bartholome left his coadjutor status behind after thirteen years and become the acting Bishop of the St. Cloud Diocese in 1953. Bartholome had a long history of contact with young people, and his interest in and commitment to Catholic education were well-established. While he never seemed to tire of warning college students at Newman meetings to beware of the dangers of "intellectual pride," he considered the young women and men at St. Cloud State to be his personal responsibility and was consistently supportive of efforts to expand and enlarge the Newman endeavor. As Illies remembers, even when times of controversy and disagreement emerged as the years progressed, and even when the Newman Center began to assert its identity and convictions in ways that sometimes produced discomfort in the diocese, Bartholome never allowed his Newman chaplain to feel alone or unsupported. At the end of every interaction, no matter how tense, Illies reports, Bartholome would always say, "You're doing a good job—I don't know how you do it." The St. Cloud bishop was not alone in his determination to support concrete action on behalf of Catholic college students studying at public universities. Leaders of the National Newman Foundation in this era openly acknowledged that the bishops of Minnesota and of North and South Dakota alike provided far more advanced leadership in Newman work than that which was operative in most other parts of the country. By 1963, in fact, the dioceses of these three northern plains states had built Newman foundations at all of their state universities and at several of their state colleges. Chaplains in the remaining schools carried out full programs for college students in parish or campus facilities.[4]

Though it was Bishop Joseph Busch who dreamed of building "our castle next to their castle," it is hardly surprising that students at the St. Cloud State Teachers College first came to have a place to call home during the tenure of Peter Bartholome and under the relentlessly energetic leadership of Will Illies and Vincent Yzermans. It certainly did not look much like a castle, and it had no moat because the guiders of the Newman movement in St. Cloud had always understood that protecting students from the challenges of the crossroads would only inhibit, not enhance, their growth as sound people of faith. But by the fall of 1956, a spacious home owned by a family named Megarry and located right on the edge of campus at 396 First Avenue South, had been purchased for $33,000 with the help of the members of St. Mary's Cathedral Parish. After spending most of that school year organizing, decorating and rearranging, Newmanites hosted an all-college open

The Megarry home (a.k.a. "The Brown House"), at 396 First Avenue South, that became "Newman Hall" in 1956. "I remember the housecleaning sessions during which everyone pitched in to mop floors, wash windows, do light maintenance work and any other chores that needed doing. Many hands made the work light, and we had a great time teasing each other and catching up on the latest happenings. I think it may have been at this time that some of the romances started. . . ."
—Joyce Warzecha Reding, '58.

Newman Hall Opens Doors To Catholic TC Students

Serves Cause of Christ On Secular Campus

NEWMAN CLUB IS A CATHOLIC ORGANIZATION established for Catholic students attending secular colleges and universities.

The Club takes its name from its patron, John Henry Cardinal Newman. Newman was chosen because of his intimate associations with university life during his days at Oxford University in England and because of his efforts by word and pen to foster the cause of Christ and the Catholic Church in the field of higher education.

Toward the end of the nineteenth century the plight of Catholic students attending secular colleges was becoming a major problem for the Church in the United States. Up to that time Catholic students had no opportunity to associate with fellow Catholic students, nor was theirs the chance to supplement their secular learning with the spiritual, intellectual and social heritage of their Faith. The need for a Catholic Club was first realized in a practical way at the University of Pennsylvania in 1892 when it formed such a Catholic Club under the patronage of Cardinal Newman. During the following decades the movement spread until in 1915 when many of these local clubs in the East formed the Federation of Catholic Clubs. In 1928 this Federation

the middle twenties with the appointment of the Reverend T. Leo Keaveny as its first chaplain by the Most Reverend Joseph F. Busch, Bishop of Saint Cloud. Throughout the following years Father Keaveny was succeeded by the Reverends Michael Kraemer, Ferdinand Falque, Leonard Galts, Frederick Kampsen, Paul Zylla, Harold Kost, John Laky, and the present chaplain, Wilfred Illies.

In 1925 the Newman Club here received its first faculty advisors in the persons of Miss Agnes Kerlin and Miss Marguerite McBride. They were succeeded in the following years by Miss Pauline Penning, Miss Robert, Mr. John Weisman, Miss Walsh, Mr. Colletti, Miss Kolb, Mr. Lynch, Mr. Donnelly, Mr. Richard Meinz, Miss Mary Louise Petersen, and Mr. Robert Wick.

The purpose of the Newman Club is to be a center of Catholic culture, learning and fraternity by fostering the spiritual, intellectual and social interests of its members. It has been chosen by the Church in America to supplement secular education with the spiritual values taught by the Church which alone are capable of bringing salvation to our troubled world. For Catholic students who take advantage of its facilities the Newman Club is a fountain of grace and a source

THIS IS NEWMAN HALL. It stands at 396 First Avenue South in Saint Cloud, overlooking the Mississippi River. It is within easy reach of the Saint Cloud Teachers College. For some 700 Catholic students at the College this is their spiritual home. **NEWMAN HALL IS THE HEARTLINE OF THE NEWMAN CLUB.** From this building will radiate the intellectual, social, and spiritual activities of Mass. Newman Hall is more than a building. It is a home, a spiritual fortress, a quiet haven where Catholic students can find the calm and peace and intellectual conviction born of a lively faith in Christ and His Church. **NEWMAN HALL IS A MANY-SIDED BUILDING.** As you open the door you are ushered into a large vestibule which immediately tells you the purpose of this the students. Many colored lamps give it a warm glow, magazines are spread about on tables and the statue of Mary over the fireplace reminds one that Mary is the Seat of Wisdom. The kitchen, used for some social functions, separates the lounge from the library. In the library two walls lined with the best in Catholic reading, the spirit of silence and the presence of desks and house so that club members could show off the new facility and the fruits of their labors. It was a grand accomplishment to have a real "Hall" and official meeting place, a building from which could, as the Newman Club paper expressed it at the time, "radiate the intellectual, social and spiritual activities throughout the school year that will make every Catholic student proud of the historical fact that Holy Mother Church is the Mother of Learning." The verbiage created to describe this exciting development was grandiose and far-reaching. The paper went on to predict with confidence that

> to this building hundreds of Catholic students will come during the year seeking consultation with a priest of God, companionship with fellow Catholics, answers to the problems and questions that will arise during the course of their maturing process. To this building many students will find their way in the early hours of the morning seeking the Life of their lives in the Holy Eucharist that will be broken and fed them at the morning Sacrifice of the Mass.

Newman Hall did, in fact, come to serve as a true spiritual home for many Catholic students who approached its doors between 1957 and 1963 and followed the instructions on the sign which hung there: "Don't knock. Walk right in." While few pictures survive of the building's interior, *Newman News* early on offered a description which captures some sense of its "feel":

> As you open the door, you are ushered into a large vestibule which immediately tells you the purpose of this home. On one

Two students visit in the lounge at Newman Hall. Note the statue of Mary on the mantle of the fireplace.

Wil Illies distributes Communion during a week-day Mass held in the second-floor chapel of Newman Hall.

wall is a large crucifix, on another is a large portrait of Cardinal Newman, and on the staircase the certificate of the federation with the National Federation of Newman Clubs. As you turn to your left you enter a large, paneled room which serves as the lounge for the students. Many colored lamps give it a warm glow, magazines are spread about on tables and the statue of Mary over the fireplace reminds one that Mary is the Seat of Wisdom. The kitchen, used for some social functions, separates the lounge from the library. In the library two walls lined with the best in Catholic reading, the spirit of silence and the presence of desks and reading tables reminds one that the life of a truly Catholic student is one of scholarship. Off the library is the Reverend Chaplain's office on one side and a classroom on the other.

The heart of Newman Hall is on the second floor. There, in a long, rectangular room overlooking the River is the Chapel where Christ in the Blessed Sacrament of the Altar remains as the Friend Guide and Enlightener of the Catholic student. Furnished simply, in the best of Catholic taste, the Chapel recalls that the Church is the Mother and Patron of the arts. Across from the Chapel are the private living quarters of the Chaplain.

Wil Illies reflected years later that it was probably the experience of the daily, half-hour mass in that simple, second-floor chapel that first sparked student interest in liturgy, gave them an authentic experience of Christian community, and inspired them to want to move toward more active involvement in the prayer of the Church.

In the fall of 1957, Bishop Bartholome relieved Wil Illies of his other pastoral duties and named him the full-time chaplain of the St. Cloud Newman Club. He thus became the first person to be given both the opportunity, and the responsibility, to devote exclusive energy to Newman ministry in the St. Cloud Diocese. Prayer and worship opportunities were expanded; in addition to the daily eucharistic liturgies held upstairs in the Newman Hall chapel, novena devotions and compline were scheduled every Monday evening. An annual retreat, replete with conferences on various aspect of the spiritual life, the celebration of a High Mass and a corporate communion breakfast took place each year on Palm Sunday, and quarterly Eucharistic Days with exposition of the Blessed Sacrament were held. The climactic spiritual event of each school year soon became the celebration of an outdoor, Baccalaureate Mass for all Catholic graduates and their parents, celebrated on the lawn of Newman Hall, right on the banks of the River of the Holy Spirit.

The 1962 Newman Student Retreat held at St. Mary's Crypt Church in St. Cloud. Tom Pluth reads to the group during dinner. Mothers of Newman Club members prepared the meal. About one hundred students participated in the retreat.

A Baccalaureate Mass held on the grassy banks of the Mississippi, right outside of Newman Hall.

More Sound Food for the Mind

As the spiritual pieces of the Newman mission in St. Cloud multiplied and grew after Illies' full-time appointment, so did its educational endeavors. In 1957, Benedictine sister Loyola (Jeannette) Klassen came on board as the Newman librarian, having just finished a new degree and ready to tackle the challenge of creating a real library for Newman students in addition to fulfilling her teaching duties at Cathedral High School. Doing so involved quite a weeding process, Klassen remembers; in its infant stage the library contained a conglomerate of donated works from priests' libraries and area schools, and it was typical for the young librarian to encounter gross errors in cataloguing. St. Augustine's spiritual masterpiece, *City of God*, for example, had been filed under "Urban Development." To Klassen was left the task of sorting, selecting, and arranging so that a decent and accessible core selection of

54

Students making use of the library at Newman Hall.

solid, Catholic literature could be established. By 1958, the Newman Hall library had grown tremendously as a result of generous donations from organizations and individuals and contained over five-hundred volumes, carefully chosen and catalogued by Sister Loyola. Thirty-nine published periodicals were also available. By 1962, the collection had grown to 2,519 and included forty-four books by Cardinal Newman and twenty-one about him, in part because Wil Illies made an effort to write to seminaries in the region and request duplicates of any Newman works that might be gathering dust on their shelves. When the new Newman Center was built in 1964, its library space included a separate "Newman Room" where all Newman works were to be housed; the long-term goal was to have that room showcase all works presently in print or previously available, by or about the Center's patron, John Henry Newman. The Newman Room remained in existence until it was converted into a "Prayer Room" in the 1970s, and the Newman collection was integrated into the main body of the library. While most of its volumes were works of philosophy or theology, the Newman Hall library also housed some biographies, fictional works, and books on "psychology, marriage, and vocations."

By the early 1960s, a student Board of Education was overseeing other components of the club's educational efforts, including a well-organized slate of classes and lectures held weekly at Newman Hall. In the fall quarter of 1960, for example, students could choose to attend a Monday evening class on "Scholastic Philosophy" with Vincent Yzermans instructing, or pursue "Instructions in the Catholic Faith," led by Wilfred Illies. If Tuesday evening proved a more convenient time, David Rieder was available then to offer a basic course

Textbook used by students taking "Modern Moral Problems" in the fall of 1961. The class met at 8:00 P.M. on Tuesday evenings and was taught by Columba Enright, T.O.R.

Outlines of
MORAL THEOLOGY

FRANCIS J. CONNELL, C.SS.R., S.T.D., LL.D.

in "Christian Theology." When winter quarter arrived, Monday evenings featured, "A Modern Approach to the Bible," taught by Daniel Taufen, and "Catholic Morality in the Modern World," offered by Columba Enright from Cathedral High School. Eventually, the academic programming proffered at Newman Hall came to be marketed in quarterly brochures as the "Newman School of Religion." Apparently, however, it was sometimes as much of a challenge to persuade large numbers of students to register for such classes in the

An evening spent at Newman Hall in enlightening and lively discussion.

1950s as it is to draw large numbers of students to many campus-ministry sponsored activities today. *Newman News* in the late 1950s is filled with regular articles, usually written by student members themselves, which scold the inactive masses for failing to make the time to come and learn about the riches of their Catholic heritage. One such article avers sarcastically that "we sympathize wholeheartedly with your lack of time to attend. Three hours a day must be devoted to card playing, and then there is the meeting of the 'Tappa-Kega-Bier Fraternity' in the evenings which are by far more important." "Where are you?" asks another pointed editorial. "Out of nine hundred Catholic students on this campus, only six of you think enough of our faith to come to a class on Church History . . . what is the matter with the rest of us?" The inactive masses must have suffered at least some twinges of guilt, or perhaps had their interest piqued; by the early 1960s class attendance was on the rise and twenty-five or more students would typically fulfill the requirements for a given course. Illies

Official club membership card and registration form, 1961-1962.

NEWMAN CLUB - ST. CLOUD STATE COLLEGE
PLEASE PRINT

NAME _____
Last   First   Middle

Parent's Name _____
Home Address _____
Street
_____ Phone No. _____
City   State
School Address _____
_____ Phone No. _____
City   State

Single	Married	Male	Female	Age	Class	Student
					Fr. Soph. Jr. Sr. Grad.	P.O. #

1. Can you help us with one or more of the following?
☐ Choir
☐ Library
☐ Workers & Marthas
☐ Gospel Readers
☐ Basketball
☐ Bowling
☐ Baby Sitting
☐ Blood Donors
☐ Servers
☐ Children's Home

2. Can you take one of our Classes?
Yes ☐ No ☐
Home Parish _____
Pastor _____

Date Paid _____
Received by _____
Amount _____

continued to work hard at promoting and advancing responsible study of the faith. In 1962, he submitted a strongly worded open letter to the diocesan paper addressed to all parents and pastors, appealing to them to urge the young women and men in their charge to enroll in the courses offered by Newman upon their arrival at the St. Cloud State campus. Pastoral care is primary in our mission, he wrote, but education is the unique reason for our existence on the secular campus; the very core of the Newman program is rounding out our students' college educations with religious knowledge and expertise so that they do not leave campus after four years being theologically illiterate. Illies did not exaggerate when he declared that the St. Cloud Newmanites had dared to fashion the most ambitious education program in the history of local Newman work, and had developed an adaptable but sturdy curricula taught by a reputable "faculty" including priests and sisters of the St. Cloud diocese and faculty members like Michael Marx, Colman Barry, and Ernest Kilzer from St. John's University. Illies' appeals bore fruit; that fall, two-hundred eighty-three students registered for at least one of the varied selection of courses offered in fundamental theology, sacred music, scripture, Christian social thought, philosophy, church history, Newman and his writings, Christian marriage, and the lay apostolate.

"Those Who Sing Well, Pray Twice"

Music also has a noble history within the St. Cloud Newman movement and the fundamental link between music and liturgy was recognized on the banks of the Mississippi long before the learning, serving and praying community which grew up there had a place of its

own in which to worship. The highly talented Harold Pavelis, who was the Director of Sacred Music for the Diocese of St. Cloud, established the "Newman Singers" in 1955. Pavelis held auditions for the forty-five-voice choir in the fall, and then divided the group into two choirs for weekday High Masses at Newman Hall. In addition to singing at these regularly scheduled High Masses and Monday night devotions, the choir usually made a series of special appearances at places like St. Mary's Cathedral, the St. Cloud Hospital and Children's Home, St. John's University, the College of St. Benedict and a few local churches in St. Cloud. The choir also combined at least once with the Newman Choir of the University of Minnesota to sing a Pontifical

Harry Pavelis rehearses members of the Newman choir.

Choir members and their leaders after singing High Mass for Station KCMT, Alexandria, Minnesota.

59

High Mass, and for several years sang High Mass over station KCMT, Channel 7, in Alexandria, Minnesota, on a regular basis. The Newman Choir established itself early on as an integral part of the liturgical life of Newman Hall and of St. Cloud; it not only gave Catholic students at St. Cloud State the opportunity to sing great Catholic music, but also enabled them to become aware of the Church's contributions to spiritual and cultural life through the art of music. It is interesting that while attendance at classes and educational events always went through ups and downs, Pavelis reported in those years that choir members were "superbly faithful" in attending rehearsals and masses.[5]

A Very Busy Intersection

By the early 1960s, the Newman movement on the banks of the Mississippi River was flourishing. The magic continued to unfold, the stars remained in alignment, and the seeds planted early on by Illies and Yzermans began to blossom with beauty and grace. The drawbridge of the castle was bustling with traffic as students crossed back and forth between the worlds that human shortsight-edness had separated into the "sacred" and the "secular," and began to learn in ever-more compelling ways that the wall of separation was thin and transparent. Numbers only scratch the surface and do not come close to telling the whole story, but it is significant to note that a self-report filled out in 1962 by the St. Cloud Newman Club records 415 dues-paying members—a number representing about one-third of all Catholic students present on campus at the time. Newman membership at St. Cloud State College in that year ranked tenth in the nation. Average attendance at general club meetings was about one hundred-sixty, and it was not uncommon for more than one hundred students to show up at

"I remember the smell of Polish sausage and sauer-kraut when Father Illies would make supper, and, usually, there was someone joining him for supper and a game of cribbage (I think it was cribbage). His hearty laughter could be heard before you got in the house."
—Mary Lou Dupre Allison, '64

60

A Parents' Day gathering held at St. Mary's Cathedral in St. Cloud, 1962.

social functions like the annual semi-formal dance. By the time the third annual "Parents' Day" was held in St. Cloud, more than five hundred parents journeyed to the campus in order to learn more about the Newman organization of which their daughters and sons had become a part. If she or he so desired, a Catholic student at St. Cloud State College could fill nearly every night of the week with Newman activity. By 1963, Mass was being celebrated twice daily at the Newman Center, at noon and at 4:45 P.M., and once on Saturday. In addition to the full and varied slate of classes on Monday and Tuesday evenings, Newman students could also choose to come to Newman Choir rehearsals on Tuesday evenings, and on Wednesday show up at the St. Cloud Hospital to donate

Newman club members, Dale and Carol Smith, enjoy becoming parents for the first time.

blood, or, if appropriate, at Newman Hall to attend a Married Couples Meeting. General club meetings took place every other Thursday and frequently included presentations by international students present on campus, missionaries from around the globe, and political figures like the administrative assistant to Senator Eugene McCarthy. On any one of three evenings each week, Newmanites could also choose to go to the

61

Missionary Matt Menger (above) speaks to Newman members about his work.

The Newman Married Couples group (above right), which met each Wednesday at 7:30 p.m. Wil Illies directed the group.

Newman "Marthas" were always hard at work. Here, Mary Pat Lerschen gives directions in the kitchen.

Early morning coffee is served up for Wil Illies and Art Yzermans. No more dedicated housekeepers could possibly be found than Ellen Winkelman and Agathe Feldhege, who served the Newman community for seven and twenty-one years respectively.

St. Cloud Children's Home to assist the Franciscan sisters in their supervision of the children's study and recreation, and at least once a week could offer their services at St. Margaret's School for Retarded Children. Young men with muscles could volunteer to be "Newman Workers" who helped with the maintenance of Newman Hall. They were also invited to be servers at daily Mass and devotions, or to read the Epistle at mass. Young women at this time, however, were still excluded from any activity taking place in the sanctuary and so were invited to become "Newman Marthas," who helped Mrs. Ellen Winkelman with the cleaning of Newman Hall. A Newman Basketball Team was formed for those interested in intramural sports on campus, and the "Newman Bowlers" was a

Carol Conoryea, Lynn Johnson, and Mary Jo Vashro take aim during a Newman bowling night in 1954.

group open to all wishing to participate in "reasonable, wholesome recreation." In the winter of 1959, Wil Illies of the "Holy Rollers" was the top bowler in the league with a high score of 172, followed closely by Joe Renn of the "Gutter Cutters" and Joe Glatzmaier of the "Klunks." Apparently, a group of "Newman Lettermen" were even organized by Wil Illies in 1959 and raised funds from their activities so that a Newman athletic scholarship could be awarded to a prominent Catholic high school athlete who wished to attend college.

A thought-provoking *Newsweek* article, written around the time that Wil Illies took over direction of the St. Cloud State Newman Club in 1953, contended that when the religious element of a culture is absent, or is neutralized to the point of ineffectiveness, a sort of social schizophrenia results that divides the very soul of society between an amoral will to power and a reactionary religious idealism that has no real capacity to influence human life.[6] While symptoms of such a schizophrenia seem to abound today more acutely than ever, those moored most authentically in the legacy of John Henry Newman knew well from that start that such debilitating divisions could be healed and overcome. If on the bustling highways that are university campuses, faith and intellect were allowed to cross over and do commerce with one another daily and freely, both would grow gradually into an ever more refined capacity to speak meaningfully to the future of the human community. Being steeped in that conviction, the leaders of the Newman apostolate in St. Cloud found themselves particularly distressed when, in 1960, the use of one of the National Newman Club Federation's publications caused an unexpected stir on the campus of St. Cloud State College. Many students and faculty took offense at a flyer distributed during the club's membership drive entitled *Broad Minded or Flatheaded?* which asked if students felt they were receiving too much education in natural sciences to the neglect of religious education and formation. The flyer was perceived by some as an anti-intellectual attack on the academic endeavors of the college and Newmanites flinched under the accusation; nothing could be farther from the truth, and the club's leaders felt they had to respond quickly, which they did by publishing a brochure entitled *For This We Stand*. The brochure was subsequently circulated to all Catholic students, to the college administration, and to the majority of the faculty; it was both lengthy and carefully crafted and began by reviewing the record of the St. Cloud Newman Club as a medium of intellectual exchange whose classes, lectures, library, and publications had never been used as "house organs" that refused to admit varying viewpoints. The Newman movement did not seek to proselytize or to set Catholic students apart from other students or from the college. Wil Illies declared on more than one occasion: "I consider myself neither an insulator nor an ecclesiastical babysitter." The Newman movement and its chaplain desired, rather, to provide specific religious information not otherwise available and to encourage students to integrate both Church and campus responsibilities in their lives. *For This We Stand* went on to clarify its charge that education is incomplete if too much emphasis is placed on "practical courses" and not enough on liberal education and religious development. John Henry Newman was quoted at length in order to underline the Newman philosophy of allowing the intellect to range with utmost freedom in the crossroads environment that is the university, but also of insisting that religion can and should enjoy the same kind of freedom, because authentic faith never shackles reason but frees it, opening it to new dimensions of reality that it would be incapable of knowing otherwise. In an atmosphere of mutual respect, faith and knowledge can interact constructively, broaden one another's horizons and contribute to the foundation of an education for young women and men that is whole and complete. Almost three years later, a guest speaker sponsored by the Inter-Religious Council on campus would echo these sentiments in a powerful way. Harold Schilling, not a minister but a professor of physics, appeared in both Stewart and Brown Halls and declared boldly that most people who reject religion do so because they have never studied the subject and have never moved beyond childish, Sunday-school apprehensions of what religious knowledge is all about. "If people were as ignorant in general about science as most of them are relative to religion they would be thoroughly ashamed," said Schilling in an interview. The physicist went on to declare that if science and religion find them-

Wil Illies interviews Harold Schilling.

selves at one another's throats, there is something wrong with us, not with the truth, because truth cannot be divided.

As Newman ministry under the deft guidance of Wil Illies continued to expand, Catholic students at the St. Cloud Beauty School and Business College were given the opportunity to become active members of the Newman movement. An interesting sign of improved Catholic and non-Catholic school cooperation in this era was the "Catholic Student Social Council" that was established, made up of student representatives from St. John's University in Collegeville, Minnesota, the College of St. Benedict in St. Joseph, Minnesota, St. Cloud State College, and the Nursing School in St.

Yet another mixer (right), held at St. Mary's Cathedral.

Which one is the trophy?

Cloud who together planned joint social activities for Catholic students from these four institutions of higher learning. In addition to the social space at Newman Hall, local assemblage places like Talahi Lodge, the St. Cloud Institute building, Wilson Park, and Sportsman's Island on the Mississippi were used for such gatherings. It was through that joint social council that Wil Illies and a student named Ludmilla Paternos from the College of St. Benedict first came to know one another; Ludmilla, or "Mil," would eventually marry Francis Voelker from St. John's University and the couple would become lifelong friends of Illies, and lifelong members of

66

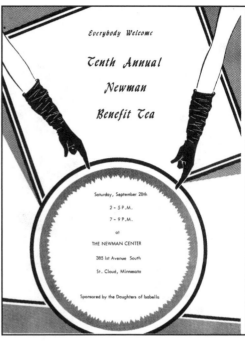

Everybody Welcome

Tenth Annual

Newman

Benefit Tea

Saturday, September 28th

2 – 5 P.M.

7 – 9 P.M.

at

THE NEWMAN CENTER

385 1st Avenue South

St. Cloud, Minnesota

Sponsored by the Daughters of Isabella

Bishop Bartholome (top, left) with some of the organizers of the first Daughters of Isabella Tea held to benefit the Newman Club in 1954.

Selling brooms (below) door-to-door for the cause.

the Newman community through all of its many stages of evolution. In those early days, however, some long-standing prejudices still persisted. Illies recalls that his sister, who was a nursing student in St. Cloud at the time, was informed that if she went out on a date with a boy from St. John's, her curfew would be at one o'clock in the morning. If she chose to go out with a St. Cloud State student, however, she would need to return by midnight.

All of this activity required funding of course; while the dues paid by students supplied some of the necessary monies to keep the club solvent, from 1954 onward the Daughters of Isabella faithfully held an annual "Tea" in support of Newman needs and the Knights of Columbus made regular donations. Yzerman's abilities as a natural promoter were often invaluable in this regard, and it was around this time, as well, that Wil Illies inaugurated "The Century Club," an invitation to Newman alums to contribute one hundred dollars to the work of the Newman Apostolate over a five-year period. Newmanites themselves would frequently do public relations presentations to local groups like "Christian Mothers" and "Legion of Mary" associations, and would peddle wares like candy and brooms on campus and in the community in order to earn a few extra dollars for the cause. In the early 1960s, the Newman Club sponsored one of its more original fund-raising efforts: the sale of "Campus-Pacs," a practical assortment of nationally advertised products for men like "Cepacol" mouthwash, "Fitch" shampoo, "Mixture No. 79" tobacco and "Old Spice" after-shave lotion, all for the bargain price of thirty-five cents. Most notably, as the years progressed an admirably cooperative rather than competitive spirit seems to have emerged in the St. Cloud area among those committed to the well-being of Catholic college students in either pri-

Washing cars for the cause, *circa* 1959.

vate or public schools; the members of the St. John's University Men's Chorus, in fact, more than once performed a benefit concert for the needs of their Catholic peers at St. Cloud State. For a number of years the club also worked diligently to pull together an annual Christmas pageant which evolved under the impetus of Art Yzermans' desire to restore the medieval mystery play tradition. After 1951, the pageant was held at St. Mary's Cathedral and was

The annual Christmas pageant at St. Mary's Cathedral.

considered the Newman Club's way of expressing gratitude and appreciation to the members of the various organizations and societies in St. Cloud who had willingly assisted them throughout the year. The pageant involved between fifty and seventy-five students cast as shepherds, angels, wise men, prophets, and women of the village, and it invariably evoked the participation of several area choirs. Through it all, Newman's own choir was skillfully guided by the familiar words of Harry Pavelis: "Sound out your words. Sopranos, you're too weak. Let's have more volume. Now let's try again."[7]

Meeting Up with Other Travelers

Perhaps because of their heart-felt conviction that living well as the Church in a crossroads environment like the university campus required the inspiration of a well-developed theology and a well-grounded vision, Illies and Yzermans worked diligently at connecting their local Newman efforts to the broader Newman movement around the country. They peddled subscriptions to the *National Newman News* and submitted stories to it for publication; they encouraged students to study, read and make use of materials coming out of the national office, and they regularly took bus and car loads of students to province and national conventions where developments in the Newman vision were honed and shared, even

When a group of Newmanites "went south" to Albuquerque for a national convention, the excursion made headlines.

Baccalaureate Mass Set For Sunday

Mass and Sermon for Graduates on Newman Hall Lawn at 11:00

Vol VI--No. 11   St. Cloud, Minnesota, Wednesday, May 20, 1959

National Convention Goes South

Aug. 31-Sept. 5

Ed Pluth

On to Albuquerque—that's the cry of the conventioneers at Newman Hall nowadays. The occasion is the 45th annual convention of the National Newman Club Federation to be held at the University of New Mexico in Albuquerque from August 31 to September 5.

Albuquerque is in the northern part of New Mexico, approximately 62 miles south of Santa Fe and in the valley of the Rio Grande River. It is the state's largest city with a population of 177,000. For those who have a historical interest in the West there are Indian pueblos located near Albuquerque along with other important monuments. Nearby also are beautiful mountain ranges where fishing, hunting, sightseeing and picnicking facilities can be utilized. The scenery in the moun-

CATHOLIC GRADUATES will start baccalaureate Sunday with Mass celebrated by Father Illies on the lawn of Newman Hall. Pictured above are students, parents

Sunday, May 24, has been set as Baccalaureate Sunday for graduates at State College.

Two years ago the College adopted the plan of having Baccalaureate Sunday celebrated in the various churches. According to President Budd and others concerned, this plan appears to have been a successful arrangement.

Newman always tries to make this a very special day for all the Catholic Graduates of the past year. As usual this year there will be an outdoor Mass at 11:00 a.m. All graduates receiving their diplomas after Spring of '58 are invited. The parents and friends of the graduates and the Catholic faculty members have also been invited. There are approximately 130 Catholic graduates.

This is the third consecutive year for the outdoor Mass. Traditionally Father Illies will again give the Baccalaureate sermon. When asked to comment Father Illies said, "I feel that this is one job I always want to reserve for myself. I always look forward to the occasion. I appreciate the opportunity to give the graduates this final send off with my best wishes and blessings. I want to congratulate all the graduates. As I observe them and bid them ave atque vale. I really feel that, despite contrary opinion, this generation is still able to die for good causes, and there are plenty of good causes left. My wish for them is they will leave college with eyes wide open to the Apostolic realities which many of their peers have either forgotten or ignored."

The Newman Singers, directed by Father Pavelis, will sing the Proper of Trinity Sunday in Gregorian psalm tones, and the Ordinary from Hassler's **Missa Secunda**. Cesar Franck's **Dextera Domini** will be sung as the offertory motet, and Mozart's **Ave Verum** at the Communion. Cardinal Newman's hymn **Lead, Kindly Light** will be the processional. Vittoria's **Et incarnatus** will be sung during Credo III.

The graduates are asked to meet at Newman Hall in time to form in procession before the Mass. They are also requested to please wear their caps and gowns.

After Mass coffee and rolls will be served

Trips to places near and far— together. Whether the road stretched all the way to Denver, Colorado (right), or only to Fargo, North Dakota (above, right), memories of laughter shared, friendships forged, and horizons broadened along the way were enough to last a lifetime.

as far away from home as Detroit, Michigan, Albuquerque, New Mexico, and Denver, Colorado. In the spring before the scheduled trip to the Albuquerque convention, *Newman News* reported with excitement that for the very reasonable fee of forty-eight dollars, students would be entitled to room and board for six days on the University of New Mexico campus as well as to participation in all convention activities and all of the planned social programming for the week, including a day at a ranch in the mountains and a show in the city featuring some top Hollywood performers whose names were still a secret at the time registrations were being taken.

It was, of course, these longer trips on which students embarked with Illies and Yzermans, who was notorious for his crazy driving, that are the ones most replete with retrospective enthusiasm and memories of laughter shared, friendships forged, insights discovered, and horizons broadened. It was the regional gatherings held closer to home, however, that became the locus of growing recognition for the ever-more vibrant St. Cloud organization. The list of tributes is long and telling. During a province convention held in LaCrosse, Wisconsin, for example, St. Cloud Newman Club President Sanford (Sandy) Banker was elected to the very important post of Province Chairman for the 1955-1956 school year. Gerald Meyer would serve as Vice-Chairman of Internal Affairs for the province just a few years later. Forty-two Newmanites attended the annual province convention in Fargo, North Dakota, in the spring of 1959. There the St. Cloud Newman Club, in recognition of its efforts to bring students into more vital contact with the ideals of John Henry Newman, received the district award for outstanding achievement in the area of a religious-educational program. At that same convention, St. Cloud's Margaret Fantini, a senior from Stillwater, Minnesota, received the "Miss Newmanite Award" and was thus recognized as the most outstanding female Newman Club member in all of the colleges from the tri-state area of North and South Dakota and Minnesota. Illies himself was reelected the district chaplain in Fargo; he was also serving in the important post of National Secretary of the National Newman Club Chaplains' Association at the time, assisting his good friend George Garrelts who guided the Newman movement at the nearby

The 1960 Minnkota Province Convention held in St. Cloud. At bottom, left, two students perform at the Saturday night variety show. Below, George Garrelts preaches, and (bottom) Vern Bartos burns up the dance floor at the semi-formal dance.

Student Gerald Meyer calls the 1960 convention to order.

At right, the Newman Choir practices for the convention Masses.

University of Minnesota and was the National Chaplain of the Federation. "George was the idea man," Illies recalls, "I was the practical German guy who helped to get things done." One year later, in 1960, the St. Cloud Newman Club hosted the Minnkota Province Convention, a significant occurrence because St. Cloud,

with its diocesan prohibition against dancing on Saturday evenings, was not a very popular choice for regional gatherings and a talent show had to be scheduled in place of the usual Saturday night fling. About three hundred and fifty Newman Club delegates as well as twenty chaplains and faculty advisors from thirty-five different Newman Clubs in the province attended the two-day convention, chaired by student Gerald Meyer. The Newman Choir premiered a series of Cardinal Newman's prayers set to music especially for them by Norman Dello Joio, eminent New York City composer. They were sung before and after all the Masses celebrated during

Wil Illies applauds convention speaker William Durkin, Newman chaplain at North Dakota State University. Sister Loyola Klassen, OSB, looks on.

Wil Illies greets the parents of Shirley Leither during Newman's "Parents' Day" at St. Cloud State.

Students work frantically to serve food at the 1960 Convention Banquet.

the convention, in a unison setting intended for congregrational singing. At a Minnkota convention in 1962, the club received the province's "External Affairs Award," Margaret Lee was named Miss Newmanite of the province, and the St. Cloud club's efforts in establishing "Parent's Day" at St. Cloud State were rewarded with the "Outstanding Club Project Award." In the fall of that year, the club won one of three national awards given in educational programming and received kudos and one hundred dollars worth of Catholic books donated by leading Catholic publishers for providing the "Best Educational Program on Newman, his life and his

Dan Taufen, right, receives a Newman Honor Key from Art Yzermans at a Newman Awards Banquet.

Miss and Mr. Newmanite, 1963. They were Julie Schneider and Clarence Mrosla.

Dick Hess (above) jokes with another award recipient, Gerry Meyer.

works." What's more, at the 1963 National Newman Convention held in Lafayette, Louisiana, St. Cloud State proudly received the award for having the "Outstanding Large Club Education Program" in the nation during the 1962-1963 school year.

The group of 1963 Newman Honor Key recipients (top, right). One awardee says today, "I still hold that key in high regard, as highly as I hold my B.S. degree." Newman secretary, Connie Kolbeck (Umerski) stands at center.

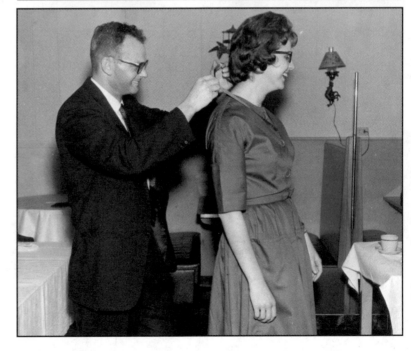

Barbara Svela receiving her Newman Honor Key from Jerry Kapsner.

Certificates were awarded annually to all students completing a required number of courses in the Newman School of Religion.

In addition to fostering broad-based connections and understandings through regional and national gatherings, Illies and Yzermans also tied the St. Cloud Newman Club into the whole structure of "awards" designed by the national office to affirm college students for various levels of commitment to the Newman apostolate. Each year, the Newman Club Executive Board made up of the elected officers and their chaplain, selected winners of a Junior Mr. and a Junior Miss Newmanite Award, a Certificate of Merit, the Newman Coat of Arms Award, the regular Mr. and Miss Newmanite Award, and the highest national honor awarded each year on the local level, the John Henry Newman Honor Key. Recipients of the Honor Key not only were required to have promoted the interest of the St. Cloud State Newman Club, the Minnkota Province and the National Newman Club Federation, they must also have brought greater honor to the name of Cardinal John Henry Newman through their lives and work in the club and on campus. Certificates for all students having successfully completed a required number of courses in the Newman School of Religion were also awarded annually.

The Castle Walls Become Too Confining

In 1962, St. Cloud Newmanites were able to win a new stereo for club use in a campus contest between student organizations to see who could collect the largest number of empty cigarette packages. The addition of the stereo, however, wasn't enough to transform

The empty cigarette packages that won a stereo for the Newman Club.

Art and Barb Grachek on their wedding day in 1964. According to legend, Barb once thought of joining the convent but was dissuaded by Illies, who told her, "Svela, you'll never make it in the nunnery unless they can guarantee you a Mother Superiorship from the start!"

Newman Hall into an adequate facility for the future. In the years following its grand opening, traffic within and around the walls of the house at 396 First Avenue South had increased steadily. It became apparent over time that the space was too small to meet the ever-expanding vision of the club and its active membership. Art Yzermans and Wil Illies began to campaign for the construction of a larger facility. Wherever and whenever the opportunity arose, Illies wrote about how the enrollment at St. Cloud State was expected to top 8,000 by 1970, which meant that a virtual army of at least 2,600 Catholic students would be present who represented many of the Church's future leaders and who deserved ample opportunity for religious care and spiritual development. He emphasized what he perceived to be an urgent need for enlarged meeting and classroom facilities, and spoke convincingly of how deep the need was for a real chapel in which to celebrate Sunday masses and provide for more profound pastoral care of college students. Newman "Martha" Barbara Svela, who would later wed the club's 1960-1961 vice-president, Arthur Grachek, now confesses that when she and other Marthas cleaned and dusted in the Newman Hall room used to hear confessions, they would often add a click or two to the counter used to keep track of statistics for the diocese in order to push up the numbers of recorded penitents and impress the diocese with the widespread spiritual hunger of Newman students.

The early 1960s was a "brick-and-mortar" period for the Catholic Church in America, but the building of new churches and Catholic schools was usually still prioritized, even though the Newman movement had steadily been gaining acceptance among the American hierarchy.[8] The baby boom, however, which had swelled birthrates since 1947, as well as the rise in percentages of young people pursuing higher education, were rapidly creating a situation in which the ever-increasing numbers of college-aged Catholics could not possibly be accommodated by existing Catholic institutions of higher learning, even if all of those students had both the means and the desire to pursue admittance to their doors. By 1960, furthermore, Newman chaplains around the country had begun to ease off a bit from that promotion of schemes for formal religious instruction that had dominated their activity for a decade and began to think of balancing those efforts with an accompanying focus on pastoral programming, a focus far less threatening to their colleagues in Catholic colleges. It was also a focus more palatable in general to bishops who, as chief pastors, would respond to advance the "spiritual" needs of students with much more unblinking readiness than they would to advance other kinds of programming.[9] During the academic year 1958-1959, bish-

The picturesque Bert Baston home purchased by the diocese in 1962 that later became the Newman rectory.

ops individually had authorized the construction of fifty new Catholic student centers.[10] While ecclesiastics around the country were thus being moved to provide the Newman movement with far less equivocal support, the passion of Illies, Yzermans, and the St. Cloud State students was more than enough to convince an already supportive Bishop Bartholome that even more could and should be done to facilitate the good work of the Newman movement in St. Cloud.

By early 1963, Bartholome initiated a massive capital fund drive in the diocese, which he christened the "New Horizons" campaign. The monies raised as a result were earmarked to finance the renovation of the St. Cloud Children's Home, to finance the building of a new gym and other needed expansion projects at Cathedral High School in St. Cloud, to support parish schools in the diocese, to establish a Newman Center at the University of Minnesota in Morris and to fund the building of a brand-new facility to house the efforts of the Newman movement on the St. Cloud State campus. The then-sizeable sum of $500,000 was allotted for the construction of a state-of-the-art Newman "Center" to replace the simple "Hall" that had provided a spiritual nexus for Catholic students since 1956. At about the same time, under Bartholome's direction, the diocese purchased a tudor-style cottage owned by one Bert Baston on the south side of Newman Hall that would later become the Newman rectory. This $57,000 move gave the diocese control of sixty-six feet of unclosed street on the river and ultimately opened up the possibility of building the center as it now stands. Bartholome justified his commitment to the creation of a far more sizable "castle" for Catholic college students eloquently, affirming that no young woman or man can have a genuine, liberal arts education without being exposed to the ideas of the greatest thinker of all, Jesus Christ. The increased Catholic student enrollment at St. Cloud State College, Bartholome reasoned with characteristic certainty, demanded that the diocese take an interest in their spiritual formation and religious

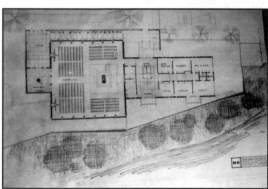

The architect's drawings and plans for the Newman facility.

education, and the erection of the center with its new facilities would place an obligation in conscience upon all Catholic students to take advantage of the instruction that would take place there, an instruction that would give purpose not only to their educational careers, but to the entire adventure of living in the world.

"We'll put the bingo tables right here." Architect Eugene Freerks shows Wil Illies a model of the new center.

Designing a Dream

The people of the St. Cloud Diocese were generous, and the New Horizons Campaign was a great success. The grand fund-raising effort generated more than six million dollars; about one-tenth of that amount would ultimately be used to construct the new Newman facility. Once the money was in hand, so to speak, Illies consulted widely with other Newman chaplains throughout the country as well as with local theologians and artists in order to craft the most effective possible design for the new building. Together, they spent hours discussing the role of the Church on campus and the ever-evolving philosophy of the Newman movement. It became clear that the construction of a chapel and of ample classroom space would have first priority; the inclusion of a gathering room with a stage and kitchen facilities that could be put to use for the hosting of Newman conventions also seemed important. In the city of St. Cloud at about this time, the Church of St. Augustine was being built on Wilson Avenue under the direction of St. Paul architect Eugene Freerks of the firm Dreher, Freerks, Sperl, and Flynn. Illies was impressed with what Freerks was doing; ultimately, Bartholome was persuaded that Freerks should be named the master craftsman in the development of the new center's design. Freerks created a building plan to fit the Newman program as it was developing under the guidance of Illies, Yzermans, and the national priorities of the Newman Club Federation in the late 1950s and early 1960s. The architectural design called for the center, which would rise up on the west bank of the Mighty Mississippi, to be divided into two sections, a church and an academic wing, a construct that was meant to reflect the Newman program's two primary concerns—the pastoral and the educational. The combined area of the two wings, fashioned in granite and reinforced concrete and accented by ebony-stained oak, covered 28,000 square feet. The academic wing measured ninety-six by forty feet and consisted of three levels with a lobby, offices, and meeting rooms on the first floor, and a library, study area, and auditorium facility on the floor below. Under the library on the third sub-level, the plan placed classrooms and lecture halls. The chapel space, situated directly south of the academic wing and adjoined to it, was a mighty square measuring seventy-five feet on each side that would seat more than four hundred and fifty people once pews were installed. The building as a whole gave shape to a dream shared by the most committed crossroads travelers. It was envisioned as a campus adjunct facility that would encourage, rather than inhibit, travel in the middle of the university highway. College students would use the center not for escape, but for very definite constructive purposes: to participate in religious services, to attend classes and lectures, to study, and to become more adept at navigating through the transforming challenges of the crossroads environment in which they lived. The plan so impressed Illies' colleagues around the nation that in 1964 he found himself elected by the National Newman Chaplains' Association to serve on the Chaplains' Advisory Board and to chair the National Committee on Newman Centers and Facilities. What's more, in a year in which it competed with eighty other projects, the Minnesota Society of Architects awarded the building one of two top honors for structure design, site utilization and use of building materials.

The whole campus seemed to share in the excitement surrounding the coming of the new Newman headquarters. Both Dr. George Budd, president of the college, and Dr. Robert Wick, dean of the School of Liberal Arts and future president of the college, expressed their delight not only that such a fine building would soon grace the campus and enhance its overall appearance, but also that the use of its facilities would enable every student to have even broader opportunities to reach spiritual as well as intellectual matu-

rity during her or his years at St. Cloud State. It was a senior student at the time named Mary Winter, however, who probably summed up best what the construction of the new castle, one with ever-more permeable walls and a drawbridge which never closed, meant in the on-going story of Newman ministry on the banks of the mighty Mississippi. Winter wrote:

Newman Hall is moved to make way for the brand new Newman Center. The house still stands at 1227 Fourth Avenue South in St. Cloud and houses "Gaetz KiddieKare."

> Instead of a club, Newmanism is now a "movement," a mainstream of students, faculty, laity, and clergy working for a common goal—the development of a secular college graduate who has matured spiritually as well as intellectually. This transition from club to movement is evidenced by the physi-

"Get in there and dig!" June 2, 1963, groundbreaking for the brand new Newman Center (above). Left to right are: Eugene Freerks, architect; student Ron Schultz, Newman Club president; Wil Illies; and St. Cloud State President George Budd.

"The White House" (right), temporary home of the Newman Club as the new center was rising up across the street during the summer of 1964.

cal move from the Hall to the Center. . . . It is significant that the Newman Center is to be completed at almost the same time as the new college student union, indicating that the movement is keeping abreast with the growth of the college.

Groundbreaking ceremonies for the new center took place on June 2, 1963, right after that year's annual baccalaureate Mass on the green and grassy banks of the River of the Holy Spirit. President Budd participated in the activity, as well as faculty members, Newman students and their parents, instructors in the Newman School of Religion, and Newman alumni and alumnae. Enthusiasm for the venture never waned through the ensuing months of construction and chaos, during which time Newman students headquartered temporarily at 401 First Avenue South, the "White House" located across the street from the old Newman Hall. The White House became the temporary locale of classes, meetings, and the celebration of religious services. On that bleak day in November of 1963 when President John F. Kennedy was assassinated, Illies recalls that students came and filled that house until its seams were bursting, and then overflowed out onto the street. They were in shock, the chaplain remembers; they came because they did not know what else to do, and they came wanting to pray.

In the Spring 1963 edition of *ERA*, former Newman Club vice-president Arthur Grachek, who was by then a graduate assistant on campus, wrote a rather prophetic article in which he mused over how extraordinary it was that the pioneering era of the Newman movement was almost ready to come to a close and culminate in a beautiful structure consisting of modern classrooms, a large library, and most important of all, a chapel in which Mass would be offered every day of the week. It is this new physical center, wrote Grachek, united with the already existing spiritual center brought to life through the unity of heart and mind that has existed for a long time among Newman Club members, that was transforming into reality something of which many had only dreamed in the past. "Not long ago I can remember the simplicity of the Newman program," reflected Grachek:

> It consisted of daily Mass, three or four classes offered each week, and the general meeting. Today, the program . . . has been widely expanded. We now have two Masses daily. The center is fast becoming a model in adapting new trends in the liturgy and exposing the student to new ideas in the Church. The educational program has developed to the point whereby a student can acquire a substantial education in the doctrines and teachings of the Church. Two semesters consisting of seventeen classes are being offered to students this year. The library has grown to be the finest of its kind in this area. Prominent men [sic] in philosophical and theological fields are brought in to lecture to the students. A program informing the parents and the public about the purpose of the Newman movement has been organized. The Newman Club itself is no longer a small-time organization.

With true prophetic foresight, Grachek went on to assert that the idea of a "student parish" on campus must be advanced that would not only serve as a good training ground for future parishioners throughout the diocese and state, but would also provide students with the opportunity to participate in the lay apostolate in the world, ready to live out a deep-rooted conviction that true world-changing conversions can happen when the sacred and the secular meet regularly and are allowed to challenge and transform one another. One can see, concluded Grachek, how the Newman movement is advancing toward the fulfillment of its goals, how it is adapting constantly to changing conditions, and how, hopefully, it will someday become an integral part of the college academic community.[11] Life in the middle of the highway for the Catholic Christian student was becoming filled with opportunities for transformation as well as for formation, and the power of the Spirit was ready to be released in new and even more compelling ways.

Notes

1 Vincent Yzermans, *Journeys* (Waite Park: Park Press Incorporated, 1994), pp. 83-84.
2 Evans, p. 113.
3 *Newman News*, Fall 1959, p. 3.
4 William Durkin, "Meeting Modern Man," *ERA*, Spring 1963, p. 16.
5 *Newman News*, Fall 1959, p. 1.
6 *Newsweek*, December 23, 1953, p. 14, as quoted in Richard Butler, OP, "The Newman Apostolate: Cultural Contribution to Higher Education," *The American Ecclesiastical Review*, June 1964, p. 408.
7 *Newman News*, March 11, 1959, p. 3.
8 "The Newman Clubs," *Jubilee*, August 1957, p. 13.
9 Evans, pp. 125-126.
10 Evans, pp. 121-122.
11 Arthur E. Grachek, "Looking Forward," *ERA*, Spring 1963, p. 3.

Chapter 3

A New Age Dawns at the Crossroads

"Christ's cross should be seen again at the center of the marketplace as well as on the steeple of a church. Jesus was not crucified in a cathedral between two candles but on a cross between two thieves—on the town garbage heap at a crossroads so cosmopolitan that they had to write his title in Hebrew, Latin and Greek."
—McLeod, quoted in the Newman parish bulletin,
March 24, 1968

*"Dissolution does but give birth to fresh modes of organization,
and one death is the parent of a thousand lives."*
—John Henry Newman

The new physical center of the St. Cloud Newman movement, constructed to embody and reflect its unique spiritual center, was impressive, indeed. The diocesan newspaper called it "striking," and as the novel structure rose, it caused more

Bulldozing begins on the banks of the Holy Spirit's River.

The Newman Center's amphitheater or gathering space (above), now known as "The Terrace," begins to take shape.

The Terrace housed a student snack bar known as "McCarthy's" in the 1960s, and a pizza restaurant in the 1970s.

than a little excitement, not only on campus but throughout the city as well. After the eighty-four-foot, "pre-stressed" concrete beams for the roof of the chapel arrived via police escort from St. Paul, a sizable crowd gathered at the construction site to watch as the eight huge beams, weighing in at eight tons apiece, were lifted into place by two gigantic cranes. For months following the first opening of its front doors, local church groups and civic organizations arrived regularly at the new Newman facility for luncheon tours and left feeling amazed and impressed.

At about the same time the brand-new Newman Center was rising up at the crossroads and creating a stir in the city of St. Cloud, a truly fascinating wrinkle was beginning to emerge on the national scene. Catholic colleges, long the nemesis of the Newman effort, were undergoing a process of soul-searching; they found themselves struggling as never before with how to maintain their integrity in the face of limited financial resources, a fragmentation of focus and duplication of effort among multiple small institutions and a student population that was becoming increasingly alienated from the institutional church and restless about the quality of the religious education they were receiving.[1] Challenged by the calls to internal renewal sounded by the Second Vatican Council and concerned about the absence of anything in their organizational structures designed specifically to serve the needs of questioning and disgruntled students, officials of the National Catholic Education Association finally began to look upon the Newman movement as a potential source of help rather than as a competitive threat.[2] In the school year 1963-1964, Catholics comprised 23.5 percent, or slightly over one million, of the 4.5 million students enrolled overall in American colleges and universities. Since the students registered in colleges operated by the Church numbered only 366,000, that meant that about two out of every three Catholics attended public, independent or Protestant institutions. By 1984, an estimated eighty percent would be receiving their education at non-Catholic colleges.[3] The editors of *America* magazine thus proposed the promotion of a "new kind of Newman Club, more on the scale of a 'Catholic Institute' . . . complete with library, lounge, study facilities, lecture halls, seminar rooms, and, above all, a faculty competent to create the scholarly climate of Christian culture" that would attract, challenge and form students. Noting that many bishops had already "provided men and money to start such centers," the magazine concluded that Catholic colleges and universities would have to be even more generous than ever about sharing their facilities, making credit courses available and even loaning faculty members.[4] These were proposals that proponents of the Newman movement had been advancing for years, and they embraced a vision that the Newman movement had endeavored to promote more than half a century earlier in those plans for Catholic foundations and campus "Halls" that had been short-circuited by short-sighted clerics in the 1920s.[5]

With the coming of a new Catholic center on the banks of the Holy Spirit's river, a new era really did dawn for the St. Cloud Newman effort, just as a brand new era was dawning for the Newman movement all across the nation. The crossroads environment of the university had produced much growth and change already, but life in the middle of the highway never truly becomes settled, and the growth and change were far from being over. Catholic Christians were only just beginning to grasp what it might mean to plant the cross in the middle of the market place, as well as on the steeple of a church. At a 1963 general meeting, St. Cloud Newman students voted unanimously to change their name from the Newman "Club" to the Newman "Association." President Ronald Schultz explained that the word "club" confused the purpose of Newmanism by "inferring that we are nothing more than a social group," and reduced the facilities of Newman Hall to "the connotation of a Newman hangout." The purpose of our association, Schultz went on to say, is not to exclude others or to preserve a ghetto mentality. On the contrary, "we students and the programs of the Newman center are constantly striving to open our doors to the truth through learning and action." On the national level, stirrings of the same sort were afoot. The famous "Ann Arbor Summit" held by the National Newman Federation in 1962 was a watershed event for the movement. The six different sectors of the Federation came together to assume a new name, the National Newman Apostolate, and that apostolate was given its own coordinating office in the Youth Department of the National Catholic Welfare Conference. The restructuring was significant; ever since the Newman movement had been admitted by the hierarchy into the Youth Department in 1940 under the rubric of "Catholic Action," it had been engaged in an on-going struggle to maintain its integrity as part of a large bureau that also monitored the activities of clubs in Catholic colleges, high schools, and parishes.[6] Now granted fuller autonomy and its own national office, and recognized as an authentic apostolate with a distinct task and mission, chaplains, students, and professors alike felt themselves sent forth under a new mandate to "bring the Church to Catholic students and Christ to their campuses."[7]

As John Whitney Evans points out, hard evidence of the newfound status of the Newman Apostolate came almost immediately. Catholic architectural magazines discovered Newman Centers as objects of artistic and financial interest. The St. Cloud Newman Center was both mentioned and pictured in the February 1965 edition of *Liturgical Arts* magazine. From 1963 to 1966, the *Catholic Periodical Index* listed seventy-seven articles dealing with the responsibilities of the Church toward non-Catholic campuses, a number nearly equaling the total published during the previous three decades. Many of these articles focused on the transformation of the old, apologetically and socially oriented Newman club into

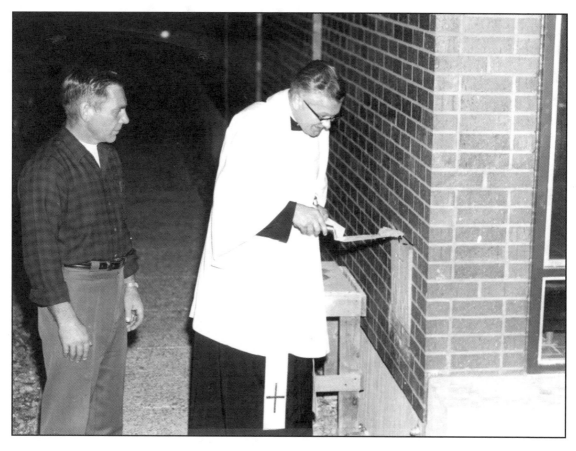

the new, pastoral and educational "mission on campus."[8] The St. Cloud Newman effort, however, had long before sown and culti-vated the seeds of such a transformation.

Laying the cornerstone, October 8, 1964.

Becoming a Center

When the St. Cloud diocesan paper announced that the new Newman Center would be ready to open in the fall of 1964, it declared that from that point on, there would be neither a Newman Club nor a Newman Association at St. Cloud State College. Though the latter was meant to be an improvement upon the former, both of these titles, the article explained, convey an inadequate impression of Newman work. Every effort was made to imprint the name "Newman Center" into the minds and hearts of all. Cardinal John Henry Newman once affirmed that "dissolution does but give birth to fresh modes of organization, and one death is the parent of a thousand lives." Those who were guiding and shaping the Newman apostolate in St. Cloud saw in these words a prophetic description of the future of their efforts. In St. Cloud, as in numerous other university communities nationwide, all vestiges of the club mentality were being erased, and no longer were Catholic students expected to pay dues in order to be a part of the Newman enterprise; at least in theory, their very presence on a college campus as baptized women and men committed them automatically to the religious and intellectual components of a Christian life, and to the apostolate of traveling through the crossroads environment of the university open to the possibilities of

Students gather in the lobby lounge of the brand-new Newman Center. Note the bust of John Henry Newman, prominently displayed.

transforming that environment, and of being transformed by it. The national office echoed these sentiments by defining the Newman mission as "doing the work of the Church in the secular campus community," a goal much broader and much deeper than protecting the personal faith and morals of a few isolated souls.[9] Newman leaders were urged to help the Church walk with finality out of the ghetto, free itself from the last vestiges of self-imposed segregation and stride boldly across campus, abandoning the alleys for the main street. "Let us not just keep the faith," the national chaplain implored, "let us share it and infuse it into the academic and the social scene of the whole campus community," because it is not enough for Catholics to maintain a high standard of religious practice within the Catholic

Students in the Newman library. Study was meant to be an important component of life at the center.

community. It is also necessary for them to build a bridge of understanding out into the secular culture and to act as interpreters of the Christian faith to the world outside the Church.[10]

One of the most interesting local signs of this shift to a paradigm for the Newman movement which promoted even more unabashed engagement with those who traveled through the crossroads called the university was the lack of recreational facilities and social space housed in the brand-new building in St. Cloud. The wall that ran in front of the center, as well as its outer courts and terraces, were all meant to provide space for quiet study and contemplation that might deepen in students a sense of the constant presence of God, help them to understand that religion and daily life cannot dwell in separate mental compartments, and make them more responsive to the tugs and the impulses of grace. But there was only one small lounge, and ping pong tables were conspicuously absent. Many students, in fact, who had been active at Newman in the years immediately preceding the construction of the center found it a puzzling omission, for socializing had been an important part of Newman life. Gathered together in warm and friendly confines, many students found their Newman Hall an excellent place to kill a few hours between classes with familiar Catholic companions. But such gathering was becoming less and less congruent with the vision that animated the heart of the evolving Newman philosophy. Illies said at this time,

> It is very important that we do not present this image of the Newman Center as a social gathering place. If we have students spending all their time here, instead of out on the campus where they belong, the Newman movement is not doing its job. We want to emphasize that the center is adjunct to the campus. We want students to come here for their spiritual needs and also for their religious education. . . . But all is lost if these same students do not take what they have gained back with them to the campus and there let their light shine.[11]

The St. Cloud State Student Senate Book Exchange was held in the Newman Terrace for many years.

Richard Butler, the national chaplain of the Newman Apostolate, summed up this latest link in the evolution of the Newman mission by describing the array of activities growing prolifically out of its renewed and refounded vision across the nation:

special programs of study for students are offered, he said, whose content and method are adapted to fit the particular conditions of the secular academic scene. What's more, liturgical life in a Newman chapel is almost always as dynamic and congregation-involved as the expanded norms permit, and programs in apostolic formation are producing a remarkably emerged laity whose skills

At top, students, clerics, women religious, faculty members, and others listen to a lecture in "Classroom A." Dr. George Forell (above), head of Religious Studies at the University of Iowa, leads the 1968 Faculty Ecumenical Seminar.

93

and maturity as well-integrated people of faith will have not only an immediate impact on their university campuses, but also a long-term effect in both the parish and professional lives they came to embrace later on. Finally, the cultural contributions made by Newman Centers to the academic community take many and varied forms and include bringing prominent lecturers to campus auditoriums, offering seminars and conferences on philosophical and theological themes, sometimes jointly sponsored by a campus department, and providing Christian art exhibits, literature displays, book and periodical libraries, sacred concerts, and dramatic productions.[12] It is to the eternal credit of the leaders and the active membership of the Newman Apostolate in St. Cloud that nearly all of the activities delineated by Butler in 1964 were already in evidence on the banks of the River of the Holy Spirit, and were continuing to expand.

Once the new St. Cloud Newman Center was ready for occupancy, a complete slate of theology courses was proffered to students each quarter as before, but enrollment was opened up to interested adults in the St. Cloud community who were not associated with the campus for the nominal fee of $5.00, and the course offerings reflected a gradual movement toward the study of ecumenism, the challenges of religion in contemporary society, and the thought and work of theologians and philosophers who broke out of traditional, scholastic paradigms, like Hans Küng and Teillhard de Chardin. The custom of inviting in fine speakers for evening lectures that attracted people from the broader community continued, as did weekly coffee-hour discussions held at the Atwood Student Center on campus. Ecumenically sponsored faculty retreats and seminars were organized annually, and the Newman Center lobby was used regularly to display the works of local artists. The amphitheater, (now known as the "The Terrace"), was even used to present the first foreign-language theater production ever put together at St. Cloud State College. Documentary films, Fellini films, and a wide range of contemporary and religious films were also shown in the amphitheater. For a fee of twenty-five cents, viewers were delighted, entertained and had their social consciences stirred by such films as "Cry My Beloved Country," "From Here to Eternity," "The Savage Eye," "The Eddie Duchin Story," and "A Time of Burning," a movie depicting the attempt at racial integration in an Omaha church.

Cornford's Law

John Whitney Evans observes with irony that many of the fashioners of the newly emerging Newman Apostolate had been so preoccupied for so long with working on the system and gaining a place within it that they failed to notice that while the the sky was indeed brightening, its color was red. A decade of student religious revival along more or less conventional lines was giving way to a period of upheaval and the apparent rejection of institutional forms, and the wisdom of Cornford's Law would soon become apparent: "Nothing is ever done until everyone is convinced that it ought to be done, and has been convinced for so long that it is now time to do something else."[13] Despite the proliferation of academic Catholic centers on public campuses across the country, Catholic educators were beginning to recognize that a heavily "intellectual" approach to religious formation might not be the most effective route, and that, when it came to passing on the faith, the primary task of the Church was more than simply informing young women and men about the religious tradition into which they happened to be born. Rather, it was to facilitate both the formation and the transformation of young women and men into true disciples of Christ.[14] Fortunately, those who guided the evolving Newman apostolate on the banks of the River of the Holy Spirit grasped the emerging horizons of this insight early on, and began to integrate it into their programming and philosophy. Wil Illies and his colleague George Garrelts from the University of Minnesota Newman Center, in fact, together drafted an article for the *American Benedictine Review* in which they suggested that Newman chaplains really ought not to be trying to run "a college outside of a college." Both of these men had been passionately invested in providing sound course offerings in theology and philos-

One of the many, many discussion sessions that became part of the life of a typical Newman member.

ophy through their respective Newman programs. By the mid-1960s, however, they were asserting with equal passion their growing belief that the Newman Apostolate, at its most authentic, mandated that theology and religion become part of the normal, academic curricula offered on state university campuses and not something on which Catholic centers should expend exclusive, or even primary, energy. They urged Newman leaders to become a true part of their colleges and universities and endeavor committedly to serve them well in those areas in which they had unique competence—liturgy, ecumenism, counseling, social action and student organization. Open interest in the intellectual life, seminars, discussions, and lectures, of course, would always be a part of the Newman program, but, most appropriately such events would be auxiliary to, rather than in competition with, university or college programs in religious studies and other related fields.[15] These two forward-looking ministers went on to muse, however, that it would be both timely and fitting for women and men from religious communities, especially those with doctoral degrees, to begin to apply for teaching positions on the staffs of state colleges or universities so that they could participate as full members in the academic life of secular campus and contribute the unique insights shaped by their faith perspective on equal footing with their faculty colleagues.[16] With typical faith in the mutual nature of all intersections taking place at the crossroads, Illies and Garrelts hinted as well at the power of the secular campus to transform religious community members in positive ways. "No one can predict," they reflected, "what the effect of such a move 'into the world' might have on religious themselves, on religious life and its rules, or on vocations. But we can at least affirm that there may be qualities in 'the world' which could enhance and even revitalize religious life and growth."[17]

Seated at center, Chair Donald Teff works with members of the Newman Council, *circa* 1966. Seated left to right, the council members are Joan Otto, Kathy Hogan, Beth Weber, and Margie Fabel.

The Transformation Continues

Newman student leaders,
circa 1967.

By 1966, many committed Newman ministers, including Wil Illies and Nick Zimmer, the man Bishop Bartholome named Illies' associate chaplain in 1964, agreed that the designation "Apostolate" was fast becoming outmoded as an effective descriptor of Newman ministry at the crossroads. For both students and college administrators alike, it reverberated with connotations of evangelizing, proselytizing and working to "bring" the Church to the pagan milieu of the campus. It also failed to respect the tone and the spirit of such Vatican II documents as *The Church in the Modern World and the Declaration on Religious Liberty.*[18] A more apt appellation needed to be given to the process of facilitating both the formation and the transformation of young women and men into authentic disciples of Christ who did not shrink from the challenges of the crossroads, who believed that the Church was already at work in the campus milieu in the persons of teachers, researchers, counselors, administrators, and students, and who understood that the sacred and the secular should meet regularly and often in a spirit of

A praying community begins to take shape at Newman.

truth and openness, trust, and celebration.[19] The word "Center" went a long way toward expressing well the locale from which this process emanated; the phrase "Student Parish" would soon be added to round out the description and make it more complete.

Illies and Zimmer early on made the decision that students who were willing to offer their leadership in guiding activity at the Newman Center would no longer be elected to "club offices." Instead, they would be chosen by their peers to serve on the "Newman Council," which in time consisted of a chair, a vice-chair, a secretary-treasurer, and social, education, liturgy, service and dorm representatives. Through the council, committees and organizations were formed as in a normal parish setting. Much of the work formerly done by the Newman Club under the heading of educational or social programming now fell under the general parish programming process and student council members were given very concrete opportunities to exercise leadership and assume responsibility in shaping the identity and mission of their Christian community. A weekly parish bulletin was published, and Illies and Zimmer came gradually to function more as "pastors" than as chaplains, pastors of a body of Catholics much larger than that found in most parishes with geographic limits. An open letter written by the advisory board of the National Newman Chaplains' Association in 1966 affirmed that worship was the starting point and goal of all Newman work, because "in liturgy we have a unique instrument for bringing together the legitimate concerns of the university with those of the Church, resulting in increased commitment to both," and, even more importantly, because liturgy was understood to be "the ultimate transforming encounter with Christ who is our reconciliation."[20] Not surprisingly, then, the most momentous and enduring effect of the shift toward envisioning the new Newman Center as a campus parish came with the opportunity that was now before its members to develop a full-fledged liturgical life. It was an opportunity, as well, for Newman members to establish their own unique spirit as a praying community touched and transformed by the kind of openness to change and challenge that the bustling highway activity to which they had committed themselves both demanded and inspired. What's more, within the Church as a whole, the spirit of reform engendered by the Second Vatican Council was now beginning to make itself felt, as well, demanding and inspiring that same kind of openness and touching and transforming Catholic Christians around the world in powerful and unexpected ways.

Notes

1 Evans, pp. 151-154.

2 Evans, p. 155.

3 Evans, pp. 156-157.

4 Evans, pp. 155-156.

5 Evans, p. 156.

6 Evans, pp. 133-134.

7 Evans, pp. 129-130.

8 Evans, p. 130.

9 *ERA*, Fall 1962, p. 6.

10 *ERA*, FAll 1962, p. 6.

11 Wil Illies, Newman Awards Banquet, May 19, 1964, at the Moose Lodge, Waite Park, Minnesota.

12 "The Newman Apostolate: Cultural Contribution to Higher Education," *The American Ecclesiastical Review*, Vol. CL, No. 6, June 1964, p. 413.

13 Evans, p. 134.

14 "Newman and a New Era," *Ave Maria*, Vol. 100, No. 9, pp. 23-24.
15 "Newman Chaplains Envision Religious Serving in the Academic Community of State Colleges and Universities," by George Garrelts and Wilfred Illies, *The American Benedictine Review*, date, p. 372.
16 Illies and Garrelts, pp. 369-371.
17 Illies and Garrelts, p. 371.
18 Evans, pp. 160-161.
19 John Whitney Evans, *Newman Past and Present*, publication of the National Newman Apostolate, United States Catholic Conference, Washington, D.C., post 1967, pp. 5-6.
20 "Open Letter Issued by Newman Chaplains Board," *St. Cloud Visitor*, 13 March 1966, p. 8.

Pope John XXIII, who led the Church from 1958 to 1963 and worked to cultivate "a flourishing garden of life."

Chapter 4

Change, Collision, and Conversion at the Crossroads

"A spontaneous resolution never to change is inconsistent with the idea of belief."
—John Henry Newman

The Second Vatican Council was called unexpectedly by Pope John XXIII, a natural optimist who did not care for those "prophets of gloom" in the Church who believed unswervingly that the past embodied perfection and were able to see nothing but falsehood, sin, and looming disaster in the modern world. Unlike the twenty ecumenical councils called before it in the history of the Church, this 1962 summoning of all the world's bishops did not have as its purpose the definition of doctrine or the defense of the Church against heresy or error. The documents it produced, notably, contained no condemnations or "anathemas." It was a pastoral council with a positive agenda, which John XIII dubbed "*aggiornamento*," bringing the Church "up to today" and sending it forth to meet the new age. We must open our windows and allow the Spirit to blow through and banish all cobwebs, the pope avowed. We must look to the present, to new conditions of life, so that our treasures can be passed on in such a way that they take root in the soil of each age and flourish. "We are not on earth as museum keepers," John declared, "but to cultivate a flourishing garden of life."[1]

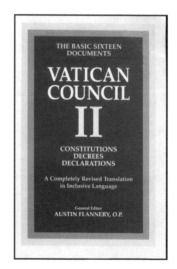

The great documents of a positive, pastoral council.

All in all, the Second Vatican Council produced sixteen documents. Of these, the relatively short *Constitution on the Sacred Liturgy*, completed in 1963, probably came to have a more potent and palpable effect on the lives of Catholics, lay and clerical, than any of the others. The public prayer of the Church had remained virtually unchanged for five centuries; the Council of Trent in the latter half of the sixteenth century had imposed strict, central control on the Roman Rite in reaction to the chaotic state of liturgy in the centuries preceding the Reformation, and, while this control served an immediately useful purpose, its effect in the long-term was debilitating and paralyzing.[2] Lay members of the Catholic faithful were robbed of that knowledge and understanding of liturgy that was their rightful legacy as baptized children of God, and over time were reduced to passive and silent spectators who watched complex rites and rubrics being acted out before them. Ritual is religion in action, the cutting edge of the tool that accomplishes what religion sets out to do.[3] For the Catholic laity, Mass had become a "hands-off," inactive matter, the exclusive preserve of the priest, his own mysterious service done publicly to and for the flock.[4] As one liturgical reformer of the period described it: "It has always been intriguing that if you brought a person into the back of church who had not been to a Mass before and asked him what he thought was going on, the last thing he would mention was an event that had anything to do with the Last Supper."[5]

The Eucharistic liturgy as presented in a pre-Vatican II missalette.

While the first seeds of liturgical renewal had been sown in the early part of the twentieth century, the *Constitution on the Sacred Liturgy* and the decrees and instructions which followed it made recommendations for reform which were strong and sweeping. The word "revise" appeared no less than twenty times in the *Constitution*, and the word "participation" twenty-six times. The intent of the document was unequivocal: "It is very much the wish of the Council that all of the faithful should be led to take that full, conscious and active participation in the liturgical celebration which is demanded by the very nature of the liturgy." It then went on to admonish pastors of souls "to realize that when the liturgy is celebrated, their obligation goes further than simply ensuring that the laws governing lawful celebration are observed. They must also ensure that the faithful take part fully aware of what they are doing, actively engaged in the rite and enriched by it."[6]

Vincent Yzermans, by then the editor of the diocesan paper and the director of the diocesan Bureau of Information, made an appointment to see Bishop Bartholome in the spring of 1962 and nervously announced his desire to attend the Second Vatican Council in Rome so that he could provide the diocese with first-hand coverage. "Pretty Good" was the highest complement that Bartholome ever paid to anyone, so Yzermans relaxed when the Bishop took a puff from his cigarette and replied: "Well, pretty good. I think it would be good for you to go."[7] When Yzermans

Peter W. Bartholome, bishop of the Diocese of St. Cloud, 1953 to 1968.

made a motion to rise, Bartholome bade him sit down again. He handed him the proposed working texts of the council and called in his secretary to write out a check for $1,000. As the two men walked together to the front door, Bartholome kept saying "Pretty good. . . . Pretty good." "I knew he was pleased as he patted me on the shoulder," wrote Yzermans, "but not half as much as I was. This day was a major turning point in my life."[8] As things turned out, it was a major turning point in the life of the St. Cloud Newman movement as well.

Yzermans did more than simply cover the momentous ecumenical council as a journalist. Once in Rome, he became one of only thirty-nine Americans appointed as counsiliar consultants, or "*periti*," through the office of the Vatican Secretariat of State while the council was going on, and, during its last session, he was also named the director of the the American Bishop's Press Panel. Yzermans was present in Rome during all of the council's sessions; as it drew to a close, he sent off the following note to the young Newmanites he had left behind in St. Cloud:

> Dear Newmanites:
>
> I would be most remiss if I did not drop you a line to let you know that you have been often in my prayers and thoughts during the past months in Rome. The longer the Council lasts the more I am convinced that you will be the ones who really create the new image of the Church in the modern world. The more I see of youth here, the more I am convinced that we have the greatest group of young people in the world. Looking forward to seeing many of you next week and with prayers for all of you —Father Yzermans.

Yzermans' words were more prophetic than he knew.

Official documents are rarely moving or poetic, but in 1972 the Bishops' Committee on the Liturgy of the United States Catholic Conference issued a document containing some simple words of great beauty and wisdom: "People in love make signs of love, not only to express their love but also to deepen it. Love never expressed dies. Christians' love for Christ and for one another, and Christians' faith in Christ and in one another, must be expressed in the signs and symbols of celebration or they will die."[9]

As a result of the Second Vatican Council, the Church embarked upon a real crossroads experience of its own. The meetings that subsequently played themselves out between the forces of reform and the forces of restraint produced disquieting reverberations felt in nearly all Catholic Christian communities. Those reverberations were felt in a very potent way, however, when it came to making decisions about how the signs and symbols of celebration should be arranged in order to express as fully and as powerfully as possible the faith and the love of the Church. It is hardly surprising, then, that in the Catholic Christian community which had built itself up in the middle of the St. Cloud State highway, it was the meetings and occasional collisions that happened around that expression of faith and love we call liturgy that produced more growth, and in some ways more pain, than any other kind of crossroads encounter ever had.

At the time of the Newman Center's construction, liturgical artist and consultant Frank Kazmarcik was hired to spend a day with architect Eugene Freerks and provide input on the design of the chapel. In typical fashion, Kazmarcik quipped, "What are you trying to build, an opera house?" and set to work offering his opinions for reshaping the draft of the chapel plan. Vatican II was in full-swing as the new building began to rise, and the Newman chapel became one of the first worship spaces crafted in accordance with the liturgical reforms ultimately approved by the council. To plan a worship space with an eye turned with such boldness toward a future that had not yet fully arrived, however, was a step that disconcerted many, including the bishop of St. Cloud. In 1962, while the plans were still on the drawing board, Bartholome sent a postcard to St. Cloud from Rome, where he was in attendance at the first session of the council. The postcard read: "Greetings to you, the staff and the students from Vatican Council. Progress is slow. How are the plans developing? Warn the architect about modernistic trends. P.W. Bartholome." The plans, in fact, were developing so well that the St. Cloud chapel space was named the recipient of a Cardinal Lercaro Bronze Medal at the 1963 North American Liturgical Week Conference in Philadelphia, one of a set of prized awards given each year to churches whose designs expressed and advanced liturgical renewal in an exemplary way. The presenter of the medal noted appropriately that it honored "not only the architect, but the chaplain and community who collaborate with their sacrifice, openness, and determination to have a fitting, vital and sacred edifice erected in God's honor and worship." But the honor of the award was far from being sufficient to quiet the fears of those who worried most about respecting the riches of the past and who turned a more cautious eye toward the coming of a renewed future. A tongue-in-cheek letter of support written by a priest-friend of Illies' at the time reveals well the kinds of tensions that were brewing:

The Liturgical Conference

3428 NINTH STREET, N.E., WASHINGTON 17, D.C.

Phone: LA 6-4541

President	*Vice-President*	*Secretary*	*Treasurer*	*Executive Secretary*
Rev. Gerard S. Sloyan	Rev. Godfrey Diekmann, O.S.B.	Rev. William J. Leonard, S.J.	Rev. John J. McEneaney	Mr. John B. Mannion
Catholic University of America	St. John's Abbey	Boston College	Church of St. Thomas More	3428 Ninth Street, N.E.
Washington 17, D.C.	Collegeville, Minnesota	Boston 67, Massachusetts	Brookings, South Dakota	Washington 17, D.C.

September 5th, 1963

Mr. Eugene Freerks
Dreher, Freerks, Sperl, Flynn, INC., Architects
410 Anchor Bldg.
116 E 4th Street
St. Paul, Minnesota

Dear Mr. Freerks:

It is with great pleasure that Liturgical Conference has the privilege
of awarding you with the bronze Lercaro Medal for your Newman Center
At St. Cloud State College. The judges were unanimous in this award
decision and at the closing day of the Philadelphia Liturgical Conference
at the presentation of the awards Father Godfrey Diekman Liturgical
Authority of St. John's Abbey, came to the stage to receive the award in
your name.

An award-winning worship space with an award-winning design.

Dear Wil,

Congratulations on your new building. I don't know how you managed to achieve as much as you did—considering the circumstances (and you know what *they* are). I see you made *Liturgical Arts*.

I would come to the dedication but I can't stand all that Protestant newfangled modernist stuff your new church and services represent . . . I'm going to tell Jesus on you. The Communists don't need the bomb, not as long as they got that Zimmer writing that liberal un-traditionalist pro-Negro stuff on the eucharist in the *Visitor*. All part of their strategy . . . I'll bet your Newman library is full of filthy literature (pardon me if a little saliva drops on this sheet as I contemplate all the filthy publications you may have).

Yours in Our Lady of Necedah and all the other conservative saints . . .

In 1964, Archbishop William Cousins of Milwaukee addressed the Newmanites of his city in a challenging way. While the prelate cautioned his students to be patient, understanding and tolerant of those who would not seem to move quickly enough in the new directions delineated by the documents of Vatican II, he also told the young crossroads travelers that they should become like an "advanced guard" in the Church, people who were able to understand intelligently the changes that were taking place, to assimilate new ideas, and to help greatly, therefore, in the transition beginning to take place.[10] The St. Cloud Newmanites were very well-prepared to assume such a mission as determined pioneers and competent shapers of the future.

A History of Openness

In the crossroads community which had grown up along the banks of the River of the Holy Spirit, efforts to reclaim and revitalize the Church's rich heritage of prayer had actually begun long before the Second Vatican Council. As early as 1936, St. Cloud Newman Club minutes report on the arrival of two monks from St. John's Abbey in Collegeville who came to give a "very interesting and educational" demonstration of Gregorian chant, one of the earliest methods employed to restore some measure of active participation in the liturgy. Just a few months later, the club attended services at the St. John's chapel in order to hear Gregorian chant live, after which they were given a "short but interesting explanation on the liturgy." In 1939, a priest-liturgist appeared to speak to the club on the "Laity and the Mass," emphasizing the crucial role of the laity in eucharistic celebration.

In the fall of 1956, Newman member Vernon Krier explained the "Dialog Mass" at a general club meeting. In the April 1959 edition of the *Newman News*, club member Edward Pluth wrote an article on this latest development in liturgy, and the impact it had on the worship experiences of students at St. Cloud State. "Come to Newman Hall some Thursday morning at 7:00 and you may see strange things happening," wrote the young journalist. He referred, of course to the Dialog Mass, or *Missa Recitata*. It would not be until several years after the Second Vatican Council closed that widespread use of the vernacular would be approved, allowing people for the first time in many centuries to worship in their native tongues and to experience a rite that acknowledged their presence and prioritized their participation. The call for less passive roles for worshipers in the pews, however, was gaining momentum long before the Second Vatican Council actually opened. In his 1947 encyclical, *Mediator Dei*, Pope Pius XII advocated increased participation for the people of God at prayer, whose voices should alternate with those of the priest and the choir. In

Ed Pluth, who brought awareness of the new "Dialog Mass" to Newman Club members.

1958, a new instruction was published by the Congregation of Rites, which echoed the *Mediator Dei* in content, affirming that eucharistic liturgy is a corporate rather than an individual offering. And so the Dialog Mass was given official sanction, a low Mass at which the laity recited out loud, in Latin, of course, the appropriate Mass texts, some in response to the priest and others in unison with him. At weekday masses held at Newman Hall, Wil Illies promoted full use of these new possibilities. Not only were the simple responses such as the *Amen* and *Laus Tibi Christe* spoken by the people, but also the *Gloria* and the *Credo,* as well as the recitation of the *Pater Noster* and the *Domine non sum dignus.* The response of students to this more explicitly two-sided way of worshiping was quite positive. The *Newman News* records a handful of negative comments like, "I concentrate much better when I can give silent praise to God." Many others, however, were enthusiastic. Student Pat Kirchenwizt reflected: "At first, when it was just introduced, I did not like it. But now, after gaining familiarity with it, I am beginning to see its greatness . . ." As student Tim Holt put it, "It brings the Mass closer, and I feel more a part of it. Takes away the idea that only the priest is participating." Betsy Stotts added insightfully that "it also gives me a greater feeling of unity with the others who are participating."

Those who are well-schooled in the legacy of John Henry Newman have marveled often over how the insights he articulated with passion and eloquence in the nineteenth century came finally to fruition at the Second Vatican Council more than a century later. In much the same manner that John XXIII adjured the church he was shepherding to update itself and to have the courage to plant its rich heritage in the soil of modern times, John Henry Newman pleaded with his contemporaries to understand that *literal* faithfulness to tradition is not necessary, or even desirable. Each age, Newman purported in his *Development of Doctrine,* needs to express the faith in a different way, appropriate to the flavor, character and needs of the time, but the *essence* of the faith itself need not thereby be placed in danger.[11] Truth is at once fixed and unchanging as a rock, yet capable of growth like a tree—a tree rooted, but growing and spreading its branches further and further all the time. It is hardly surprising, then, that Newman centers, which had attempted from the start to transplant the spirit of that great nineteenth century thinker to the North American Church, would be among the first to welcome the spirit of reform that John XXIII's pastoral council spawned. And the Newman Center in St. Cloud embraced that spirit with extraordinary enthusiasm.

A Chapel Carefully Crafted

A very early liturgy celebration at Christ Church. Note the absence of pews.

"Welcome to all. Welcome to Christ Church. Welcome to the Newman Center. Today we begin the full schedule of Masses, Confessions and Devotions in our new church . . ." Thus read the parish bulletin on September 27, 1964, the Sunday on which the first liturgies were celebrated in the brand new chapel of the brand new center, christened "Christ Church" in honor of a chapel at Oxford University in England, John Henry Newman's beloved alma mater. The parish's first baptism also took place: Stephen Neal, son of Mr. and Mrs. Gregory Weiler, became a member of Christ's Body on that notable fall day. The Decree of Erection, given by Peter Bartholome on August 6, 1964, established Christ Church as a semi-public oratory, meaning that while only specific categories of people could become official members, all persons were welcome to attend mass and other religious services held at the chapel. Those permitted to enroll as full-fledged parishioners at Christ Church if they so desired were single or married full-time students at St. Cloud State and all faculty and staff members of the college. Baptisms could be celebrated at the oratory, weddings and confirmations could not. From the start, the chaplains at the new

Newman Center parish prompted those members of Christ's body who worshipped there to move beyond the fears and inhibitions that may have characterized their experiences of worship and ritual in the past and to begin to pray as full participants in a spirit of joy and freedom. The second bulletin published in 1964 offered the following simple, but important, challenge: "Christ said, 'Take and eat,' and that is exactly what you have to do with the hosts that we use for Communion at Christ Church. There is still a *mistaken* notion in the minds of some that the host is not to touch the teeth and not to be chewed. Whatever the source of this idea, it is false. Chew the hosts, as the apostles certainly did at the Last Supper."

The chapel space in which student and faculty worshipers gathered each week in those early years to begin their schooling in "full, conscious and active participation" was, on the surface, a very plain and uncomplicated space. But every detail of its design was, in fact, deliberate, including its simplicity. The renowned Trappist monk, Thomas Merton, once lamented that for hundreds of years people had been building churches as if a church could not belong to the present age—as if a church had to look like it was left over from some other age in order to be a true church. "I think," Merton went on to say, "that such an assumption is based on a kind of atheism—as if God does not belong to all ages and as if religion were only a pleasant, necessary social formality preserved from past time in order to give our society an air of respectability."[12] The liturgical reformers of Vatican II agreed, admitting that while the old basilica-style churches where very beautiful, they did not work well for promoting active participation in worship in the latter-half of the twentieth century. A church, said the reformers, is not primarily an architectural monument built to symbolize God's glory, but a functional space created for the worshiping community that must help people to feel at home, free them to pray and invite them to participate. The most worthy needs of modern humankind must find their fulfillment in church spaces: the urge toward community life, the desire for what is true and genuine, the demand for clarity and intelligibility, and the longing for quiet and peace, for a sense of warmth and security.

The St. Cloud Newman Center's unadorned, square-shaped chapel space was meant from the start to foster a sense of community, to promote wide participation in worship, and to encourage people present to focus on one another as the living Body of Christ gathered together to pray. Peter Hammond, author of a book entitled *Liturgy and Architecture*, noted aptly that reduced to its bare essentials, a church is nothing more than a building to house a congregation gathered around an altar. The Newman

Center church, externally and internally, was designed to be simple, honest, humble, earthy and straightforward.[13] There are no statues, there are no paintings, and while there are Stations of the Cross along the walls, they are small and unobtrusive. When empty, the chapel seems plain, bare and colorless, but, pour a praying community into its pews and the space becomes filled with life and color. The chapel is designed purposely so that *the people* provide the life and the color, and so that the people focus upon one

A simple but beautiful space brought to life by the people who gather within it.

another and upon their act of gathering around the tables of the Word and Eucharist, instead of upon ornaments and icons. The Gothic architecture of the medieval cathedral encouraged worshiping communities to focus vertically—to elevate their eyes and ele-

vate their minds in order to contact a majestic and transcendent God and to commune with the holy in the heavens. The simple space of Christ Church chapel, on the other hand, encourages the community gathered to focus horizontally, not in order to minimize the transcendence of God, but in order to maximize awareness of the Christian mystery called Incarnation, our shared conviction that, through Jesus, the human and divine have wed and holiness has thus become close and immanent enough to be discerned all around us. By far the greatest challenge for most of us as human beings is not to train ourselves to look upward in search of God; it is, rather, to train ourselves to look directly and lovingly at the people sitting next to us, the people we pass on the streets every day, the people with whom we live and work and struggle, and to learn to see in them the face of Christ and the presence of God. The Newman chapel space makes the unadorned demand that its worshipers look at one another in such a way, and search determinedly for glimpses of the holy.

An integral part of the Newman Center chapel design was the large granite ambo, or lectern, installed to serve as a massive and compelling Table of the Word equal in nobility to the Table of the Eucharist with which it shared space in the sanctuary. Unfortunately, the granite ambo had to be removed in later years and

The Table of the Word and the Table of the Eucharist (below) were designed to be equal in nobility.

replaced with a wooden one because of logistical problems associated with its original placement. By 1968 a free-standing tabernacle, designed by Frank Kazmarcik, had also been installed in the sanctuary to replace the one that had been situated temporarily on top of the eucharistic table, a move that had to be approved by the diocesan Liturgical Commission because it had not yet been widely embraced as a valid practice. The wooden cupboard resting unobtrusively atop a stately marble column in the right, rear corner of the Newman sanctuary allowed the tabernacle to be restored to its original function: providing a secure storage space for eucharistic bread and wine that can later be taken to the sick if need be. The ornate structures that had served as tabernacles for centuries prior to the Second Vatican Council were designed primarily to inspire veneration of the eucharistic elements and did little to help the Christian community remember that, as a fifteenth-century cardinal quipped, the bread and wine were "instituted as food, not as a show piece."

The free-standing tabernacle.

The ambo and the simple tabernacle disconnected from the altar were highly progressive elements in the chapel's design, but an even more compelling component of the Vatican II-inspired space was its baptistry. "To be a Christian," John Henry Newman wrote, "is one of the most wondrous and awful

The baptismal font at the chapel entrance.

gifts of the world. . . . Let us remember that Baptism, though administered once and long since, is never past, and always lives as a blessing or a burden. We have a right to cherish it only when we are doing our part towards fulfilling it." The forecourt, or atrium, of the Christ Church chapel was designed to provide a transitional space between the street and the Church, and also to serve as a place for enjoying conversation and communion with others after religious services. Once the doors of the chapel are opened, however, the baptistry is encountered immediately. The smooth granite baptismal font centered there is much more than a giant holy water dish, a magnified version of the saucer-sized receptacles gracing the entry ways of most churches of the era; it is the holy place where infants, children, and women and men of all ages come in order to "put on Christ" for the first time. The font, constructed like both the ambo and the altar by the Kollman Monumental Company in St. Cloud, was placed prominently in the entry area of the

church because baptism, as one of the three sacraments of initiation, marks entrance into the Christian life. The earliest Newman parish bulletins are filled with admonitions to worshipers to dip their fingers into the font and trace the cross on their foreheads upon entering the church instead of upon leaving it. The baptistry's positioning was meant to make a strong statement and to serve as a potent reminder to community members of where they had begun, of who and what they claimed to be, and of what they had committed themselves, through baptism, to keep on striving to become more fully.

On July 30, 1964, Peter Bartholome sent off a rather testy set of instructions to Will Illies that foreshadowed the nature of some of the tensions over the novel liturgical space at Newman, which would become magnified in years to come. His letter began as follows:

> Dear Father Illies,
>
> Judging from the make-up of the Chapel at the Newman Center as it is laid out at the present time, I deemed it necessary to lay down a few regulations in regard to the fixtures that are to be installed and services that are to be conducted, and the manner in which they are to be conducted.
>
> The Altar platform covers about one-fourth of the space of the chapel. It is evident that the intent is to say Mass facing the people and sacrificing space for additional pews. No doubt in not too many years when the number of students increases it will be necessary to remove the platform and put the altar against the wall in order to accommodate the students. The following instructions are to be observed:
>
> 1. Mass facing the people is not to be offered by any priest at the Newman Center chapel.
> 2. What I think is a seat at the rear of the altar is to be taken out. . . .
> 5. The liturgical program to be followed at the Newman Center is not to be different from the program adopted by the parishes. In the course of the year the liturgical program will be duly announced.

Bartholome had been supportive of Illies and his decisions with respect to the shape and direction of Newman ministry in the diocese for many years. The nature of his participation, as well as his voting record at the Second Vatican Council, placed him squarely with the progressive majority. But the bishop was disquieted by the manner in which the liturgical traditions of the past, which he had long safeguarded, were coming into collision with the spirit of change and reform sweeping through the Church as a whole, and especially through the Catholic Christian community he had helped to construct at the crossroads. He began to counsel caution and to worry over the chaos, confusion, and potential disunity that change typically engendered.

A free-standing altar had been incorporated into the Christ Church chapel, which would one day allow for mass to be said facing the people, and a presider's chair had been placed at the rear of

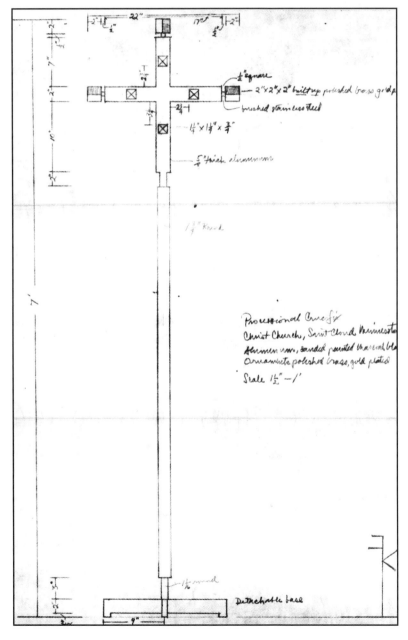

The original artist's sketch of the design for the Newman's Processional Cross.

115

the sanctuary. Both of these moves were considered radical at the time. The letter reprinted in part above was prompted by a surprise visit Bartholome had made one day to the newly-erected center; Illies' recollections of that visit are worth reproducing in full. As Wil describes it, Dan Taufen, who was living in the diocesan-owned house across the street and assisting with daily liturgies at Newman at the time, came bursting into Illies' office and informed him that he had better get into the chapel immediately, because Bishop Bartholome was there and didn't look happy. Says Illies: "I went into the chapel, and we had a big argument—a set-to of sorts about the altar and the chair." The bishop was displeased with the small size of the altar, which at the time was only wooden and was not connected to the wall. He also did not approve of the small size of the tabernacle then situated on top of the table. "You've got to have a big altar in here," he told Wil with characteristic gruffness, "a six-foot altar at least, and a tabernacle—a big tabernacle. I'll buy it." Then he noticed the chair placed in the rear of the sanctuary behind the altar and barked: "What's that?" "That," Illies informed him, "is the president's chair" "My God!" exclaimed Bartholome, "Do you want me to put a mitre on you too?" "Some day," Wil told the bishop in exasperation, "this Church will be used in the way it was meant to be used." "Yes," Bartholome retorted, "after you're dead." "No," said Wil in reply, "after *you're* dead." "Yeah, I know," the bishop flung back without missing a beat, "You hope that I die."

Though Illies and Bartholome parted from that encounter, as they parted from all encounters, with their relationship in tact, the inevitable tensions that would arise for members of the Church as they confronted the challenges of their own, internal crossroads experience would be a part of the relationship between Illies, his bishop and his peers in ministry for some time to come. The altar

The table around which the Newman community now gathers is moved into place. Its length measures exactly five feet, eleven inches, not six feet as the bishop desired.

around which the Christian community gathered at Christ Church remained free-standing, and the 9,000-pound granite table which replaced the temporary wooden one so distressing to Bartholome measured in finally at five feet, eleven inches in length, not six feet, as the bishop had requested. Donated by the Kollman Monumental Works, designed by Kazmarcik and fashioned from granite quarried in Ortonville, Minnesota, the altar was dedicated on April 10, 1965, and contains the relics of Sts. Peregrina and Ignotus. Fred and Rosemary Petters donated the first cloths for the new altar and Newman housekeeper Agatha Feldhege sewed them. An October 18, 1964, piece in the parish bulletin urged parishioners not to give up hope, as their requests that presiders face the congregation from behind the altar would certainly be met in due time. It would be May of 1967 before the bulletin was at liberty to announce that Newman presiders would, in fact, be facing the congregation within the next few months, and that the Mass would soon be celebrated entirely in English. From the start, however, the free-standing altar went a long way toward enabling the community to understand that in coming together around a common table for a meal which anticipated the Kingdom, they were expressing their willingness to be transformed themselves into the living, breathing Body

Visiting song writer Joe Wise plays and sings as bread and cup are shared around the table at Newman.

of Christ in the world. The focus for many years in eucharistic liturgy had been upon the elements resting *on* the table—the bread and
the wine—as well as upon the mystery of faith involved in believing that those elements were transformed into the body and blood
of Christ. After Vatican II, theologians worked hard to engender in
the people of God the sense that *who* is gathered *around* the table,
and *what happens* to those who are gathered around the table, is a
mystery every bit as important, and every bit as awe-inspiring. Not
just the bread and the wine, but women, men, and children are to
be transformed into the body and blood of Christ—into people who
see one another as sisters and brothers, into people who try to
crumble all the walls that keep them separate from one another,
into people who feel one another's hurts and experience one another's joys, into people who are willing to be broken and poured out
for one another in love, and into people who work daily to become
more reconciled, more united and more responsible for one another as members of one Body in the Lord.

Though the free-standing altar was of monumental significance, in some ways it was "The Chair" that finally came to serve as
the clearest symbol of the spirit that defined and animated the Christ
Church Newman community coming to birth on the banks of the
Holy Spirit's river. *The General Instruction on the Roman Missal*, first
published in 1969 to guide the Church in its use of the liturgical
reforms inspired by Vatican II, suggests that the best place for the
presider's chair is "at the back of the sanctuary and turned toward the
congregation," as a symbol of the office of presiding and directing the

A view of the president's chair at the rear of the sanctuary.

assembly. The granite presider's chair that once graced the Newman sanctuary was inspired by the spirit of that instruction, but it was an instruction that had not yet been formally given at the time the chair was installed. Bartholome was displeased with it for that reason, and also because he thought it inappropriately reminiscent of a bishop's throne. The chair remained, but over time the presiders making use of it in Christ Church came to feel that it placed them at too great a distance from the assembly and separated them, emphasizing their "differentness," rather than accentuating their oneness, with the community. In making its recommendations regarding the placement of the presider's chair, the *General Instruction* qualifies its preference for positioning at the rear and back of the sanctuary by adding sensibly: ". . . unless the structure or other circumstances are an obstacle (for example, if too great a distance would interfere with communication between the priest and people)." It was Bill Vos, pastor at Christ Church Newman Center between 1969 and 1979, who first made the move to abandon the chair and sit in the front pew as part of the main

Presider Nic Dressen and preacher Linda Wall sitting in the front pew as part of the main body of the assembly during a liturgy. (Photo courtesy of the St. Cloud *Visitor.*)

119

body of the assembly, thus inaugurating a tradition that has persisted to this day. From this position in the pew, the presider is confronted with the Word in precisely the same fashion as are all the other members of the gathered community, and he is able to do precisely what lectors, music, and eucharistic ministers serving the community do: remain in the place of greatest importance—the midst of the assembly—until it comes time to come forward in order to offer one's particular service.

The organ which now stands in the Newman Center chapel is a wonderful piece designed by Eric Fiss from Fargo, North Dakota. The total cost of the organ was $9,000, and, while the Knights of Columbus, other local church groups and some Newman parishioners made donations toward its cost, 1967 had dawned before sufficient funds were in hand to order and install it. Fiss sat for hours at a drawing board and created a compact, custom organ that would work effectively with the Newman chapel's unique acoustical space. Unlike most other organs, the pipes were set with the instrument instead of separate and away from the keyboard; real tones would always be heard by the congregation, not echoes. Fiss then sent his plans to an organ factory in Germany where the instrument was built, then taken apart with great care, boxed, shipped across the ocean and then reconstructed by the North Dakota craftsman. A March, 1967 parish bulletin announced:

Eric Fiss at work.

You may want to stop in periodically to see what the "entrails" of the organ are and how they fit into place, and to meet Mr. Fiss. . . . It is by no means the "grandest" organ in the world, nor is it for "grand" concerts. It will usually be played by non-professionals, and is to be an instrument of "service." For a very good lecture on the concept of "service" in worship, talk to Mr. Fiss.

When Fiss finished putting the organ together, he proclaimed simply: "Anyone who hears my organ hears the truth. After all, isn't that what people come to church for; to find the truth?"

And Music Fills the Sacred Space

In 1972, the Bishops' Committee on the Liturgy of the United States Catholic Conference issued the document *Music in Catholic Worship*, which affirmed eloquently that the quality of joy and enthusiasm music adds to community worship cannot be gained in any other way. In addition to expressing texts, music also unveils a dimension of meaning and feeling, a communication of ideas and intuitions, which words alone cannot yield.[13] "Song is a sign of the heart's joy," wrote the author of the Acts of the Apostles, and "to sing belongs to lovers," said St. Augustine of Hippo.

Students praying through music and song at Christ Church Newman Center.

Even though the truth of the proverbial saying, "one who sings well, prays twice," has long been acknowledged, in the history of our Church the story of music in liturgy for many centuries was but one more unfortunate chapter in the larger story of how people in the pews were gradually edged out of recognized roles and active participation. When music was employed at all in the Tridentine liturgy, acclamations, chants, and complicated mass settings performed by choirs and by clerics dominated. From the early decades of the twentieth century onward, however, reformers were hard at work developing ways to redefine the integral relationship between music and liturgy, and to underscore music's power and identity as a critical element of ritual action that expresses and shapes the faith of the praying community, enhancing its ability to participate prayerfully and fully.

Truth was communicated beautifully and often through Fiss' instrument from the moment it was completed; it wasn't long, however, before new instruments and new sounds were being added to the repertoire of truth-enhancing, and prayer-enhancing, music in the Newman community. An "experiment" started at the 5:00 P.M. Wednesday Mass, which soon grew to include the 8:30 P.M. Mass on Sundays. "Anyone who can play guitar, banjo, bass, flute, recorder, or bongos and would like to play for Mass occasionally, please leave your name," advertised the Newman Choir director, David Marthaler. The choir director began using some Alexander Pelaquin pieces composed for a variety of instruments at a time when the use of any instrument other than the organ, but especially the use of the guitar, was considered dangerously avant-garde. In 1967, in fact, the Newman Choir under Marthaler's direc-

David Marthaler (front) works with the Newman choir, *circa* 1967. Note the presence of guitar and bass.

Sebastian Temple comes to Newman.

tion presented a program entitled, "Meeting the Musical Challenge of Our Times," which featured the very modern "Mass for Joy" composed by Peloquin. It was a combination of jazz, folk and rock-style music arranged for solo voices, choir, and congregation and accompanied by string bass, trumpets, trombone, guitar, timpani, and organ. Committed to helping the crossroads community explore the cutting edge in liturgical music, in 1967 the Newman Center also invited the composer and singer, Sebastian Temple, to lecture and perform in the chapel. Born in South Africa of Jewish parents and a new voice in liturgical folk music, Temple's song "All That I Am" was quite a popular choice for liturgies in the late 1960s and early 1970s, and his "Prayer of St. Francis" is still sung widely today. In 1969, the "well-known black priest," Clarence Rivers, arrived at the Newman chapel to present a lecture on the place of music in the liturgy of the church to a packed audience of more than five hundred. He directed the Newman choir and a delighted audience through some works of his own composing, including his Mass dedicated to "The Brotherhood of Man," a particularly relevant theme in an era which found itself struggling with race relations and civil rights.

Reverend David Marthaler had taken over direction of the Newman Choir in time to prepare the group to be a part of the official dedication of the new Newman Center and chapel on April 25, 1965. The parish bulletin that day reported playfully on the decorative flags hung outside the building, a tradition that has continued this day as a way of marking special occasions. "No," said the bulletin, "we are not setting up a miniature United Nations. The flags outside the Newman Center and Christ Church are simply decorative; they do not have any deep, dark, mysterious symbolism." Dedication Day activities began with the blessing of the academic wing and chapel, followed by the celebration of a Pontifical High Mass at which the choir sang a large repertoire of music that they had worked long and hard to prepare and would later use as material for an album they recorded with great pride.

Clarence Rivers speaks stirring words to the Newman community.

Dedication Day Program, April 25, 1965.

NEWMAN CHOIR

DIRECTED BY:
REV. DAVID J. MARTHALER

NEWMAN CENTER
ST. CLOUD STATE COLLEGE
ST. CLOUD, MINNESOTA

Album cover of the choir's proudly recorded LP.

Bishop Bartholome presided and preached the sermon, and former Newman chaplains assisted and participated in a variety of ways. Leo Keaveny was the "presbyter assistant," while Frederick Kampsen and Leonard Gaida served as deacons of honor and Harold Kost as deacon for the Mass. Paul Zylla was the master of ceremonies. Though rain poured down and the skylights leaked during the service (much to the delight of those naysayers who insisted that one end of the building would surely sink into the Mississippi before long), the celebration was a great success. Marthaler has two significant memories of the event, one being Bartholome's characteristically gruff yet oddly endearing way of responding to the unique Newman spirit already manifesting itself in liturgy. "We did a piece of a very beautiful Mozart Gloria which would have been rather long in its entirety," Marthaler recalls, "and at one point Bishop Bartholome looked over at us wryly and asked, 'Are you done?'" Later, the bishop would bark to Illies, "Thank God they didn't sing all of it!" Marthaler's second significant memory is of how he smashed his first glass into the fireplace at the rectory after the day was over, a practice that had become customary for his predecessor, Harry Pavelis. Wil Illies' fondest recollections of the day, however, center around the banquet held at Garvey Commons on campus following the celebration of the Dedication Mass. Speakers at the banquet included St. Cloud State President George Budd, Newman Student Council President Donald Teff, Mr. Fred Hughes, co-chair of the New Horizons Campaign and long-time friend of the Newman effort, and Newman member Robert Wick, dean of the School of Liberal Arts at the college, who would, just three years later, be named Budd's successor as president of St. Cloud State College. What Illies remembers with most delight, though, is that as all of the invited guests and dignitaries came streaming into Garvey Commons for the meal, some of the crimson-clad monsignors found themselves bereft of direction and sorely perplexed; there appeared to be no head table set up in the room. "Where do we sit?" they asked Illies in confusion. "Wherever you want," Wil told them in reply. "We were trying," Illies explains, "to get away from some of this triumphalism business in the Church," which separated people out according to rank and status and always placed clerics in a more elevated position than laity, a practice that lead to unbecoming divisions within the Body of Christ and created an aura of pomp and circumstance certainly unbecoming in individuals who claimed humble servanthood as a chosen vocation.

The Best of Times and the Worst of Times

Nick Zimmer arrived in St. Cloud to become Wil Illies' partner in Newman ministry in 1964, just as the new center was completed. Zimmer quotes Charles Dickens when he looks back on the five years he subsequently spent living and working in the middle of the highway called St. Cloud State College: "It was the best of times, it was the worst of times." It was certainly a time of great hope and excitement about the future. Vatican II had triggered the emergence of a new atmosphere of openness and a new wave of optimism in the church; the election of the young John Kennedy had caused a similar wave of optimism to swell over the nation. But it wasn't long before other forces began to make themselves felt, and as the decade of the sixties progressed, there also emerged much chaos, confusion, conflict, and pain, both in the church and in society as a whole. There was Kennedy's assassination in Dallas and the escalation of American involvement in the Vietnam War. There was the great "March on Washington," the Civil Rights movement as a whole, and the intensification of the cry for authentic liberation for women. There was a mass exodus of priests and women religious from the ranks of the Church, and there were revolutions in fashion, in music, in youth culture, and in social mores. And there was 1968, bringing with it the infamous Democratic National Convention in Chicago, the publication of the Church's controversial document banning artificial contraception, *Humanae Vitae*, race riots in the streets, and the unspeakably tragic assassinations of both Robert Kennedy and Martin Luther King, Jr. The causes and characteristics of this volatile era in our collective history are complex, and they have been pondered, analyzed and categorized by many, but Nick Zimmer's summary reflection on those years will probably always, to some extent, hold true. "If you lived through it," Zimmer avows, "then you know. If you didn't, I can't explain it to you."

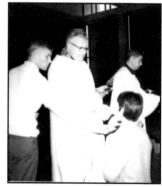

In the middle of a crossroads environment like the university where ideas, influences, and people of varied backgrounds and convictions are all brought into confluence, the social, religious and political upheaval going on throughout the nation was, of course, often magnified. Fortunately, the leaders of the Newman effort in St. Cloud were wise enough to navigate well through the perils of the upheaval, and to allow themselves and the ministry they guided to be touched and transformed through the experiences of conflict and tension that were emerging in and around the highway community to which they were committed.

Illies and Zimmer (right) distribute communion, working side by side as they did in all things.

In 1967, Illies, Zimmer, and their colleagues Richard Lewis from the Wesley Foundation and Raymond Anderson and Joseph Ottoson from the Lutheran Student Association together composed a moving piece of text for the local newspaper on the modern college student in which they expressed their shared conviction that the uncertainties and restlessness of their age were necessary and valuable and that the welter of thought, controversy, and confusion through which people were wending their way was, in fact, merely the turmoil always caused by newness and rebirth. Further, in the newsletter published biannually in those years by the Newman staff as a means of communication with parents, associates, and alumni, Zimmer and Illies placed prominently in the layout a quote from Maurice Oliellet which read: "Youth is a time of rebellion. Rather than squelch the rebellion, we might better enlist the rebels to join that greatest rebel of his time—Christ himself." And the front of the Newman Center brochures printed in the late 1960s featured John Henry Newman's declaration that "a spontaneous resolution never to change is inconsistent with the idea of belief." Inside, the Newman chaplains wrote:

> This is the era of the "new breed," the "restless generation," the cool and the committed. These are not labels to be scorned, for campuses include thousands of young people who are questioning, challenging, demanding, and taking nothing for granted. Apathy is present, too, but the general atmosphere is one of serious, active concern with all aspects of human existence.
>
> It is essential for the informed college man and woman of today not only to be *in* the campus community, but also to be *with* that community. . . . Each person has a significant contribution to make. . . . The college encourages free inquiry and religious involvement: involvement with liturgy, theology, ecumenism. The Newman Center exists with the college for that purpose.

In a "Parent's Day" homily delivered on May 4, 1969, Wil Illies explained to the fathers and mothers of college students assembled before him that, in large part because of the crossroads environment of the university that by its very nature fosters openness to diversity and growth, the implications of those ideas and changes launched for Catholics by Pope John and the Vatican Council had been welcomed and embraced by most of their children. Unfortunately, many of the parishes from which students came and to which they returned when at home had refrained from proclaiming those principles very boldly, or had backed away from their ramifications once they had been enunciated. Because of the resulting disappointment and disillusionment that students experienced, Illies continued, "I would sense that the attitude of many of our young people is that they are simply kind of waiting to see if they are going to remain with the church or not. The young or at least many of them, I believe, will remain only if we can show them that in the church, and by the church, they will be heard and they will not be tuned out."

Illies and Zimmer were not by any stretch of the imagination unthinking radicals who advocated change for the sake of change. The commentaries they offered were balanced, and they chastised both "liberals" and "conservatives" alike who became so fanatic in their viewpoints that they displayed a sorry lack of ordinary courtesy in their dealings with others.[14] A quote from India's Mahatma Gandhi reprinted in one bulletin even reminded parishioners that "when you think the world is all wrong, remember that it contains people like you." But the Newman ministers of the crossroads understood that, as Illies once reported to a local

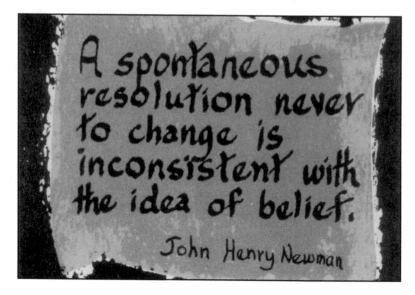

A spontaneous resolution never to change is inconsistent with the idea of belief.

John Henry Newman

Council of Catholic Women, the knowledge of the penny cate-
chism simply could live up no longer to the soul-searching of people today. Zimmer and Illies did their best to listen well, to encourage openness and growth and to model a certain refreshing sanity
and perspective when it came to matters religious. The weekly bulletins from 1965 onward, for example, are full of thought-provoking quotes and repartees from people like Dag Hamarskjold,
Simone Weil, Karl Rahner, Hans Küng, and John XXIII. Letters
from a presumably fictitious character called "Aunt Ermalinda"
appeared for a while, providing an amusing and non-threatening
way for challenges, commentary, and gentle chiding to be offered.
Aunt Ermalinda, the 1965 bulletins reported, had lived for a while
among the Irish in Boston to get away from the ordinary "hoi pol-
loi" of the Midwest. But after returning to live on the farm with
Uncle Louie, she started to read voraciously and then report to her
"nephews" in St. Cloud on what she was learning. "She threatened
me with perpetual ignorance," one bulletin announced, "if I didn't
read 'The Christian Adventure—Risk and Renewal' by Gregory
Baum in the April-May *Critic*. . . . The author treats the rather perplexing question of change in the Church, with shades of
Newman's *Development of Doctrine* in modern dress. It reminds one
of Will Roger's statement that things aren't what they used to be,
and maybe never was. With our simplistic approaches to things, we
tend to forget the 'maybe never was' part."[15] An even better report
on Aunt Ermalinda's progress described her recent discovery of
ecumenism, "a rather huge and progressive interest for Auntie."
She was fearful, the bulletin reported, "that her anti-Protestant
prejudices might be tarnished with the truth. But she kept reading.
. . . Auntie said that she is getting confused. I wrote to tell her I
thought confusion was better than complacent error, and that
unlearning is usually more difficult than learning."[16]

Five years after the opening of the Second Vatican Council
and three years after the opening of the new Newman Center,
Zimmer and Illies wrote a bulletin piece offering some telling com-
parisons between "then" and "now" for the community. Five years
is actually a very brief period of time, but the contrasts which they
were able to draw are revealing, and give some indication of why
that period in the Church's history was a trying and tension-filled
one, despite the excitement and hope also in the air. That October
15, 1967, bulletin summed it up in this way:

> Answers and definitions in '62; questions and reformulations
> in '67.
> Optimism and hope in '62; tension and wondering and trying
> in '67.

128

Clerical celibacy was settled in '62; it's open for discussion in
'67.

Sins and limits were neat in '62; conscience is stressed in '67.

Liturgy was Latin mystery in '62; Liturgy is English with more
basic questions in '67.

Protestants were "the others" in '62; Protestants are fellow-
Christians in '67.

Closed attitudes in '62; open attitudes in '67.

Collisions as Well as Conversions at the Crossroads

Transformation happens when the power of the Holy Spirit
is released and women, men, and institutions are led to new levels
of self-discovery, eye-opening shifts in perspective, and changed
ways of understanding. But, as Rosemary Haughton wisely reminds
us, transformation occurs most powerfully when formation in some
way breaks down, comfortable patterns are disrupted, and time-
honored structures are unsettled because they are no longer adequate to embrace the demands of love as these are issued forth in
a changed and changing environment. The challenge of that paradox presents itself as a matter of course in a crossroads environment like the university, where many and diverse ideas, values and
visions constantly and inevitably interact, influence and stretch
one another's parameters. The paradox is much less comfortably
encountered, however, in a very settled environment like the
Church, always a catalyst, hopefully, of spirit-guided transformations in individuals and in communities, but also an institution
whose mission it is to proclaim the unchanging deposit of faith and
to safeguard the structures designed to support formation in that
faith. Accustomed to adopting a posture of openness, born under
the star of a watershed moment in the modern history of the
Church and exposed from the start to the theological and liturgical
foundations of the steps toward renewal the Vatican Council would
parent, the Newman Center campus church became a transformed
and transforming "Vatican II community" without hesitation. Not
only in the way its worship space was designed and used, but in
other areas of programming and decision-making as well, those who
guided the community implemented reforms and welcomed needed change with enthusiasm. There were many students, many faculty members, and many members of the St. Cloud community at
large who were delighted at the way the Catholic Christian community planted in the middle of the St. Cloud State highway was
evolving and saw in its life a true manifestation of the Spirit
released and at work on the banks of her river. There were others,
however, who did not.

Illies chats wtih a young
church-goer in the Newman
Terrace.

129

Whenever he had the opportunity, Wil Illies would commend and compliment the parents of college students who came to visit their daughters and sons at St. Cloud State and then venture over to come and see the campus parish of which their children had chosen to become a part. "I'm afraid," Illies would say to them sadly, "that it's generally just those who do not come and see who perhaps are doing most of the vicious complaining and backbiting." And complaining and backbiting there were, especially among the ranks of the clerics who were Zimmer and Illies' colleagues in the diocese of St. Cloud. "We had all been brought up in one way, where everything was secure and authority figures took care of all problems," Nick Zimmer reflects. "Then, suddenly, we were alone, left on our own to figure it all out in the midst of all different kinds of views. . . . It was like watching everyone try and paint a room a different color." Zimmer affirms without hesitation that the evolution was a necessary one, but the process was painful. "Our faith and our ministry was intimately connected to a very firm structure, and, when that structure got shattered, for some people there wasn't always a whole lot left." For a 1989 pictorial directory of the presbytery of the Church of St. Cloud, Vincent Yzermans wrote a brief but insightful introduction detailing what he perceived to be some of the typical virtues and foibles of the men who had chosen to serve the diocese over the years. Fidelity and charity were their most conspicuous virtues, Yzermans purported, while a certain parochialism and distaste for anything that unsettled the known and the familiar was, in general, their most grievous fault. That parochialism often enabled them to serve as highly committed local pastors, but at the same time it led some of them into smugness and complacency. In Yzermans assessment: "The range of their reading was much too narrow. The cultivation of the arts was too often neglected. The difficulty many experienced in accepting the teachings of the Second Vatican Council indicated that they were babes in the woods in understanding the philosophical and theological explosion going on well before the Second World War." Whether or not one accepts that assessment as accurate, Yzermans is certainly correct in observing that in the first decade of the administration of Bishop George Speltz, who officially took over the reigns from Peter Bartholome in 1968, the bonds between "priests and priests" in the diocese were strained as they never had been before, and tensions surrounding the age of reform and renewal that had emerged in the Church, and in society at large, had not a little to do with that strain. Illies and Zimmer came to suffer the effects of the quagmire more poignantly than many.

By the late 1960s, a group of about twelve or so diocesan clergy had become increasingly outraged by what they believed was going on "over there" at the Newman Center, even though the most vociferous of the objectors had never really been "over there," or taken the time to converse respectfully with Zimmer and Illies about their management of Newman ministry. Some few pastors were angered because their parishioners were being "stolen" by Newman, and others were made uncomfortable by the anti-war demonstrations and civil rights protests that were a part of campus life at the time, and thus came to be associated with the life of the campus church as well. But for the most part, the dissatisfaction of Zimmer and Illies' colleagues centered around liturgy. "When you look back on it now it was so ridiculous, really," Illies reflects. The innovations he and Zimmer were adopting were actually quite minimal, and they never blatantly ignored rubrics or moved irresponsibly beyond approved liturgical norms, despite vocal and ill-informed accusations to the contrary. It was just that, as Zimmer puts it, any deviation from standard practice was considered major at the time, so that small things like serving communion in the hand, or adding guitars to the organ and the choir, or sharing wine at weekday masses, or turning around to face the people at certain moments in the liturgy before such practices had been officially adopted, caused monumental consternation. The greatest tragedy of all, of course, is that such consternation was handled dysfunctionally, and that little or no open and constructive conversation ever happened. Dark letters were sent and secret conversations were held with the bishop; the bishop's housekeeper would even

Illies presiding over the prayer of a community he loved.

come over to the Newman chapel for Mass and then return to the chancery with "reports" on what she had observed. Prodded on by one or two men with particular axes to grind, the group of clergy who were most disgruntled and suspicious decided to make their displeasure known by withholding the assessments they were supposed to pay yearly from their parish treasuries in support of diocesan-sponsored ministries like Newman. The tension reached a critical point.

In the summer of 1969, long-time Newman chaplain George Garrelts at the University of Minnesota found himself lamenting the resignation of James Shannon, auxiliary bishop of St. Paul/Minneapolis and a long-time personal friend of Wil Illies. Garrelts asked urgently in a tribute written for his own parish bulletin that Wil reproduced in the St. Cloud Newman bulletin: "What can we do to create a climate in which able, gentle, jovial, attractive men can exercise their ministry without fear or undue restraint?" Nuns, priests, and sometimes bishops left their work in the Church in record numbers during those years; their reasons were many, but more often than not it was because under the liberating influences of the post-Vatican Council world, they had found the internal freedom to reexamine their personal motivations, their desires and hopes for the future, and the theological foundations of those ecclesiastic structures to which they had previously felt themselves bound without the right to question. Many also became frustrated by the resistance to change they encountered all around them, and by the oppressive efforts to control and to contain that consistently emerged in reaction to the forward movement Vatican II had generated. David Marthaler muses today that the most apt and abiding image he carries with him of those tumultuous years following the council is of people "driving off." Because of Wil Illies' openness and hospitality, Marthaler recalls, the rectory at Newman was often a "last stop" and transitional sanctuary for fellow members of the presbyterate who had made a decision to leave the diocese, or the priesthood altogether, because they knew they would be received sympathetically and respectfully by Illies while the details of their departures were finalized. Sadly, in March of 1969, it was Illies' trusted colleague in Newman ministry, Nick Zimmer, who found himself "driving off" and away to begin a new assignment as pastor of St. Mary's Church in Chokio, Minnesota. Less than six months later, Illies himself would be driving off as well.

It was the practice of the diocesan personnel board in those years to send out a form each February in which members of the presbyterate were asked to indicate whether or not they were con-

Bishop George Speltz, left, celebrates the Feast of Christ the King with Illies, Zimmer, and the Christ Church Newman community.

tent in their current assignments, and what their feelings were about the possibility of movement. Zimmer had become increasingly disheartened by the hostility targeted at Newman by some of his colleagues in the presbyterate, and by the minimal backing he and Illies received from Bishop Speltz. In a moment of frustration, he pulled out the form one day shortly after it arrived and wrote with a flourish: "Yes, I'm willing to move; let some of those doing the complaining come here and take the job." Less than a month later, right before Holy Week, he found himself on the way to Chokio. When Zimmer's reassignment was made public, the campus community exploded in protest. Letters of support for Zimmer were sent off to the bishop, petitions appeared in the press, and the protestant clergy with whom Zimmer and Illies had come to work closely penned moving letters to the editor. Zimmer himself had to sit up one night into the wee hours of the morning in order to talk a well-intentioned supporter out of organizing a march on the chancery. Illies was furious and stomped over to see the bishop, demanding to know why he had allowed Zimmer to resign. Speltz responded by asking Illies: "What do you think I should have done, given him a vote of confidence?" "Yes, absolutely," Illies retorted. "Do you think I should give you a vote of confidence?" the bishop inquired. "Yes," Illies replied without hesitation, "I think you should." "Well, I can't do that," Speltz said curtly, "because I've lost all confidence in you."

Biship Speltz greets church-goers at Newman.

From that moment on, things went from bad to worse. Illies was angry, but he was also deeply hurt. Years later, Illies and Speltz would be able to talk about that painful time in their relationship and achieve some level of mutual understanding. But, at the time, it seemed to Wil that Speltz was far too quick to suspect and far too reluctant to trust; he could not help but be offended that the bishop gave so ready an ear and lent so much credence to the complaints of the critics, who actually were proportionally quite

134

small in number, and at the same time gave him and Nick Zimmer so very little credit for being responsible, competent and trustworthy facilitators of a unique and important ministry in which they had spent years developing expertise and wisdom. "Too many forgot, in that era," Illies reflects now with a certain sadness, "that you have to let people be a little bit, and let students be who they are as they grow." Newman ministry is very important to the life and to the future of the Church, because the posture of respectful openness it assumes enables people who would never come near a church otherwise to approach the doors, and begin to explore. From the very start, searching and questioning students found a refuge at Newman, and countless others who had become disillusioned, dissatisfied, disappointed or just plain apathetic found themselves saying, "If it weren't for Newman, I wouldn't go to church at all now—I would have given up completely long ago." Pastors and bishops, affirms Illies today, should never be nervous about that; they should be grateful for that, and endeavor to understand.

But both gratitude and understanding were in short supply in those tense and painful years at the end of a tense and painful decade. Illies and Speltz had a few more curt conversations; Speltz asked Illies to provide him with a week's schedule so that he could see exactly what Illies was doing, and Illies complied caustically by providing a detailed listing not just of Mass and confessions, not just of the numerous appointments he had with students and the countless engagements he had on campus, but also of the precise times at which he rose, brushed his teeth, drank his coffee and took his meals. Worn out by the constant

Wil Illies

Nick Zimmer

tension, exasperated at having to play "Mickey Mouse games" and tired of feeling mistrusted and unsupported, Illies finally told Speltz he didn't think he could work at Newman under such circumstances much longer. Speltz asked him if he would be willing to take another parish; by August Illies agreed. The announcement that Illies would be leaving St. Cloud as of August 22 to become pastor of St. Marcus Church in Clear Lake, Minnesota, shocked, saddened and enraged the community. Once again, letters poured into the chancery and to the local newspaper from students, faculty members, ecumenical colleagues, and others. The Civil Liberties Union on campus was ready to go to bat for the man of the cloth they had come to know, respect and trust as a colleague at the crossroads. But the die was cast and there was no turning back. On August 17, 1969, Wil Illies celebrated his final liturgies with the Newman community he had sustained and nurtured with love and great commitment for sixteen years. Later he told the St. Cloud State student newspaper: "I have to admit that I did ask to be reassigned, but I did so because of the pressure. . . . For my own good and Newman's, I asked to go."

The many parting words spoken by and about Illies and Zimmer probably sum up as well as anything else could the legacy they left behind, and the Spirit-filled ways in which they themselves had been touched and transformed as a result of travels and encounters that became a part of their lives in the crossroads community called St. Cloud State. In a farewell letter written "To members of Christ Church, the college community, and friends," Zimmer concluded by saying this:

> In my opinion, my experience at the Newman Center and my association with a college community has been one of the greatest experiences in my life. I don't know how to express all of this, but the following statements may indicate something of my feeling. I have learned that there is a growing moral sensitivity among young people, which I can only admire. I have learned that the young are too wise, too honest, and too aware, to be satisfied with simplistic approaches to complicated problems, I have learned that there is great confusion and searching, but that in this there is a great reason for hope. I have learned that an old and quite describable world is dying, and that a new and quite indescribable world is being born. I have learned that people want to be treated as persons, and not simply as statistics or cogs in a machine. I have learned that the Catholic Church must become more catholic. I have learned that many people are threatened and angry and that the great task for Christians is to bring love and reconciliation into the world. I have

learned that of the many scriptural strains from the past, the words "apocalyptic" and "prophetic"—vague though they may be—can best describe the world in which we live, and struggle and hope. My most appropriate button reads: "Old hippies never die, they just trip away."

Shalom to all,
And keep smiling,
Nicholas M. Zimmer

Of Wil Illies, Ward Trautz, the custodian engineer at the Center, remarked simply: "Words cannot express my appreciation towards Father Illies. If there were more men like him in this world it would be a much better place to live in." And Ray Anderson, Joe Ottoson, and Merv Repinski, Illies' colleagues in ecumenical campus ministry, wrote movingly:

> How does a body say farewell to its right arm? For those who know of the close relationship which has existed among the campus clergy here at St. Cloud State, it should not be necessary to elaborate in detail the tremendous loss that the "reassignment" of Father Illies will mean to each of us personally, and to the campus in general. Perhaps it would be sufficient for now to express our thanks for the past, and our anticipation of his continuing contributions at the redemptive, reconciliatory, and revolutionary activity of the Church of Christ on earth.

It would be twenty years before two of Illies' successors in Newman ministry, Nic Dressen and Frances Nosbisch, would pen their first reflections on how the people of God who open themselves up to the challenges of the crossroads almost inevitably come to grace-filled milestones on their journeys "over tough roads, through construction zones, by way of detours and wrong turns." With the departure of Zimmer and of Illies, the Newman community arrived at another important milestone in its journey; a bit older and a bit wiser now, that community knew that it would undoubtedly face many more tough roads and construction zones in the years ahead as it dedicated itself anew to the continuing search for signs of grace, and to both the legacy and the mission which had become its own. On his last Sunday at the Newman Center he had done so much to build, before the unique Catholic Christian community to which he had given so many years of his life, Wil Illies offered the words of Teilhard De Chardin as a parting plea and prayer: "May the Lord preserve in me a burning love for the world and a great gentleness. May God help me to persevere to the end in the fullness of humanity." It

The Newman custodian (top), Wil Illies (middle), and secretary Yvonne Honer (bottom).

137

was a prayer and a plea to which the members of the Newman community living and loving on the banks of the mighty River of the Holy Spirit would always endeavor to be faithful.

Notes

1 Pope John XXIII, *Opening Address to the Second Vatican Council*, October 1962.
2 Monica Hellwig, ed., *The Modern Catholic Encyclopedia*, "The Liturgical Movement," by J. Leo Klein, S.J., p. 512. (Collegeville, Minnesota: The Liturgical Press, 1994).
3 Quoted in Evans, p. 161.
4 Evans, p. 161.
5 Quoted in the Newman parish bulletin, October, 1967.
6 Documents of Vatican II, Constitution on the Sacred Liturgy, No. 11.
7 Yzermans, *Journeys*, pp. 178-179.
8 Yzermans, pp. 180-181.
9 United States Catholic Conference, *Music in Catholic Worship*, 1972, no. 4.
10 "Newman Students Called on to Pioneer Council Changes," *St. Cloud Visitor*, 20 September 1964, p. 7.
11 John Henry Newman, *Conscience, Consensus and the Development of Doctrine: Revolutionary Texts by John Henry Cardinal Newman*, commentary and notes by James Gaffney (New York: Doubleday, 1992), pp. 33-118.

12 Thomas Merton, as quoted in "Newman Center's Plan Determined by Purpose," *St. Cloud Visitor*, 14 April 1963, p. 6.

13 "Newman Covers Plan Determined by Purpose," *St. Cloud Visitor*, 14 April 1963, p. 6.

14 Christ Church Newman Center bulletin, 26 February 1967.

15 Bulletin, 20 June 1965.

16 Bulletin, 4 July 1965.

Chapter 5

Going My Way—And Yours
Catholicism Meets Other Faiths at the Crossroads

*O Lord Jesus Christ . . . look down in pity on the manifold division among those
who profess thy faith and heal the many wounds which the pride of man and the craft of Satan
have inflicted on thy people. Break down the walls of separation which divide
one party and denomination of Christians from another . . .*

— John Henry Newman

I n 1947, about three years after he left his post as spiritual advisor to the St. Cloud Newman Club to become pastor of a small church in Elizabeth, Minnesota, Frederick (Fritz) Kampsen was playing baseball, as he loved to do, for Elizabeth's town team. It happened, one day, that some men from Grand Forks, North Dakota, who did scouting for the St. Louis Cardinals were passing through town and stopped to watch the afternoon game. They were impressed with Kampsen's pitching abilities and asked some people in the stands the name of the fellow who was working the mound. "That's our priest," they replied. Surprised, the scouts returned wryly, "Your priest! Well then, where's your minister?" Without missing a beat the good people of Elizabeth responded truthfully, "He's the umpire." That small-town interfaith baseball game and the harmony it appeared to reflect between Protestants and Catholics in the community so impressed the scouts that they told their tale to the local newspapers; shortly thereafter, *The Catholic Digest* picked up the story and gave it national exposure. From almost the earliest of times, then, ecumenism in many forms has been a part of the Newman journey.

A hat contest during the Minnkota Province Convention, held in St. Cloud at Cathedral High School. Gerald Meyer (sporting a hat) stands at left.

Fr. Illies (left) and Fr. Durkin (right) with Newman Club students involved with the Minnkota Province Newman Convention hosted in St. Cloud in 1960.

The restoration of unity among all Christians, affirmed the Second Vatican Council, is a principal concern because Christ the Lord founded one church and one church only. Although many Christian communions present themselves as the only true inheritors of Jesus Christ and condemn all others, such exclusiveness and division openly contradicts the will of Christ, scandalizes the world, and damages the sacred cause of preaching the Gospel to all peoples.[1] The immediate occasion for the start of the ecumenical movement in the twentieth century was the scandal of rivalry between Christian missionaries and among Christian student organizations.[2] The spiritual foundation of the movement, however, was the desire to respond to the wish of Christ formulated in Scripture that became the dying prayer of Pope John XXIII, "that all may be one . . ." That wish, interestingly enough, became the theme of the first convention of the newly formed "Minnkota" Province of the National Newman Federation held in St. Cloud in 1960. Newman members from college campuses in Minnesota, North Dakota and South Dakota gathered for three days in April to focus on the theme of Christian unity on the banks of the River of the Holy

Robert Fixmer delivers his keynote address to the Minnkota Province Convention in St. Cloud. William Durkin sits to his left, George Garrelts and Wil Illies sit at right. "That All May Be One" was the convention's hopeful theme.

143

Spirit, and the results were impressive. Chaired by student Gerald Meyer, its speakers included William Durkin, George Garrelts, Robert Fixmer, Robert Schulzetenberg, Paul Halloran, Kilian McDonnell, Gerald Potter, Vincent Yzermans, and Bishop Peter Bartholome. At the opening mass of the convention, Bartholome told the students before him: "You are the Church! Don't you forget that. If you live in accordance with the teachings of Christ, you will make a tremendous contribution toward unity." The inside

Bishop Bartholome addresses the Minnkota Convention, "You are the Church!"

cover of the convention program contained an eloquent affirmation of the Christian vocation to learn to live in one household of faith, of the Christian hope that unity is possible and every effort toward it worthwhile, and of the importance of Christian charity, which ought to prompt women and men of faith to act as neighbor toward all with the love of Christ. That love, the program went on to say, is a love alike for "Protestant, Oriental Dissident, Catholic, Jew, for Muslim, Hindu, Buddhists, and primitive worshiper." Just five years later, the Fiftieth Anniversary Congress of the National Newman Federation held in New York City would also make "That All May Be One" its theme. In a papal message sent to the 1,000 student representatives at that Congress, Paul VI stressed the need for charity as well, and told students that "the realization of this prayer of our Blessed Lord may well be possible through the fulfill-ment of the motto of Cardinal Newman, your inspiration and model: 'Heart Speaks to Heart.'"[3]

After decades of protective isolationism and a defensive refusal to allow sanctioned discussions of denominational differ-ences lest the Church appear to be advocating "religious indiffer-entism," John XXIII opened the door to extensive ecumenical activity when he called the Second Vatican Council and created the Pontifical Secretariat for the Unity of Christians. Paul VI later took another major step forward by initiating the first bilateral ecumenical dialogues in which the Catholic Church officially par-ticipated. The Catholic principles of ecumenism articulated in the documents of Vatican II are really quite extraordinary. They are based upon both loyalty to the Catholic tradition and upon respect-ful trust that the yearning for Christian unity comes from the Holy Spirit who continuously guides the Church and should not be ignored. The *Decree on Ecumenism* strongly recommends "spiritual emulation" as the proper attitude to be adopted between divided members of the Body of Christ and advocates frequent prayer in common with other Christian communions as well as trust in the power of that prayer to foster mutual reconciliation.[4] The *Decree* also insists that Catholics should become familiar with the outlook of separated churches. Study is affirmed as an essential prerequisite to authentic understanding, and the document even goes so far as to point out that theology must be taught with due regard for the ecumenical point of view, so that it may more accurately corre-spond with the facts. One of Vatican II's most striking avowals, in fact, is that "future pastors and priests should have mastered a the-ology that has been carefully elaborated in this way and not polem-ically."[5]

In 1961, Catholic lay scholar William Whalen wrote a guide for Catholic students in secular colleges and universities in which he described the reality of their lives very bluntly:

> You may expect to encounter a wider spectrum of humanity on a secular campus than you would on a Catholic one. A state university faculty may include agnostics, Christian Scientists, Moslems, secularists, Catholics, ex-priests, paci-fists, retired army officers, Unitarians, Freemasons, funda-mentalists, Socialists. Among your classmates you may meet Texans, Mormons, country boys, Hindus, Jews, idealists, sophisticates, Anglo-Catholics, prudes, and libertines.[6]

Such is the crossroads environment of the state university. To its credit, even though it emerged originally from a desire to provide support for Catholic students who sometimes felt besieged and alone in such an environment, from its very beginnings the Newman movement was determined not to become "clannish" in any narrow, religious sense and really did attempt to speak "heart to heart" with others encountered at the crossroads. As former Newman chaplain Harold Kost notes, throughout most of the twentieth century it was not unusual for St. Cloud State students to have come from small, homogeneous communities and to have had very little experience of diversity in any form. But, unlike their peers in Catholic institutions, these Catholic students had no choice but to rub elbows with professors, administrators, and other students whose religious beliefs were quite different from their own; they came face to face, daily, with the reality that good women and men abounded who did not share a frame of reference they took for granted. Being thrust into the middle of a highway where such diversity of thought and belief existed led them, in general, to an authentic appreciation for the necessity of openness, no matter how sheltered their backgrounds had been. In an article written for the *Minnesota State Monthly,* a St. Cloud Newmanite named Jane Lang, in fact, adamantly underlined Harvard theologian Harvey Cox's conviction that any work which is not radically ecumenical has no place on the university campus, or indeed, anywhere else. Christians succeed in strengthening and enriching the crossroads environment of the university, Cox had asserted in *The Secular City,* only when they live with responsibility within it and for it, and not in and for the denominational churches that weaken and fragment it.

Christ Church　　　　Newman Center

Community

The Church is not a building, a budget, a program, an organization. It is a people in motion, an 'eventful movement' in which barriers are being struck down and a radically new community beyond the divisiveness of inherited labels and stereotypes is emerging. — COX

146

True ecumenism—true and active fidelity to the desire to restore unity among the divided Christian Churches—depends for its success and its life upon a genuine conversion, or *metanoia,* in both individuals and communities that produces truth, charity, and humility. As a Newman parish bulletin expressed it in 1968, "We can pass through the door of ecumenism only on our knees." The Vatican II documents avowed strongly that no ecumenism worthy of the name can ever exist with interior conversions, for "it is from newness in attitudes of mind, from self-denial and unstinted love, that desires of unity take their rise and develop in a mature way."[7] Over time, the meetings that emerged out of inevitable intersections at a crossroads like the St. Cloud State campus proved to be genuinely converting encounters for both Catholics and non-Catholics alike, and the spirit of ecumenism took root and blossomed on campuses throughout the nation in ways much more powerful and far-reaching than those that emerged in other environments. The documents of Vatican II also refer often to the necessity of the Holy Spirit's guidance in prompting the kind of conversions that make ecumenism possible; perhaps we should not be surprised, then, that on the River of the Holy Spirit conversions of heart and mind leading to a true spirit of ecumenical cooperation between the Christian churches were taking place almost from the very beginning.

A History of Heartfelt Meetings

The Newman Club was actually the very first religious group to organize itself on the campus of St. Cloud State Teachers College. The Lutheran Student Association followed six years later in 1929, as did campus chapters of the YMCA and YWCA. By 1932 the Calvin Forum and the Wesley Foundation had also been established, followed in succeeding years by the Westminster Fellowship, the Canterbury Club, the Baptist Student Fellowship, the Missouri Synod Conference of Lutheran Students, and the Covenant Club for members of the Mission Covenant Faith. By 1959, the inter-denominational United Campus Christian Fellowship, or UCCF, consisting of members of Presbyterian, Congregational, Evangelical, United Brethren, and Reformed faiths, had been added to the ranks. The various religious groups on campus shared periodic frustrations with an environment that did not always take their common concern about the importance of things spiritual as seriously as they would have liked. But, from the earliest of times, cooperative efforts between them seem to have been rooted in something much deeper. By 1932, an "Inter-Religious

Council," made up of representative student members from all religious organizations on campus had been formed. Similar councils were not uncommon at other secular universities throughout the country.[8] Although ease in interaction between separated Christians was not part of the climate of the times, all evidence suggests that fairly warm relationships existed among the religious organizations that came to be established on the campus of the St. Cloud Teachers College. The October 7, 1937, minutes of the Newman Club report, for example, that the Lutheran Student Association, as well as members of the general public, were the guests of the Newman Club at a lecture given by the ever-popular priest-geologist, Henry Retzek. Such invitations were returned in kind. In May of 1938, the Newman Club held a brief business meeting and then adjourned to the W.C.A. Room where they were the guests of the Wesley Foundation for some unrecorded event. In 1939, all religious organizations of the college and the English Club were guests at a program held in the auditorium and given by Miss Helen Bottum, supervisor in the Primary Department of Riverview. Miss Bottum read the play, "Shadow and Substance," by John Vincent Carroll. On May 24, 1945, the Newman Club minutes report that a trip to the St. Cloud Orphanage replaced their regular meeting, and that "many Protestant students went along as our guests." It seems, too, that joint meetings of all religious organizations on campus were held regularly, at least in the 1930s and 1940s, and that such meetings, featuring speakers of various denominations, were well-attended and well-received.

While the Inter-Religious Council at the St. Cloud State Teachers College was organized initially simply to coordinate religious activities on campus, by 1954 *Talahi* felt justified in reporting that an additional goal of the council was to work for "cooperation and harmony" among the seven religious groups then functioning at the college. Cooperation and harmony appear to have been the norm rather than the exception, however, in inter-denominational relations on the banks of the Mississippi, and shared fun became as much a part of the agenda for students of differing denominations as shared meetings, speakers, and planning efforts. As early as 1934, *Talahi* reports that the council sponsored a party in the Social Room for all religious organizations at which each club presented an entertainment feature, the whole group participated in a "sing-a-long" and former Newman chaplain Leo Keaveny addressed the group as a whole. Joint "Caroling Parties" often happened in the holiday season, and in 1938 the religious organizations on campus together constructed their first joint float for the homecoming parade.

There were times in these years, unfortunately, when the national leadership of the Newman movement slipped into a more cautious mode when it came to ecumenism and actually discouraged interfaith activism on its many campuses because of the fears and the warnings of the hierarchy. A truly sad moment came in 1954 when the executive secretary of the National Newman Federation proudly announced that most Newman chaplains "kept joint activities to the lowest possible minimum," and were participating in the popular Religious Emphasis Weeks and other interreligious discussion groups "rather reluctantly."[9] Less than a decade later, the Second Vatican Council would baptize and advocate such pioneering, ecumenical efforts. Even in the face of opposing winds, however, the dual influences of the River of the Holy Spirit, and the crossroads encounters that are an inevitable part of life on a university campus, continued quietly to produce the kind of conversions of heart and mind that made ecumenism an unshakeable part of the Newman way for Catholics at St. Cloud State. Catholics at public universities throughout the nation were likewise prodded toward ecumenical conversions by the highway environs in which they lived, and by 1964, national structures had begun to catch up with the lived learnings of their grassroots membership. Notably, a 1964-1965 booklet printed by the National Newman Club Federation, which provided suggestions for the planning of Religious Emphasis Weeks on campuses, strongly encouraged the adoption of ecumenism as a theme for such weeks. That booklet offered to Newman students ten "Practical Suggestions" for promoting wider ecumenism on campus that still have considerable worth today and could benefit people of faith in all ages. The booklet counseled:

1. Try to develop a theology which is more relevant to the needs of our times and needs . . .
2. Try to develop the theology of baptism of desire, of implicit or virtual faith as in the criterion of the last judgment ("I was hungry . . ."), of the religion of sincerity and commitment to justice and goodness ("not everyone who says, Lord, Lord . . .") . . . of the new Jerusalem and of heaven when the Church will be seen as one Bride of Christ and when distinctions of faith, hope will have disappeared and charity alone will remain.
3. Study other religions, their sacred texts, preferably with them.
4. Cultivate a spirit of ecumenism towards them; dialogue not polemics. Seek the things that unite rather

than what divides. Respect ideas, things and persons sacred to them.

5. Pray and meditate together with them concerning the common truths we might hold and the common ideals and needs of our peoples.

6. Work together for the social good—of the university, of the city and of the country. The sanctification, especially of the laity, has to be realized in and through daily life: work and labor. Our engagement in building the city of man [sic] on earth is also our contribution to the building of the new Jerusalem.

7. Invite and welcome non-Christians to as many of our meetings and functions as possible.

8. Participate in their activities as much as possible.

9. Seek to understand the noble inspirations that may animate even those who do not profess any religion at all.

10. Try to develop an ecumenical approach towards non-Christians in the so-called "Christian" countries also.

By 1981, those who guided crossroads ministry at the national level had grown even more bold. In that year, the national Catholic Campus Ministry Association formed an Ad Hoc Committee for Ecumenical Concerns at the Joint Lutheran/Catholic Conference held at St. John's University in Collegeville, Minnesota, and unequivocally defined their task and mission as follows:

> To present to the United States Catholic Conference Office of Ecumenical-Inter-Religious Affairs a vision of the Church rooted in our ecumenical perspective on college and university campuses; a vision which will allow us to share a more common religious life with Lutheran brothers and sisters, including:

> A. Full recognition of each other's ordained ministries, and

> B. Celebration in Eucharist of our growing unity in the deep hope that we shall there find ourselves to be more and more built up into the one body of the risen Lord and thus become a sign of unity within our churches.

That ad hoc committee included two members of the pastoral staff at the Newman Center in St. Cloud at the time, namely, Sam Jadin and Gigi Mooney, as well as one future member of the staff, Bill Dorn, who was employed in Bemidji at the time.

Religious Emphasis Weeks

It was during the 1935-1936 school year that the Inter-Religious Council at St. Cloud State first began to sponsor "Religious Youth Week" on campus, an event which sought to focus student attention on the spiritual dimension of life and later came to be called "Religious Emphasis Week." Over time, the major task of the Inter-Religious Council seems to have become the planning and executing of these weeks, which evolved into inter-denominational endeavors to encourage in all college students the development of a personal relationship with God, to impress upon students and faculty alike the importance of religion in their daily lives and in higher education and to demonstrate the intellectual respectability and relevance of religion in a rapidly changing world. These abiding shared concerns, as well as a history of playing, living and learning well together on campus, provided the impetus for efforts that cut across denominational lines and did much to foster a spirit of unity among the disparate members of Christ Body dwelling on the banks of the Mississippi.

Religious Emphasis Weeks usually centered around a theme and included the presentation of a lecture by a speaker as well as other events designed to have broad appeal. In 1948, for example, the movie "God of the Atom" was shown in Eastman Hall as one of the week's activities. As Religious Emphasis Week evolved over the years into "Religion in Life Week," it occasionally experienced rough going, but not because of a lack of cooperation among campus religious organizations. In February of 1959, *Newman News*, expressed concern and sadness that that year's conferences were not better attended. The opening convocation, student editorialist Gene Casey pointed out, was scheduled for 10:00 A.M., a free hour, and it is deplorable that "a college permits a cup of coffee or the atmosphere provided by a snack bar to be more appealing than a renowned speaker." Mr. Casey went on to decry the lack of courtesy, common decency, and support for Religious Emphasis Week displayed by the college administration because it allowed so many other activities to interfere with the programming of the mere three days of focus granted to religious organizations on campus each year. The student body, too, was implicitly scolded for being apathetic about prioritizing attendance.

In 1958, the theme chosen for Religion and Life Week on the banks of the Mississippi created a bit of controversy; apparently, "Christ the Hope of the World" carried with it connotations uncomfortable for those concerned with the rights of non-believers and members of non-Christian religious communities at the college. Due to conflict over that theme, and over the quality and types of meetings held during religion weeks in general, President George Budd appointed a team of three faculty members to study the nature, scope, and legal ramifications of religious activities on campus. The results of that study were published in 1959; it was a well-balanced report that included an overview of relevant state and federal law as well as a survey of religious activity on more than one-hundred other secular campuses in forty-four states. The authors of the report concluded by affirming their belief that, with competence and maturity, it would certainly be possible for a faculty to avoid a dogmatic approach to religious activity at St. Cloud State College. They wisely advocated an approach for the future that would be characterized by neither an undeviating invocation of the separation of church and state principle nor an emotional, doctrinaire interpretation of religious values. Two years later, in 1961, a rather impressive "Religion in Life Week" was organized around the theme "Religion and Power in the World." St. Cloud State President George Budd penned an eloquent message for student participants that appeared in the printed schedule for the week. True students of religion, he averred, draw attention to the fact that there are more concepts common to all the great religions in the world than there are differences among them and that students had a responsibility to learn how to understand the values held by others. Religion in Life Week, Budd concluded, is an opportunity to study and think, to raise questions and seek information, and then to achieve understanding based on knowledge. That year, the program included a showing of the Ingrid Bergman film, the "Inn of the Sixth Happiness," as well as lectures given by a Baptist minister, a Jewish rabbi, and George Garrelts, the well-known National Newman chaplain from the University of Minnesota. A closing music concert was held in the Stewart Hall Auditorium featuring the St. John's Choir. In subsequent years, as "Religion in Life Week" evolved into an annual "Conference on Religion," its planners became even more firmly committed to offering a program of events that would be relevant to the entire academic community; thus it was that physicist Harold Schilling from Penn State University came to offer his views on the relationship between religion and science, and mathematician Charles Hatfield from the University of North Dakota was invited to share his views on the topics: "Faith and Reason," "Evil, Suffering, and God," and "Life's Most Urgent Questions." Perhaps it was because of consistent exposure to such cooperative efforts to educate and enliven the faith of students on campus that the 1963 edition of *Talahi* was able to offer a description of student religious organizations of which John Henry Newman would have been proud:

152

The religious organizations on campus give the interested student a focal point in his [sic] search for meaning. United by a common bond of faith, members are shown that a passive acceptance of religion is not enough. Instead, by joining an informal company of peers in an extensive range of activities, social and intellectual, recreational and religious, each individual is encouraged to become a total person and led to make an active declaration of belief by works as well as words.

Vatican II Lights a Fire

When the doors to ecumenism were opened officially by the Second Vatican Council, Newman leaders throughout the country were more than ready to walk through with enthusiasm, and those who were guiding Newman ministry at St. Cloud State were no exception. In July of 1963, the St. Cloud Newman Center and the *St. Cloud Visitor* jointly secured a visit from Gustave Weigel, a noted Jesuit who, as Art Yzermans put it, was an ecumenist in the United States before most American Catholics could spell the word. Weigel served as the official interpreter for the observer-delegates from non-Catholic churches at the first and second sessions of the Second Vatican Council. Prior to his arrival in St. Cloud, Weigel had been banned from speaking at the Catholic University of America, together with Hans Küng, John Courtney Murray, S.J., and Godfrey Diekmann from St. John's University in Collegeville, other ecumenically-minded theologians imbued with the spirit of Vatican II who would later become quite famous. At

Third from the left is Gustave Weigel, noted ecumenist who visited the St. Cloud State crossroads community in 1963.

an evening lecture held in Brown Hall, Weigel announced that American Catholics now realize that they can and should engage in ecumenical conversations with other Christians without seeking their conversion to Catholicism. The local paper noted that many protestant clergymen were in the audience. In that same year, after learning that the archbishop of St. Paul and Minneapolis had canceled a scheduled address by Hans Küng at the Newman Center of the University of Minnesota, Bishop Bartholome courageously invited the young Swiss theologian to the Diocese of St. Cloud to deliver his address "Freedom and Unfreedom" before a standing room only audience at St. John's University.[10] Ecumenism at the crossroads which is St. Cloud State took on a very practical face in the summer of 1964, when Catholic students had to vacate the old Newman Hall so that its site could be cleared and construction could begin on their new center. The Lutheran Student Association under the direction of Reverend Joseph Ottoson graciously agreed to allow Catholic students to hold and attend mass in the assembly room of LSA's "Luther Hall," located just a block away from Newman Hall. Bishop Bartholome approved of the arrangement, and Wil Illies expressed his deep gratitude to the Lutheran Student Foundation and their director for such a tangible display of the true ecumenical spirit at work on campus.

The Lutheran Student Association agreed to allow Newman to share its worship space while the new Newman facility was under construction. From left to right are W. Birch, LSA's president; Wil Illies; Ron Schultz, Newman's president; and Reverend Joseph Ottoson, LSA's director.

By 1967, two national student groups had embraced the spirit of ecumenism so unabashedly and unequivocally that they took bold action. The Council of the Lutheran Student Association of America adopted a resolution at its annual meeting calling on the nation's Lutheran churches to seek organic reunion with the Roman Catholic Church, and to "explore the possibility that Lutheranism and Roman Catholics need not regard themselves as separate churches or denominations but merely as different points of view within the Western . . . Church." The resolution was forwarded to the National Newman Conference meeting at Northwestern Illinois University coupled with a "Message of Greeting." Newman students in attendance at that conference unanimously endorsed the Lutheran resolution and called upon the Catholic bishops of America, the bishops' Committee on Ecumenism, and the bishops' Committee on Education for Ecumenism "to seriously consider the recommendation of LSAA and to explore all avenues which may lead to an organic reunion of the Lutheran and Roman Catholic churches." At the local level in St. Cloud, a similar determination to work intrepidly for the restoration of unity in the fragmented Body of Christ was at work. The Newman Center's own Wil Illies was appointed to the newly-formed, three-member diocesan Ecumenical Commission in the mid-sixties, and often found himself invited to speak about ecumenism at local Catholic and non-Catholic gatherings. He was also given official accreditation to the Fourth Assembly of the World Council of Churches meeting in Uppsala, Sweden, in July of 1968, a gathering at which representatives of 232 Protestant, Anglican, Old Catholic, and Orthodox churches were present.

As campus ministers, both Illies and Zimmer were confident, convinced and unwavering in their determination to explore the possibilities for ecumenical cooperation and renewed unity at the crossroads, and their enthusiasm was shared by their non-Catholic colleagues. A brochure published jointly in 1967 by the Newman Center, Lutheran Campus ministry, the United Campus Christian Fellowship (which would in later years be called "United Ministries in Higher Education") and the Wesley Foundation declared boldly that "ecumenism is the real hope for religion on the state college and university campus," and that anything else would "fail to provide meaning for the college we are meant to serve and are able to serve." As "Christians in Cooperation," these groups announced further in their prophetic brochure that the Church is really people who move and care for each other, not static structures that divide people from each other. Since the leaders of the religious organizations active on campus at the time were courageous enough to believe that it was

Page 5   The College Chronicle   September 26, 1967

Christians In Cooperation Classes Begin This Week

Classes in the Christians in Cooperation will begin this week. Christians in Cooperation is the title of a coordinated effort of Gamma Delta, Lutheran Christian Ministry, Newman Center, United Campus Christian Fellowship, and Wesley Center at St. Cloud State. In addition to other programming, Christians in Cooperation will sponsor the following classes during the fall quarter.

CATHOLICISM TODAY taught by Revs. Illies and Zimmer, and stressing current theological trends among Catholics, will meet on Mondays at 7 p.m. and be repeated on Tuesday at 10 a.m.

THE LUTHERAN CHURCH PAST AND PRESENT will meet on Tuesdays at p.m. This class, with Rev. Joseph Ottoson and guest lecturers, will discuss Lutheran Confessional statements within a 20th century context.

PROBLEM AREAS IN THE OLD TESTAMENT, with Revs. Ray Anderson and Nicholas Zimmer, will meet at 7 p.m. on Tuesdays (not Wednesdays as previously scheduled) to discuss Genesis, the creation stories and evolution, the Bible and myth, exodus and the miraculous, the prophetic message, and related areas of present concern.

All classes will meet in the Newman Center once a week beginning the week of Sept. 25 and continuing through the week of Nov. 13. Classes are free, and open to all students, faculty, and the public.

The cover of a joint brochure (right) published by St. Cloud State's "Christians in Cooperation."

time "to move . . . to come out . . . together," they made some fairly significant decisions about refusing to fragment their efforts along denominational lines and worked deliberately to combine their programming efforts for the year. Because of its "exceptional facilities," most of the classes developed were offered at the Newman Center. There was a Ecumenical Study Group and a joint scripture class offered, as well as a class in Christian economics and a roundtable discussion focused on Teillhard de Chardin's book, *The Phenomenon of Man.* On Sunday evenings, there were also joint programming offerings ranging from the showing of such films as *La Strada, The Parable,* and *A Time for Burning,* to panels, discussions, and shared services. Each week a "Coffee Hour" was sponsored by all the campus ministries at the Atwood College Center, and during the Week of Prayer for Christian Unity in January, daily evening prayer services were held at Newman. Joint service opportunities were explored and many other ecumenical discussion and dialogue oppor-

156

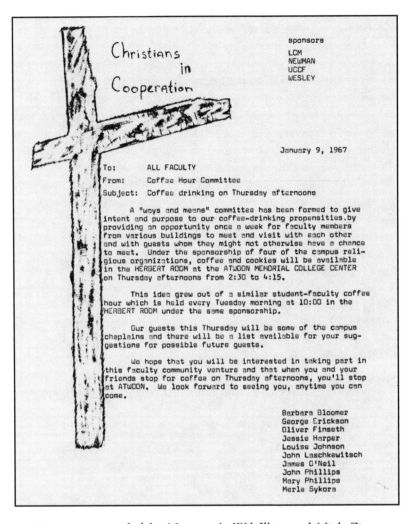

Faculty involvement has been a highlight of ecumenical activity at St. Cloud State.

Within the image:

Christians in Cooperation

sponsors
LCM
NEWMAN
UCCF
WESLEY

January 9, 1967

To: ALL FACULTY

From: Coffee Hour Committee

Subject: Coffee drinking on Thursday afternoons

A "ways and means" committee has been formed to give intent and purpose to our coffee-drinking propensities.by providing an opportunity once a week for faculty members from various buildings to meet and visit with each other and with guests whom they might not otherwise have a chance to meet. Under the sponsorship of four of the campus religious organizations, coffee and cookies will be available in the HERBERT ROOM at the ATWOON MEMORIAL COLLEGE CENTER on Thursday afternoons from 2:30 to 4:15.

This idea grew out of a similar student-faculty coffee hour which is held every Tuesday morning at 10:00 in the HERBERT ROOM under the same sponsorship.

Our guests this Thursday will be some of the campus chaplains and there will be a list available for your suggestions for possible future guests.

We hope that you will be interested in taking part in this faculty community venture and that when you and your friends stop for coffee on Thursday afternoons, you'll stop at ATWOON. We look forward to seeing you, anytime you can come.

Barbara Bloomer
George Erickson
Oliver Finseth
Jessie Harper
Louise Johnson
John Laschkewitsch
James O'Neil
John Phillips
Mary Phillips
Merle Sykora

tunities were provided by Newman's Wil Illies and Nick Zimmer, Reverend Joe Ottoson of Lutheran Campus Ministry, Reverend Ray Anderson of UCCF, and Reverend Richard Lewis of the Wesley Foundation. Notably, beginning as early as 1964, the campus ministries also sponsored a faculty retreat together, and for several years in a row beginning in 1965 planned and implemented an "Annual Faculty Ecumenical Seminar." In 1966, that seminar was entitled "The Sacred and the Secular," and consisted of presentations and discussion sessions spread across two days on such provocative topics as freedom, prophecy, and service. Alfred McBride, O. Praem., conducted the seminar, after which he wrote a note to Wil Illies and Nick Zimmer exclaiming like Boy Wonder in the Batman series: "Holy Barracuda! . . . I have probably never done so much thinking or been more aware of the need for greater competence than in my experiences especially with the ecumenical group." Christians in

157

Re-Formation Talk Set at Newman Center

Dr. Donald R. White will speak on "Society, the Church and Re-Formation" Tuesday at 8 p.m. at the Newman Center, St. Cloud State College Campus.

Dr. White

His visit is sponsored by the Christians in Cooperation, on the campus.

Dr. White took M. A. and Ph. D. degrees at the University of Chicago in 1962 and 1964. He is now a visiting professor of religion at Carlton College and assistant professor of historical theology, United Theological Seminary of the Twin Cities, New Brighton, Minn.

A discussion will follow.

The program is in commemoration of the 450th anniversary of Luther's posting of the 95 theses on the door of Wittenberg.

Above, a community ecumenical event sponsored by Christians in Cooperation.

Opposite page, the ecumenical campus ministry staff at St. Cloud State, *circa* 1974.

Ecumenical cooperation at work in very concrete ways.

Cooperation also celebrated the Forty-fifth Anniversary of the Reformation together on October 31, 1967, with a speaker, a question, dialogue and discussion session, and a closing prayer service in which all participated. On the Sunday following that celebration, the Newman parish bulletin contained this announcement: "THANK YOU! to the ecumenical Lutheran member of the faculty who sent us flowers on the anniversary of the Reformation. If more people on all sides of the church issue had 'said it with flowers' during the past 450 years, we wouldn't be in quite the trouble we are."

By 1969, "Christians in Cooperation" or "CIC" actually served as a structure for the organization of ministry efforts on campus for all the mainline Christian denominations. Bill Vos, who succeeded Illies and Zimmer at the St. Cloud Newman Center, describes ecumenism as a highly significant piece of how he experienced and framed his ministry at the crossroads throughout the decade of the 1970s. Areas such as administration and finances, the Coffee House, community relations, commuter students, counseling coordination, faculty relationships, minority students, noncredit courses, retreats, service projects, publicity, the annual joint brochure, shared worship experiences and many others, were divided up between the combined staff people of all of the denominational ministries. As a 1971 brochure articulated it, sharing in per-

TASK RESPONSIBILITIES OF CLERGY to June 15,1970		
ITEM:	PRIMARY:	SECONDARY:
Administration and Finances	Marv	Joe
Area Clergy	Ray	Bill
Area Schools and Colleges	Marv	Bill
Coffee House	Marv	Joe
College Structures & Orgzt'n	Ray	Marv
Community Relations	Ray	Bill
Commuter Students	Joe	Bill
Conveniener	Marv	
Counseling Coordinator	Joe	Bill
Crises Intervention	Bill	Joe
Draft Counseling	Marv	Joe
Faculty Relationships	Ray	Bill
Fine Arts - Film,Drama,Art	Marv	Bill
International Students	Joe	Ray
Inter Religious Council	Marv	Ray
Married Students	Bill	Marv
Minority Students	Marv	Joe
New Student Days	Marv	Ray
Non Credit Courses	Ray	Marv
Professional Relationships	Ray	Joe
Publicity and Brochures	Bill	Ray
Religious Studies	Joe	Bill
Retreats and Trips	Marv	Joe
Service Projects	Marv	Bill
Sports	Joe	Marv
Summer School	Ray	Marv
Worship	Bill	Joe
Y.M.C.A.	Joe	

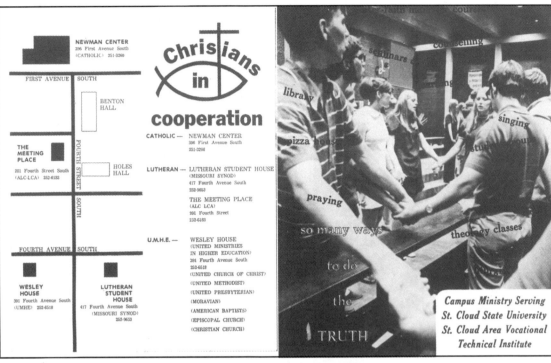

NEWMAN CENTER
396 First Avenue South
(CATHOLIC) 251-3260

FIRST AVENUE SOUTH

BENTON HALL

THE MEETING PLACE
201 Fourth Street South
(ALC-LCA) 252-6183

FOURTH STREET SOUTH

HOLES HALL

FOURTH AVENUE SOUTH

WESLEY HOUSE
391 Fourth Avenue South
(UMHE) 252-6518

LUTHERAN STUDENT HOUSE
417 Fourth Avenue South
(MISSOURI SYNOD)
252-9653

Christians in cooperation

CATHOLIC — NEWMAN CENTER
396 First Avenue South
251-3260

LUTHERAN — LUTHERAN STUDENT HOUSE
(MISSOURI SYNOD)
417 Fourth Avenue South
252-9653

THE MEETING PLACE
(ALC LCA)
201 Fourth Street
252-6183

U.M.H.E. — WESLEY HOUSE
(UNITED MINISTRIES
IN HIGHER EDUCATION)
391 Fourth Avenue South
252-6518
(UNITED CHURCH OF CHRIST)
(UNITED METHODIST)
(UNITED PRESBYTERIAN)
(MORAVIAN)
(AMERICAN BAPTISTS)
(EPISCOPAL CHURCH)
(CHRISTIAN CHURCH)

library pizza nous praying so many ways to do the TRUTH seminars singing theology classes

Campus Ministry Serving
St. Cloud State University
St. Cloud Area Vocational
Technical Institute

"Joe"
Rev. Joseph Ottoson, A Lutheran Campus Minister to statewide Lutheran Campus Ministries.

"Vonnie"
Vonnie Olsen, Executive Secretary for Lutheran Campus Ministry. Vonnie serves as receptionist at Meeting Place.

"Gordy"
Gordon Phelps, A Lutheran Campus Minister serving students at St. Cloud State University.

"Marv"
Rev. Marvin Kuhlman, Lutheran Campus Minister serving Lutheran students at St. Cloud State University and St. Cloud Area Vocational Technical Institute.

"Bill"
Rev. William Vos, A Newman Campus Priest serving Roman Catholic Students at St. Cloud State University.

"Ray"
Rev. Raymond Anderson, A UMHE Campus Minister to statewide UMHE Ministries.

"Pete"
Rev. Peter Fribley, UMHE Campus Minister who teaches Scripture and ministers to Protestant students.

"Kathy"
Ms. Katharyn Waldon, A Newman Campus Minister who teaches Systematics, Philosophy and works with Social Action Programs.

"Ade"
Rev. Adrian Lederman, A Newman Campus Priest serving Roman Catholic Students at St. Cloud State University and St. Cloud Area Vocational Technical Institute.

"Katie"
Sr. Katherine Kraft, Campus Minister who teaches Scripture and works with Liturgy.

159

sonnel and resources allowed for more efficient fulfillment of the common goals of campus ministry. Though CIC staff members continued to work as representatives of their respective religious organizations, diversity as well as the reduction of unnecessary duplication was made possible through their efforts to provide a "united" service to the academic community. Individuals like Peter Fribley, Joseph Ottoson, Ray Anderson, Marvin Repinski, Peg Chamberlain, Darius Larsen, and many others became highly valued colleagues and trusted friends for members of the Newman Center staff. Beginning too, in this era, United Ministries in Higher Education, which coordinates outreach to students and faculty on behalf of the United Methodist, Episcopalian, United Church of Christ, Disciples of Christ, Presbyterian, and Moravian churches, actually operated out of rented office space within the Newman Center building and continued to do so for more than a decade.

As the 1970s unfolded, however, a gradual shift occurred in the flavor of those cooperative efforts embraced so enthusiastically in the wake of the Second Vatican Council and in the wake

In a humorous ecumenical moment of shared laughter, Newman minister Adrian Ledermann demonstrates Methodist prayer-meeting activities by removing his collar, rumpling his hair and leading the audience in whooping and hollering.

of that transforming upheaval and reform that swept institutions of all sorts in that era. While the warmth of relationship and the level of mutual respect and regard to this day has not declined or become compromised among the campus ministers serving the St. Cloud State campus, in the late seventies a slow movement away from united programming and back toward individual activity emerged. Most of the shift occurred more for practical than ideological reasons; the novelty of shared activity passed, and many students seemed to respond to denominationally-based activities more readily than they did to diffuse, ecumenically-focused ones. Those who have traveled in ecumenical circles for many years reflect, too, that once the earliest hurdles of polemical attitudes, stereotypes and inbred biases are overcome and differing Christian communions discover that they can work comfortably together with mutual respect, a complacency of sorts set in. Enthusiasm for discovering, and then moving to the next level in the search for unity often dissipates. For these or other reasons as yet unrevealed, even though both the reality and the depth of the ecumenical spirit prevailing at the crossroads that is St. Cloud State remained beyond dispute, it eventually slowed in its pace and fervor. As the 1970s and 1980s progressed, the "CIC" brochure, which for a few years clearly presented campus ministry as a jointly sponsored and jointly run activity, advertising its "staff people" as part of one, cooperative organi-

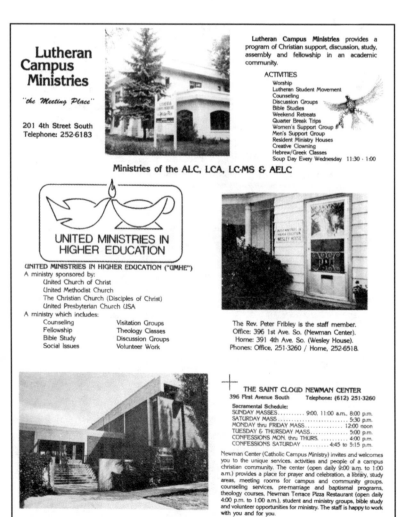

Lutheran Campus Ministries

"the Meeting Place"

201 4th Street South
Telephone: 252-6183

Lutheran Campus Ministries provides a program of Christian support, discussion, study, assembly and fellowship in an academic community.

ACTIVITIES

Worship
Lutheran Student Movement
Counseling
Discussion Groups
Bible Studies
Weekend Retreats
Quarter Break Trips
Women's Support Group
Men's Support Group
Resident Ministry Houses
Creative Clowning
Hebrew/Greek Classes
Soup Day Every Wednesday 11:30 - 1:00

Ministries of the ALC, LCA, LC-MS & AELC

UNITED MINISTRIES IN HIGHER EDUCATION

UNITED MINISTRIES IN HIGHER EDUCATION ("UMHE")
A ministry sponsored by:
    United Church of Christ
    United Methodist Church
    The Christian Church (Disciples of Christ)
    United Presbyterian Church USA
A ministry which includes:

Counseling	Visitation Groups
Fellowship	Theology Classes
Bible Study	Discussion Groups
Social Issues	Volunteer Work

The Rev. Peter Fribley is the staff member.
Office: 396 1st Ave. So. (Newman Center).
Home: 391 4th Ave. So. (Wesley House).
Phones: Office, 251-3260 / Home, 252-6518.

THE SAINT CLOUD NEWMAN CENTER
396 First Avenue South   Telephone: (612) 251-3260

Sacramental Schedule:
SUNDAY MASSES.......... 9:00, 11:00 a.m., 8:00 p.m.
SATURDAY MASS............................ 5:30 p.m.
MONDAY thru FRIDAY MASS.............. 12:00 noon
TUESDAY & THURSDAY MASS.............. 5:00 p.m.
CONFESSIONS MON. thru THURS. .... 4:00 p.m.
CONFESSIONS SATURDAY .... 4:45 to 5:15 p.m.

Newman Center (Catholic Campus Ministry) invites and welcomes you to the unique services, activities and people of a campus christian community. The center (open daily 9:00 a.m. to 1:00 a.m.) provides a place for prayer and celebration, a library, study areas, meeting rooms for campus and community groups, counseling services, pre-marriage and baptismal programs, theology courses, Newman Terrace Pizza Restaurant (open daily 4:00 p.m. to 1:00 a.m.), student and ministry groups, bible study and volunteer opportunities for ministry. The staff is happy to work with you and for you.

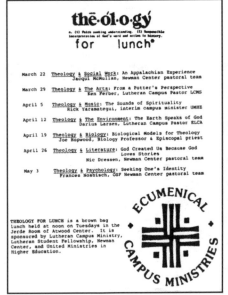

zation, began to allot a "panel" for each participating denomination in which a whole array of worthy, but separate, activities were described. Only one panel of the brochure continued to be reserved for the advertisement of joint, CIC programming, and over the course of the decade, these programs declined in number. Theology courses, faculty luncheons and seminars, social concern efforts, and Interfaith Marriage Seminars seemed to have had the greatest lasting-power.

When the 1980s arrived, ecumenical campus ministry leaders created a successful faculty luncheon program which was dubbed "Theology for Lunch." Once each week the Newman Center, United Ministries in Higher Education and Lutheran Campus Ministry sponsored a "brown bag" lunch meeting in the Jerde Room of Atwood Center from noon until 1:00 P.M. at which someone would speak on a timely topic with theological implications and then invite discussion among all present. Speakers included St. Cloud State faculty members, members of the various campus ministry staffs, and other professionals invited in from the surrounding community. Over the three academic years, 1979-1980, 1980-1981, and 1981-1982, a series of fall luncheon presentations inspirited in a special way by Dr. Peter Fribley of United Ministries in Higher Education focused on reflective responses to the theme "Whence Cometh My Help? Roots and Support Systems for Excellence and Ideals in Teaching and Administration." The series was well-received, and some of the responses it generated were published in the winter of 1982 by David Johnson, then Vice-president for Academic Affairs. These responses from an inter-departmental cross-section of faculty members provide some very stimulating reading and give valuable voice to the feelings of SCSU faculty on such varied questions as: "What are your criteria for excellence and how did you come by them?" "How do you keep these convictions alive and honor them other than in the breach?" "How do you avoid, when you can, being numbered among those who no longer really give a damn?" "How do you fight burn-out?" "What do you most respect around this place? What least?" "Is our work here largely a plus or a minus for your family?" and "What role has a specific religious community or community of purpose had in your life?" These poignant and provocative reflections included the thoughts of members of the biology, sociology, art, speech communication, English, physics, foreign languages, astronomy, and other departments. Other "Theology for Lunch" topics covered the gamut, from civil disobedience, to psychology, to myths, to sports and storytelling in theology, to literature, to criminal law, to pacifism, to ethics in business, to women in the church, to science and religion, and to reflections on North American involvement in Central and South American politics. As time went on, it was not uncommon, in fact, for well-known peace and justice activists to be invited to speak at these brown-bag sessions, including the Reverend Jonathan Nelson, who participated in the 1982 blockade of the first Trident submarine commissioned for active duty. "Theology for Lunch" persisted for almost ten years and represents one of the best efforts—ecumenical or otherwise—made before or since to involve the faculty of St.Cloud State university in active dialogue about how faith and life cross over and interact in the crossroads environment of a university.

The 1980s also brought with them a continued commitment to ecumenical programming in the marriage preparation process, and for many years the Newman Center, Lutheran Campus Ministries and United Ministries in Higher Education sponsored a joint, two-day Marriage Preparation Course featuring workshops on budgeting, communication, human sexuality, the Christian understanding of marriage and last, but certainly not least, the challenges of an ecumenical marriage relationship. These sessions included presentations by several couples in ecumenical marriages who were also members of the Newman Center parish, like Jerry and Sylvia Mertens, Steve and Joan Vincent, and Bette and Vern Bartos. In fact, as Christ Church Newman Center took root and grew as a parish community with ever-increasing membership, it became a real haven for couples in inter-denominational relationships searching for a place to worship where their diver-

Registration fee is $10 per person, payable in advance of the weekend.

Registration fee includes all materials, coffee breaks, and Saturday lunch.

<u>TO REGISTER</u>

1) Fill in pre-registration form
2) Tear off and mail or leave with

   Newman Center
   396 So. 1st Ave.
   251-3260

   United Ministries in Higher
      Education
   396 So. 1st. Ave.
   251-3260

   Lutheran Campus Ministry
   201 So. 4th St.
   252-6183

For further information:

   Contact any of the above sponsoring ministries.

MARRIAGE PREPARATION COURSE

NOVEMBER 8 & 9, 1985
ST. CLOUD NEWMAN CENTER

Sponsored by

Catholic Campus Ministry

United Ministries in
Higher Education

Lutheran Campus Ministries

Children from several different Christian congregations in the southeast corner of St. Cloud come together to sing, learn, pray and play as part of an annual ecumenically run Vacation Bible School.

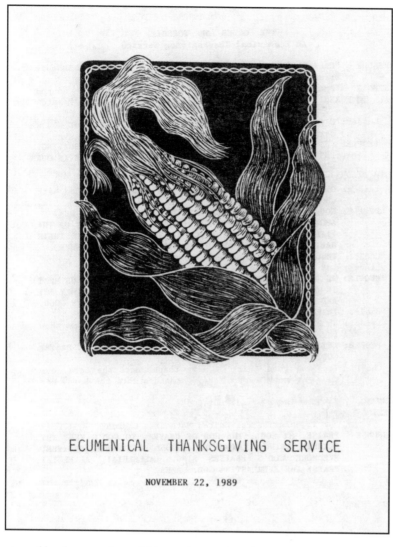

ECUMENICAL THANKSGIVING SERVICE

NOVEMBER 22, 1989

sity of background would be welcomed and respected. In addition, after 1972 the Newman Center's newfound status as a parish also gave it reason to participate in ecumenical efforts taking place between the "neighborhood churches" in the southeastern corner of St. Cloud of which it is a part. Those efforts have taken a variety of forms over the years, but the two most enduring traditions to emerge from them have been an annual ecumenical Thanksgiving Service, held on the Wednesday night before Thanksgiving, and an event of some sort in January designed to highlight the Week of Prayer for Christian Unity. At Thanksgiving time, the participating Catholic, United Methodist, Lutheran, Presbyterian, Episcopalian, United Church of Christ and Covenant churches agree not to hold their own denominational services but instead encourage their members to participate in a common, ecumenical one. Presiding, preaching and music ministry are rotated and shared among the churches, and for the people in the pews the Ecumenical Thanksgiving Service provides one of the few opportunities available on a regular basis to participate in prayer and worship with members of other Christian denominations. The Week of Prayer for Christian Unity has also inspired the planning of joint prayer and song services, joint theology lectures, the trading of preachers and, more recently, the sending of "good will" ambassadors from one church to another to extend greetings and prayerful support from sisters and brothers in Christ who would otherwise not be encountered in the context of Sunday worship.

Sadly, among some few Christian individuals and communities, a reactionary "traditionalism" has emerged in recent years quite contrary to the spirit of true ecumenism that would seek once again to accentuate differences rather than commonalities and to insist with uncompromising certitude upon customs and practices that do not truly belong to the unchangeable deposit of our shared faith. By and large, there continues to grow a widening gap between cautious official directives and bold behavior at the grassroots level.[11] In the United States, for example, ecumenism is taken for granted on many college campuses and parishes. Eucharistic sharing is often practiced with no reference to official guidelines. The ecumenical spirit is spreading rapidly, moreover, because most marriages in the majority of American dioceses are now "mixed," or as they ought to be called, "ecumenical," unions.[12] Individual Christians in all churches have been impatient with the slow motion of their institutional leadership, and ecumenism has increasingly become a de facto, if not a de jure, reality.

The level of enthusiasm for broadening the reality of true ecumenism and for moving very deliberately toward unity may have waned a bit among church leaders at St. Cloud State as the decades after initial rapprochement passed, but the Spirit persists in prodding those dwelling on the banks of her river to broaden both their hearts and their horizons. Campus ministers from the varying mainline Christian denominations continue to meet regularly together to this day, and notably in 1995, Newman pastoral minister Linda Wall was invited by Signe Gray, Darius Larsen, and the members of the University Lutheran community to preach at their Sunday service commemorating the Reformation. The crossroads encounters that Christian individuals and communities have had with one another since the 1930s on the edge of the Holy Spirit's river have, beyond a doubt, been authentically converting. In and through those encounters, the structures of formation embraced by members of many and various denominations have given way to the process of transformation, and to the demands of love and charity in ways not demanded in more sheltered environments off the beaten path, so to speak. But on the bustling highway that is the "secular" university, constant interaction and heart-to-heart conversation have produced in clergy, staff members, faculty, and students alike a degree of openness and humility that might otherwise never have emerged. In the process, many, many people of faith living and working on the highway have moved closer toward recognizing how deep is the scandal of disunity, how tragic the arrogance and sinfulness that produces it, and how truly urgent is the need to reestablish our connectedness as members of one Body in the Lord so that, one day, that Body might fully accomplish the reconciliation it is meant to accomplish in the world.

Notes

1 *Decree on Ecumenism,* Second Vatican Council, November 21, 1964, paragraph 1.

2 *The Modern Catholic Encyclopedia,* Monica Hellewig, editor, p. 273.

3 "Pope Reminds Newman Students of Their Need for Christian Charity," *St. Cloud Visitor,* 12 September, 1965, p. 4.

4 *Decree on Ecumenism,* paragraphs 7-8.

5 *Decree on Ecumenism,* paragraph 9-10.

6 William J. Whalen, *Catholics on Campus* (Milwaukee: The Bruce Publishing Company, 1961), pp. 20-21.

7 *Decree on Ecumenism,* Second Vatican Council, November 21, 1964, paragraph 7.

8 "Religious Activities in Public Colleges," *Bulletin,* St. Cloud State College, May, 1959, Vol. 14, No. 4.

9 Annual Report, 1954, Executive Secretary, National Newman Club Federation, n.p., ANNA, Executive Secretary. (Evans, p. 108).

10 Vincent A. Yzermans, *The Spirit in Central Minnesota* (St. Cloud: Sentinel Printing Company, 1989), p. 389.

11 Monika Hellwig, *Encyclopedia of Catholicism,* pp. 274.

12 *The Modern Encyclopedia of Catholicism,* ed. Monika Hellwig, p. 274.

Chapter 6

Meetings at the Middle Station
The Lay Church Emerges at the Crossroads

I want a laity, not arrogant, not rash in speech, not disputatious, but people who know their religion, who enter into it, who know just where they stand, who know what they hold, and what they do not, who know their creed so well that they can give an account of it, who know so much of history that they can defend it. I want an intelligent, well-instructed laity . . .

You will be doing the greatest possible benefit to the Catholic cause all over the world if you succeed in making the University a middle station at which laity and clergy can meet, so as to learn to understand and to yield to each other . . .

— John Henry Newman

The modern term "laity" is derived from the Greek word "laos," which means "people." The term was originally used to refer to all Christians as the new, "chosen people" of God. Jesus called most of his disciples from the ranks of the Jewish laity, and Christianity was, in fact, a lay movement from the beginning. Laity held key leadership roles, presided over communities, preached, taught and celebrated rituals of worship.[1] Almost two hundred years passed before some of the laity began to be called "priests," and three hundred and fifty before others organized themselves as monks or religious. Eventually, the term laity came to refer to the nonclergy, identifying them as the common, uneducated dependents of a clerical, governing elite. Today, the term is applied to over ninety-eight percent of the Church's membership, Catholic Christian women and men who have not considered the sacrament of orders but are, nonetheless, consecrated to the Lord by virtue of the sacraments of initiation.[2]

Baptism: the entryway to life in Christ for all people.

169

Every year in August, a group of Newman alumni still gather in St. Cloud to rekindle memories and to renew their ties with one another and with Wil Illies, who was was once their chaplain. They are nearly all adults with grown children of their own, and grandchildren as well. But, to a person, they look back on the years they spent as members of the St. Cloud Newman Club as foundational ones in their lives, years that not only gifted them with a strong sense of belonging and an invaluable set of lasting friendships but also made an indelible imprint on the ways in which each of them came to perceive themselves and their faith. At times they border on eloquence as they describe how their Newman involvement had an enduring impact on them as Catholic women and men, prompting them to embrace a mature commitment to the Church and shaping the ways they chose to work and to live as lay members of the Catholic Christian community throughout the course of their life-

Newman students in the 1950s, learning to laugh and learning to lead.

times. Rose Kelly, Sandy Banker, Dennis John, Bruce Perrizo, Mary Jo (Vashro) Russ, Bob Myers, Monica (Myers) Meyer, Marie O'Connell, Harry and Karen (Holwell) Larson, Gene and Pat Wasbusch, Gene and Shirley (Leither) O'Neill, Mike and Judy (Buck) Trepanier, Bruce and Pat (Devereaux) Perrizo, Chuck and Pat (Walker) Ernst, Art and Barb (Svela) Grachek, Marty and Pat (Devereaux) Rossini, Ed Pluth, and many others have one important thing in common: they all attribute the faith commitment they have lived and the leadership they have assumed in the life of the church in the thirty plus years that have passed since their graduations from St. Cloud State to the enduring influence of Yzermans, Ilies, and the

Newman Club where they learned how heart can speak to heart on the highway, and lives can be transformed forever.

Today, these individuals are religious educators, liturgical ministers, church committee and parish council leaders, and keen and dedicated participants in countless other facets of the Church's life. As 1964 graduate, Karen Larson, puts it, "those skilled in leadership, church involvement, participation—we all developed them at Newman. . . . Wil could see the gifts of everyone; he helped us all to believe in ourselves." Most notable of all, however, is the fact that that fostering of Christian identity, maturity, and leadership that flourished under Illies and Yzermans, did not cease in the decades that followed their tenures as Newman ministers. With steadily increasing frequency, in fact, St. Cloud State students who came into contact with the Newman crossroads community emerged with a transformed sense of who they were as "laity" in the Church, and of what they were capable of accomplishing.

Awakening the Church

The Second Vatican Council, responsible for so many significant shifts in the life of the Catholic Christian community, is also credited with returning to the laity their long-obscured dignity and proper place within the Church. It was in and through the documents of the Council that the whole People of God regained their proper significance, and that the distinct role and mission of lay women and men as priests, prophets, and kings in their own right was affirmed as something much more than a participation in the apostolate of the hierarchy. A hundred years before the Second Vatican Council opened, however, John Henry Newman was working to awaken in the Church its sluggish and slumbering sense of the laity by defending the importance of non-clerical members of Christ's Body with both eloquence and passion.[3] In 1867, a monsignor named George Talbot with whom John Newman often found himself at odds fumed over Newman's ideas. "What is the province of the laity?" Talbot asked angrily. "To hunt, to shoot, to entertain. These matters they understand, but to meddle with ecclesiastical matters they have no right at all. . . . Dr. Newman is the most dangerous man in England . . ."[4]

Over and against the opinions of those like Talbot who had definite qualms about granting respect to lay members of the faithful, Newman pointed out with disarming simplicity that "the Church would look foolish without them!" Christ, Newman avowed over and over again, is one whose likeness has been implanted in the minds and hearts of millions. Newman's book, *Grammar of Assent*, was written, in fact, to illustrate that ordinary women and men, without particular qualifications in theology or philosophy, can discover a truly reasonable way to faith. Newman was emphatic about the ways in which the laity share in the offices of Jesus Christ, and Newman's work on the development of dogma affirmed that the "Sense of the Faithful" should be consulted with care and consistency by the Teaching Church. It was Newman's unwavering conviction that there dwells within even the most ordinary and unsophisticated members of the faithful—deep in the bosom of the mystical Body of Christ—a collective intuition, an instinct for truth, and a continuous growth in intelligence and familiarity with Christ that can be traced to the presence and work of the Holy Spirit. "The hidden saints," affirmed Newman, "are enough to carry out God's noiseless work."[5]

Remarkably, fully one hundred years ago, John Henry Newman affirmed the potential of the university campus as a crossroads locale where clergy and laity could meet, interact and intersect in new and more grace-filled ways. Only at such a "middle station," Newman believed, could lay and clerical members of Christ's Body, who often found themselves at odds with one another, undergo some necessary conversions of heart and work out together a transformed understanding of how they might work in harmony to live and to spread the gospel. Newman wrote to one of his contemporaries:

> So far as I can see, there are ecclesiastics all over Europe, whose policy is to keep the laity at arm's length, and hence the laity have been disgusted and become infidel, and only two parties exist, both ultras in opposing directions. . . . You will be doing the greatest possible benefit to the Catholic

Father James T. Burtchaell

Presents a Major Address
in the area of Moral Theology

THE EXPERIENCE OF THE LAITY:
THE SOURCE OF MORAL DOCTRINE

TUESDAY, JANUARY 26 at 7:30 p.m.

BROWN HALL, ST. CLOUD STATE UNIVERSITY

Fr. Burtchaell is a professor
of theology at the University
of Notre Dame, a former
provost of the University,
and the author of Rachel
Weeping: The Case Against
Abortion, and other books.

If you find rules, checklists
and historical statements to
be inadequate when it comes
to making moral decisions,
Fr. Burtchaell's address may
be just the thing you are
looking for.

Free Admission

An educational event sponsored by the Newman Center in the 1980s very much in keeping with the spirit of John Henry Newman.

The "middle station" called St. Cloud State University.

cause all over the world if you succeed in making the
University a middle station at which laity and clergy can
meet, so as to learn to understand and to yield to each other,
and from this, as from a common ground, they may act in
union upon an age which is running headlong into infidelity .
. . [6]

    As the nineteenth century came to a close and the twenti-
eth was about to dawn, the Catholic Church in North America was
itself at a significant crossroads that would have ramifications for
Catholics on secular university campuses and the kind of middle stations they would be able to create for many years to come.
Catholicism in the nineteenth century had been the religion of a
struggling and sometimes isolated immigrant population; it had gradually come to be accepted, however, as a formative force in a plural-
istic society and educated Catholic lay people were now regularly
making significant contributions in intellectual, cultural and social
fields. They had become capable of taking their place in the world
and of assuming their own part in the apostolic work necessary to
spread the Kingdom of God upon the earth.[7] Two great lay conferences were held in the last decade of the nineteenth century, one in
Baltimore and the other in Chicago, both of which affirmed the need
for ordinary Catholic women and men to become involved in
addressing social needs and alleviating social problems. Spiritual
leaders of the Roman Catholic Church in the United States, furthermore, emerged from World War I ready to turn their attention
toward discerning what the American experience of religious pluralism, democratic forms of life, breakthroughs in science and technol-
ogy, interfaith cooperation, religious liberty and higher education
might mean for Catholic structures and piety. These bishops believed
that unless they updated and adapted their church, it would fail not
only to convert America, but even to survive as a source of life and
hope for the modern world.[8] Unfortunately, this promising reappear-
ance of lay leadership coupled with a new willingness to engage the
Church with modernity was threatening to many; by the early years
of the twentieth century it came to an abrupt halt. Pope Leo XII
wrote a letter to the leaders of the American hierarchy condemning
what he called "Americanism" and eight years later Pope Pius X
issued his scathing condemnation of "Modernism." The final blow
came with the promulgation of the 1917 Code of Canon Law. Made
up of over two thousand canons, only one of these, Number 682,
applied to laity, and it did no more than assure them of the right to
receive from clerics the helps needed for salvation.[9]
    During the 1920s many exclusively lay organizations, as well
as other groups that united clergy and laity in various worthwhile
efforts, did come into existence. *The Commonweal* appeared, a lay-
edited weekly on politics, religion, and the arts, and associations of
Catholic historians, philosophers, anthropologists, writers, doctors,

and lawyers emerged, as did the Knights of Columbus night schools, the Lay-Retreat Movement, the Catholic Association for International Peace, and the American Federation of Catholic Alumni.[10] But cautious counter-forces were ever at work, and the arrival of the officially-sanctioned Catholic Action Movement in the United States at the end of the decade virtually assured future clerical control over most lay movements.[11] Not all, however, were equally willing to be controlled. The tenacity of those lay members of the faithful who came to be influenced by the philosophy of John Henry Newman, and by their powerfully transforming experiences at the crossroads, would not easily hand over their baptismal integrity. They understood quite clearly what Newman lay minister Jacqueline Landry would affirm many years later in 1987: "Lay people do not operate in a vacuum, so that if the laity are not being used effectively, one can bet that neither are clergy or religious. Any question of the laity must call into account an entire ecclesiology. A laity that is not being used effectively is indicative of a Church that is ineffective."[12]

Catholic newspaper of the Diocese of St. Cloud MN

DIOCESAN PASTORAL PLANNING

The Lay Ministry Factor

In the closing decade of the twentieth century, the Diocese of St. Cloud has realized with increasing clarity how essential lay ministry is to the health and growth of the Church.

The Laity Move the Newman Movement

The very idea of the Newman Club, from the start, implied that laity had unique responsibilities as members of Christ's Body and could not simply be the passive recipients of a faith passed on, interpreted, defended and promoted for them by bishops and priests. The very birth of groups dedicated to deeper study, understanding and application of the faith suggested that the lay Church had a role to play in the evangelization of the world beyond that defined by the parameters of "participating in the apostolate of the hierarchy," and that preparation for that role was a task important enough for time and effort to be devoted toward its development. Perhaps James McGuire, CSP, said it best in 1950 when he emphasized the vital importance of the Newman apostolate by pointing out that "we have here a direct contact of the Church with the naked reality of the secular mind . . . we have an apostolate that depends from its very inception on a highly developed sense of lay responsibility."[13] Even in the earliest decades of the St. Cloud Newman Club, local chapters of groups like the Ladies of the Grail, the Daughters of Isabella, and the Knights of Columbus did all that they could to pass on their sense of being charged with a unique apostolate to Catholic students at the St. Cloud Teachers College and often offered financial support to help keep the club alive. Before long, this unfledged sense of lay mission fomenting within the ranks of Newman students would be honed and developed in surprising new ways.

The Newman Movement, as we have seen, originated in the United States as the result of purely lay initiatives. Public university students John McAnaw and Timothy Harrington conceived the idea and established the first prototypes for the Newman clubs, which would later spread to campuses across the nation. As Evans points out, these clubs were truly pioneering efforts made on the part of some of the Church's most youthful and inexperienced lay members. They came to birth without any clerical initiative or guidance and, when it came to efforts to bring these foundling clubs into a national federation that would support and encourage their growth, lay members of the flock again took nearly all of the initiative.[14] As far as the birth and early evolution of the Newman movement is concerned, in other words, the Catholic Church clearly *followed* its students, and for the first time in many, many centuries, the ordinary faithful preceded the priests and cried for them to come out to them.[15]

Catholic lay advisors and members of college and university faculties were absolutely instrumental in sustaining Newman clubs in the earliest years of their existence. The first two advisors of the St. Cloud Newman Club, established in 1923, were two women named Agnes Kerlin and Marguerite McBride. A Miss C. Sheehan and a

176

Mrs. A.J. Tschamplin also appear to have volunteered their support in the club's very first years, and then in 1927 a member of the art department, one Pauline Penning, began what would evolve into a long-term and extraordinarily generous commitment to the St. Cloud Newman Club. While the St. Cloud clerics who were assigned to be the club's spiritual advisors were quite dedicated to the task and accomplished many fine things, until 1957 they all had other jobs in addition to their Newman chaplaincies. As more than one of these early chaplains admits with great readiness, they would have been lost without the aid of the club's faculty supporters. In 1995, former chaplain Fritz Kampsen reflected with great admiration that "Miss Penning never missed a meeting. . . . She knew all of the students, she knew speakers and people who would be good, she was tremendously helpful in getting things organized and in helping me get started." The May 2, 1940 minutes even report that "Miss Penning gave a talk on the subject: 'Do Catholics Find it Hard to Get Jobs?' She gave many interesting experiences to illustrate the points she wished to bring out, and also many suggestions." John Weissman was also extremely active in the early years of the club, as former chaplain Harry Kost attests. Weissman, Kost insists, "is someone I just can't say enough about. He was a well-respected teacher, a great liaison to the faculty and administration on campus, and a fine man in every way." Weissman and Penning were succeeded in later years by numerous other dedicated and generous faculty mentors like Miss Robert, Miss Walsh, Mr. Kolb, Edward Colletti, George Lynch, William Donnelly, Richard Meinz, Arthur Erler, Mary Louise Petersen, Robert Hall, Donald Netzer, Mary Russell, Charles Ernst, Robert Wick, and many others.

Seated together at a Newman affair were one-time Newman advisors Robert Hall (left forefront), Bob Wick (at the table's end next to his wife, Alice) and John Weissman (right forefront).

In its early decades, the Newman movement produced of necessity a working laity. On many campuses under-staffing and under-funding propelled even reluctant students into leadership, forcing them to become responsible for planning, carrying out and evaluating much of their own programming. The 1950s gave birth in new ways, furthermore, to an increasing emphasis upon student responsibility for the health, growth, and direction of the Newman presence on college campuses throughout the country, initiated in large part by the older, tougher, post-war students who began to fill campuses at this time and were often less than patient with clerics.[16] These searching, self-directed students were instrumental in advocating efforts to broaden the concept of "Newmanism" and its mission on the secular campus. In 1947, "The Responsible Catholic Program" was developed in the New York Province of the National Newman Federation and was adopted nationally in 1950. It focused on forming "mature, prayerful and socially conscientious Catholic graduates of secular colleges."[17] New educational programs such as these, as well as the increased emphasis upon serious intellectual study that began to pervade both national Newman literature and local club efforts at this time, reflected, in part, the initiative and concern of students themselves. Students active in the national structures of the Newman Federation in this era also demonstrated a fascinating determination to take responsibility for the direction and development of their own apostolate. They argued that a priest should not hold the most influential position in their federation—that of Executive Secretary—and worried that the Federation's affairs would be knit more and more tightly into the clerical bureaucracy and eventually be wrested from the grasp of the lay women and men to whom it rightfully belonged.[18] A feisty, and rather admirable, unwillingness among students to allow themselves to be ignored, sidestepped or minimized by the clerics in charge persisted within the movement. In 1962, for example, a student committee dedicated considerable time and effort to the raising of money that could be used to produce a documentary film on the nature and needs of Newman work. The St. Cloud Newman Association, in fact, was later chosen to be one of the groups visited by a film crew gathering footage for use in the picture. The student committee had agreed to transfer their collections to the National Newman Foundation, but a press release issued by the Foundation's treasurer indicating that $15,000 had been earmarked for the motion picture did not acknowledge the students' financial contribution. What's more, invitations to view the rough footage and determine the final content of the film excluded students. Student members of the apostolate were outraged and did not hesitate to make their feelings known.[19]

An Intelligent, Well-Instructed Laity Arises

Whether it was during ping pong games in the basement or on long drives in the car with Illies and Yzermans, St. Cloud Newman Club members under their tutelage remember experiencing welcome, unconditional acceptance, warmth, laughter, stimulating conversation, compassionate counseling, and persistent encouragement from the "gold dust twins," who invested themselves so unselfishly in the building up of those young women and men they encountered at the crossroads. Those two men, affirms one Newman alum, loved the Church but they were open, and so they enabled others to grow because "we could argue, discuss, explore and say anything, without being censored or scolded." Several years after leaving the St. Cloud State campus, 1954 graduate Joan Schmid wrote an article for *Newman News* in which she offered similar reflections on what Newman involvement had contributed to her maturation as a Christian adult; her musings are music to the ears of any who have desired to stir into flame the latent embers of lay investment in the mission of the Church. The strong sense of identity, the opportunities to grow in self-awareness, and the truths she studied and absorbed in her mind and heart as a result of her involvement with the Newman Club carried over, Schmid wrote, into her vocation as a teacher and member of a religious community. They contributed greatly to the formation within her of a deep concern for social justice, a sense of direction, meaning and focus in life, and a keen awareness of her membership in the Mystical Body of Christ.[20]

Paul Hallinan, the Bishop of Charleston and the Episcopal Moderator of the National Newman Club Federation in 1961, wrote that "in almost all Newman Clubs there is an intellectual and spiritual ferment that characterizes one of the finest lay apostolates in the Church."[21] Intellectual ferment and the emboldening of the lay Church that it inevitably fosters already had a long and noble history within the St. Cloud Newman movement. As we have seen, from the start a great deal of effort went into encouraging students to question, to explore, to discuss and to embrace serious, intellectual study of the faith. St. Cloud State students were provided with many valuable opportunities to grow into the kind of "intelligent, well-informed" laity for which John Henry Newman passionately hoped. As 1964 graduate Mary Lou Dupre Allison remembers it: "I was challenged to think for myself on topics I didn't know I had a choice on. This has proven invaluable to me over the years and . . . perhaps more than anything else, has kept me in the Catholic Church when obstacles presented themselves, for I knew why I was a Catholic and had information to help me figure out moral dilemmas."

The steady diet of theology classes and the countless lectures given by renowned scholars that eventually came to be an everyday part of life at the St. Cloud Newman Center also

179

enhanced the expertise, competence, and rootedness of lay women and men both on campus and in the St. Cloud community at large. The motivation behind such intellectual offerings, however, was not merely a paternal desire to instruct an uninstructed laity on the basics of their faith; more often than not it was an ardent and authentic wish to spark in them an appreciation for the fascinating science of theology, and to ignite within them a sense of the potential they possessed to grow into "lay theologians" in their own right.

As early as 1954, club minutes reveal that in an era when it was not common for anyone other than a cleric to be considered a legitimate student of theology, the St. Cloud Newman Club was holding discussion groups for college students interested in "lay theology." These meetings were structured not as classes but as opportunities for the mutual exchange of ideas, and club members themselves took turns at leading and facilitating the meetings. In 1966, an individual named Don Waite came to speak at the Newman Center. In addition to the intrigue he created as a missionary headed to do agricultural community training work in East Africa, Waite also stirred interest because of his status as a "lay theologian," a term that for many centuries had been considered an oxymoron. Waite was one of twenty-eight people selected out of 1,200 applicants to participate in the Lay Theologian Program at the University of San Francisco and to complete the usual array of courses that a seminarian would complete, from Dogmatic and Speculative Theology to Philosophy. As Waite explained, his interest and that of his fellow lay theologians was not primarily in the polemic aspects of the theology they would study, but, rather, in its power to ground, motivate, inspire and guide their active involvement in the world.

1976-77

Newman Center, SCSU

Credit Courses in Theology

Wil Illies was never able to realize his dream of establishing a formal Religious Studies Department on the St. Cloud State campus. But, in the fall of 1972 under the direction and inspiration of Bill Vos and Katherine Kraft, the first theology courses for academic credit at St. Cloud State College were offered through the Newman Center. Credit was granted through St. John's University in Collegeville and then transferred to St. Cloud State through the cooperation of both institutions. Katherine Kraft was the instructor for the inaugural, three-credit theology course entitled "God and the Human Predicament," billed as an introduction to fundamental religious questions such as the meaning of faith, the "problem" of God, the reality of evil and death, the nature of the human person and the meaning of salvation. The tuition charged for that first class was $21.75. Credit courses continued to be offered through the Newman Center until 1989 and included such irresistible billings as "The Person of Jesus Christ," "Dimensions of the Church," "Christian Freedom and Personality," "Religious Themes in Literature," "Women in the Judeo-Christian Tradition," "Belief

180

THEOLOGY COURSES
at
NEWMAN CENTER

FOR CREDIT OR PERSONAL ENRICHMENT

WINTER QUARTER 1986-87

WOMEN IN THE JUDAEO-CHRISTIAN TRADITION   3 CREDITS

INSTRUCTOR: JACQUI McMULLAN, M.DIV.   THURSDAYS, 7-9:30 P.M.

This course will investigate the biblical, theological, and historical positions of women in the Judaeo-Christian tradition with the purpose of assessing the implications for Christian women today.

COLLEGE CREDIT WILL BE GIVEN BY ST. JOHN'S UNIVERSITY, COLLEGEVILLE. CREDITS ARE TRANSFERABLE TO SCSU.

FOR REGISTRATION AND TUITION PAYMENT, COME TO THE NEWMAN CENTER, 396 SOUTH FIRST AVENUE, ST. CLOUD, MONDAY THROUGH FRIDAY, 9-4:30 p.m.

SCSU TUITION RATES PER CREDIT ($91.35) THIS COURSE CAN ALSO BE TAKEN FOR PERSONAL ENRICHMENT ($35).

CLASS BEGINS DECEMBER 4, 1986 AT NEWMAN CENTER.

FOR FURTHER INFORMATION, CALL NEWMAN AT 251-3260.

and Unbelief," "Christian Moral Issues and Process," "Christian Spirituality and Mysticism," and "The Book of the Apocalypse," as well as more traditional overviews of scripture, and Christian worship. Peter Fribley, Ph.D., a UMHE campus minister, as well as Katherine Kraft, Paul Johnson, Edith (Edie) Reagan, Regina (Gigi) Mooney, Nic Dressen, and Jacqui Landry from the Newman staff served as instructors over the years and brought the gifts of their impressive theological backgrounds to the classroom, helping both college students and other members of the community to grow in knowledge, understanding, and commitment as novice lay theologians. Gale Maxwell, Newman's music director from 1979 to 1989, recalls that in a Christology class she attended taught by Edie Reagen, she became nervous one day because she was certain that the relatively novel and progressive ideas being put forth by Reagan in her lecture would certainly "blow the mind" of a little old lady from the small town of Foley, Minnesota, who was taking the course with her daughter. When Edie had concluded her class presentation, that elderly woman raised her hand and remarked: "You know, Edie, I've always thought just that, but I never could have said it!" Chagrined, Maxwell remembers saying to herself at that time: "So much for you clerics, too, who think that the people in the pews aren't 'ready' for things!" Non-credit opportunities for theological grounding also continued to be a regular part of the fare at Newman; in the 1980s "Introduction to the Catholic Faith," "Heaven is a Playground: A Theology of Sports," and "Personal Prayer and Spirituality" were consistent favorites. In 1992, a Sunday night program consisting of informal, theological discussion sessions for students named "Salsa" was introduced. "Salsa," the promotional flyer explains, is a spicy sauce made up of tomatoes, onions, and chili peppers, eaten with tortilla chips. "Salsa at Newman," the flyer continues, is a spicy conversation session made up of ideas, questions and curiosities about being Catholic, shared

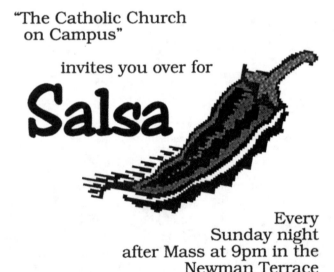

"The Catholic Church on Campus"

invites you over for

Salsa

Every
Sunday night
after Mass at 9pm in the
Newman Terrace

Salsa:

A spicy sauce made of tomatoes, onions and chili peppers, eaten with tortilla chips.

Salsa at Newman:

A spicy conversation made of ideas, questions and curiosity about being Catholic, shared informally over tortilla chips and regular salsa with the Newman staff and other SCSU students after the 8pm Mass.

The Sunday evening education program for St. Cloud State students introduced in 1992.

informally over tortilla chips and regular salsa with the Newman staff and SCSU students after the 8:00 P.M. Mass.

In 1992, too, a formal, adult education program was established for the Newman community dubbed "Made Not Born," a title borrowed from the noted liturgist Mark Searle who contended that fully-developed Christian disciples are not "born" that way but are "made" over the course of a lifetime of action and reflection. The "Made Not Born" series presents input and discussion sessions on a wide variety of topics designed to stimulate both formation in faith, and that constant openness to transformation which is such an integral part of the Christian life.

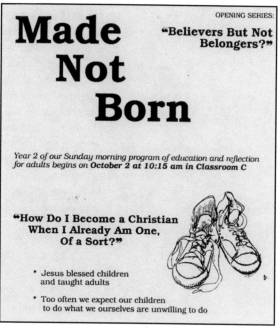

OPENING SERIES:

Made Not Born

"Believers But Not Belongers?"

Year 2 of our Sunday morning program of education and reflection for adults begins on October 2 at 10:15 am in Classroom C

"How Do I Become a Christian When I Already Am One, Of a Sort?"

* Jesus blessed children and taught adults

* Too often we expect our children to do what we ourselves are unwilling to do

The adult education program at Newman launched in 1992.

Learning What It Means to Lead

Appropriating faith by growing in knowledge, understanding and commitment, however, is but a piece of the journey toward becoming a mature member of the lay apostolate. Learning to assume leadership with readiness, and then exercising that leadership in an authentically Christian way, is also an integral component of the lay mission in the world. In 1986, the Newman Pastoral Team composed of Nic Dressen, Bill Dorn, Francis Nosbisch, and Jacqui Landry sent a letter to Catholic students on the St. Cloud State campus at the opening of the school year, informing them that there exist three different kinds of souls in the world distinguished by the three different kinds of prayers they typically offer:

1. I am a bow in your hands, Lord. Draw me, lest I rot.
2. Do not overdraw me, Lord. I shall break.
3. Overdraw me, Lord, and who cares if I break!

The Newman Center on the banks of the Holy Spirit's River, the letter went on to suggest, would seek to assist students in discovering who they were in relation to All There Is, and to encourage in them the willingness to be overdrawn in service to the gospel, to those in need, and to the ways of Christ. That encouragement to assume leadership, as we have seen, began in a particularly powerful way with Wil Illies and Art Yzermans, but it certainly did not end with them.

In 1963, a fascinating handbook for students on "Newman Leadership" was published by the National Newman Apostolate. Catholic students, the handbook suggested, must be competent thinkers in sociology, chemistry, history, or whatever field they chose to make their own, and must work tirelessly to become balanced and integrated individuals. They should be "with it" and take care not to behave as "aliens" on campus, because while Newman centers are always built on the fringe and will remain there, Newman students can be at the very center of campus life if they become active and contribute positively to that life. The handbook adamantly avowed, in addition, that a critical component of the campus lay apostolate for students must become the modeling and practice of a truly Christian style of leadership, one which engages in responsible, respectful discussion at all times, one which is neither dogmatic nor demeaning, and one which builds up rather than tears down. The handbook's introduction affirmed the importance of following five simple principles when participating in discussion

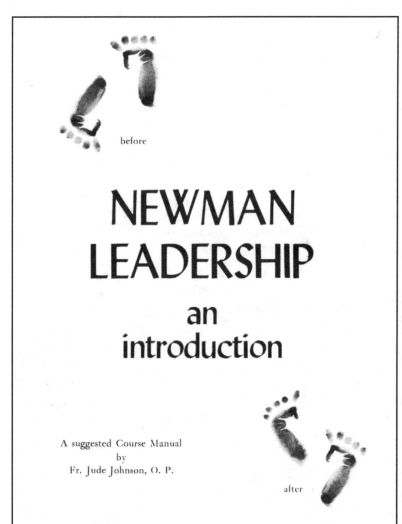

before

NEWMAN LEADERSHIP

an introduction

A suggested Course Manual
by
Fr. Jude Johnson, O. P.

after

The Newman Leadership
Handbook published in 1963.

of any kind, and, because the well of public and Church debate continues in our age to be poisoned by the absence of standards to discipline it, direct it and refine it, those principles are still quite relevant today:

> 1. Keenness of intellect, wit and the ability to persuade are all worthless without charity. Only informed, intelligent love has something of value to give.

> 2. One mark of educated people is their ability to differ without becoming angry, sarcastic or discourteous. They know that they are not infallible themselves and presume that others have something worthwhile to say. This respect for the person and the intellect of opponents dissuades the educated Christian from using cheap tricks, caustic comments or personal attacks in discussion, no matter how forceful, unjust or unfair the adversary may be.

> 3. In all discussions, those exchanging viewpoints should be confident that truth can defend itself and state its own case without specious arguments, emotional displays and personal pressures. This large view of truth leads to inner freedom and expansiveness of mind and heart. It allows people to suffer apparent defeat when they know their position is right and not feel shattered, embittered or without hope for the future.

> 4. None of us should be angered or shocked by new evidence of public vulgarity or blindness. We should, rather, be prepared to see in these expected human weaknesses a compelling reason for more compassion, better dialogue skills and stronger evidence. We must seek always to persuade and seldom to denounce.

> 5. To lack firm conviction is to be rootless. To lack respect for the differing position of others is to be haughty or ignorant or both. And, to lack conviction of the power of truth to state its own case is to be unworthy of intellectual combat.

The handbook on Newman Leadership ends by saying: "Women and men who lack one or all of these talents clearly reveal in public and private discussion the limitations of their education and the extent of their personal insecurity."[22] Almost four decades later, that conclusion remains pretty much on target.

In 1977, some twenty years after that compelling handbook was published, pastoral team members Paul Johnson, OP, and Adrian Ledermann instituted a "Peer Ministry" program at the Newman Center, which in many ways built upon the primary principle advanced in the pages of Newman Leadership: leadership is exercised most powerfully when students dare to moved to the center of campus life and interact in healthy, holy ways there, bringing with them their unique perspectives and sensitivities as Christian disciples and thus assuming ever-greater responsibility for the ministry of the Church in ways for which they are uniquely equipped as lay women

The Peer Ministry program thrived for more than a decade at Newman.

PEER MINISTRY

PEER MINISTRY IS PRIMARILY A TRAINING PROGRAM IN THE FOLLOWING SKILLS:

1) PRAYER LEADERSHIP
2) DISCUSSION LEADERSHIP
3) LISTENING/UNDERSTANDING
4) OUTREACH TO NEW STUDENTS

IT IS A 9 WEEK PROGRAM WITH WEEKLY MEETINGS OF 1½ HOURS. THE APPROXIMATE FORMAT OF EACH MEETING IS:

PRAYER - 5 min.
LISTENING TIME (IN GROUPS) - 15 min.
INPUT (BY STAFF LEADER) - 15 min.
DISCUSSION (IN GROUPS) - 20 min.
PRACTICE (IN GROUPS) - 30 min.
ASSIGNMENT - 2 min.
PRAYER - 3 min.

ONE OF THE BOOKS WE USE IS PEER COUNSELING IN THE CHURCH.

AT THE END OF EACH QUARTER THERE WILL BE A COMMISSIONING CEREMONY FOR THOSE WHO HAVE COMPLETED THE PROGRAM.

PEER MINISTRY HAS BEEN HELPFUL TO STUDENTS AT NEWMAN FOR NINE YEARS. THIS TRAINING LOOKS GOOD ON RESUMES, TOO! THERE IS NO COST FOR THIS PROGRAM.

FOR FALL 1987 THE PEER MINISTRY MEETINGS WILL BE ON TUESDAY NIGHTS, 7:30-9:00. SISTER FRANCES WILL BE THE STAFF LEADER.

CHRIST CHURCH
NEWMAN CENTER

OFFICE   251-3260

and men. With that presumption as a backdrop, then, Ledermann and Johnson devised a training program for students selected for their personal stability, leadership potential, concern for people, and faith as Christians (though students with a "Super Christian" or "Holy Joe" attitude were never considered).[23] These "Peer Ministers" were guided in the development of basic listening, counseling and discussion leadership skills and, after being formally commissioned, simply went about their business on campus with ears and eyes attuned to the needs, concerns, joys, and struggles of other students, offering assistance, empathy, and further information when necessary about religious and/or community resources available. The program continued for a decade, in later years under the direction of pastoral team member Frances Nosbisch, OSF, and the training of peer ministers grew eventually into a nine-week program which included prayer, study, and practical training. Countless St. Cloud State students learned poignantly through their experiences as peer ministers that the call to "go forth and do likewise" was directed to *all* followers of Jesus. *Empowered by the Spirit*, the 1985 pastoral letter on campus ministry promulgated by the National Conference of Catholic Bishops, insisted that "developing leaders for the future" was one of six essential aspects of campus ministry; the NCCB's "Letter to College Students" issued ten years later, however, was much more explicit in its affirmation of the universal call to discipleship and leadership. In that 1995 letter, the bishops begin by declaring to students that "we write to you as coworkers in Christ." They go on to remind them of their baptismal call to make the love of Christ present to other people, to make contributions toward peace and justice, to aid and serve the local community, and to model simplicity, responsible stewardship and gospel values in their lifestyle choices. The bishops conclude by avowing:

> You have so many gifts and talents to offer the Church: your faith, your desire to serve, your spiritual hunger, your vitality, your optimism and idealism, your talents and skills. We can all learn from you, so we ask you to expand your leadership role in witnessing to the Gospel on campus. We promise you our prayerful support and encourage your future involvement in the mission of the Church through a parish faith community. We look forward to working more closely with you to make the Church ever more effective in announcing the reign of God.

Newman students are not the only ones who have been challenged over the years to take the lay apostolate seriously, to become coworkers at the crossroads with clerics and other Christians, and to take to heart the universally directed summons of Jesus to "go forth and do likewise." Members of the St. Cloud State faculty and of the St. Cloud community at large who began to make the Newman Center their spiritual home in the 1960s also demonstrated a growing awareness of their dignity, identity, and vocation as lay members of Christ's Body. In 1967, for example, five couples from the St. Cloud area started a monthly "Layman's Forum" group after returning from a "National Association of

Newman students Mary Richter and Theresa Kantor listen to a presentation on listening at a peer ministry training session.

A peer ministry installation in the Newman chapel, May 4, 1986.

John Nevins Dwyer
1921 to 1986

Laymen" meeting in St. Paul. Their goal was to "get people to talk to each other" and to foster more open communication between lay people, pastors, and bishops. On the Steering Committee of the newly-founded Forum were two individuals who ultimately became dedicated members of the Newman permanent community: Edwin Hark and John Massmann. John Dwyer, furthermore, who worked for the Liturgical Press in Collegeville, Minnesota, at the time and whose family would grow into a long and intimate association with the Newman community, was a member of the panel that led the second Laymen's Forum meeting on liturgy. While helping to guide discussion on the notion of the priesthood of the laity, Dwyer pointed out how difficult it is for ordinary women and men of faith to become cogent and active participants in the Church when they had been trained for so long to act as silent and passive spectators, not just in the liturgy but in so many facets of life. Far from being either passive or silent in his lifetime, when Dwyer died suddenly twenty years later he was eulogized and lauded as a shining personification of the ideal Catholic lay person. "He was devoted to his family but also to the larger family of the Church," attested Daniel Durkin, who was then the director of the Liturgical Press. "John personified the kind of leadership and the qualities the lay person in the Catholic Church is trying to do now. . . . We've passed the area where priests and sisters are the leaders, and we're all waiting to see what they'll do."[24]

At that early discussion meeting on liturgy that Dwyer helped to guide, a parishioner from St. Mary's Cathedral in St. Cloud spoke passionately about how more changes were need in the liturgy in order to highlight and encourage the priesthood of the laity, suggesting that lay people ought to speak the words of consecration with the priest and to take the host and give it to themselves. "Why should it be wrong to touch the host with our fingers if we touch it with our tongue?" that impassioned parishioner asked, "If we are to fulfill the role of priesthood in our everyday lives, then we should know a real feeling of priesthood within our church." While lay women and men have yet to begin speaking the words of consecration, in the Newman community, at least, they began early on to assume both liturgical and administrative leadership roles.

Professional Ministry Expands at the Crossroads

Early in the 1960s, it became increasingly apparent that facilitating the constructive and mutually converting intersection of the sacred and the secular at the campus crossroads required some special levels of expertise and sensitivity. In 1962, the first "Newman Chaplain's Training School" was established, and plans were drawn up that called for the foundation of four additional schools in four regions of the country, each one accommodating about fifty individuals. In format, these training institutes brought prominent chaplains and guest lecturers from the fields of psychology, history, philosophy, theology, and university administration to present theoretical and practical aspects of campus religious work. The schools sought to confer on Newman ministers a semi-professional status and to instill in beginning chaplains a common perspective on campus life while supplying them with a handful of helpful how-tos.[25] Promoters of the schools were somewhat dismayed, however, that about forty percent of the ordained Catholic priests who graduated into the apostolate were then reassigned to other work three or four short years later.[26] That reality, along with many others, served to inject lay ministerial leadership into the Newman apostolate in very forceful and fruitful ways. Religious women led the first wave of a lay-embrace of ministry at the crossroads that would prove to be compelling and contagious in the decades to come.

In 1965, the Bishop of Manchester, New York, declared publicly that "there are literally hundreds of highly trained, wonderfully zealous" nuns who could help carry out the Church's mission on secular campuses.[27] In 1966, a Sister M. Peter, CSJ, who was serving with one other sister at the Catholic Student Center at Louisiana State University, wrote a delightful reflection for *The Catholic Commentator* on her experience as a ministry pioneer. Involvement in those converting encounters at the crossroads that make up the Newman apostolate, Sister Peter noted astutely, was forcing "wonderfully zealous" nuns from all over the country to make greater distinctions between the essence of the religious life, which remains unchanged, and the expression of it, which can and should change to meet the needs of the times. It was helping many religious communities move beyond rules of enclosure and garb that had kept them confined for decades, and was prompting them to live, work and behave less anachronistically in the world. Sister Peter went on to describe the expanding parameters of her identity as a minister:

> We don't say Mass of course—at least, not yet—and we don't give absolution. But confession we hear, often by the hour! Without casting aspersions on the competence of priests as counselors, and without drawing conclusions about the competence of women in the same direction, we can report that many students, with and without problems have a definite preference for consultation with a woman. . . . It surprises many people to learn that the sisters who serve at Newman Centers do not confine their counseling to the female students. On the contrary, they probably spend more time in conference with the young men. . . . Sisters at Newman Centers rarely suffer from boredom or a surplus of spare time. Add to the counseling several theology classes a week, some discussion groups, several meetings, and some get-acquainted interviews, and the hours in a week are pretty well accounted for.

189

Katherine Kraft in 1971.

Katherine Kraft, OSB, who began traversing the bustling highway along the Mississippi's banks in the summer of 1970, was the first of women religious to serve as a full-time member of the staff of the St. Cloud Newman Center. The bulletin announced her arrival in the following way:

> Sister Kathryn Kraft became the latest addition to the Newman Staff about a month ago. She has just returned from Stanford University and is now 'officially' on the job. We are very fortunate to have Sister with us. Over and above her excellent background in theology and her fine teaching record she possesses many personal gifts which will be a great boon to all involved at Christ Church and the Center.

Kraft would be the first in a long line of women religious and other lay professionals who would change the contours of the crossroads and the lay of the land at Newman forever; she and those who followed after her would transform both minds and hearts profoundly as a result of the gifted and grace-filled ways they came to teach and to touch other travelers on the highway.

Becoming Co-Responsible for the Community at the Crossroads

The July 13, 1969, bulletin that welcomed Bill Vos to the Newman community contained a providential piece reproducing six criteria formulated by the noted theologian and preacher, Walter Burghardt, SJ, as necessary for the successful establishment of "co-responsibility" within the Church and elsewhere:

The Newman Pastoral Team in the fall of 1978: Adrian Ledermann and Bill Vos are seated behind Trudy Schommer and deacon intern Jude Verly.

190

1. as much freedom as possible, only as much restriction as necessary
2. the readiness to take risks
3. the freedom to be wrong
4. dialogue before decision
5. respect for law without enslavement to law
6. openness to new solutions

The publication of these criteria foreshadowed a very definite commitment the Newman community would make to the mutual sharing of responsibility and authority in the years ahead. The professional ministerial staff serving the Newman Center began to grow after 1970. Bill Vos was alone as chaplain for only one year when Katherine Kraft came on board, and Harry Pavelis returned to offer assistance for a brief period of time. This group began having small staff meetings that eventually grew in sophistication and in dedication to collegial functioning. When a like-minded Adrian Ledermann, especially concerned about the inclusion of women in Church decision-making, was assigned to serve as associate pastor of the Newman Center in the fall of 1971, the staff as a whole stood ready to make a statement. They modified their titles and their *modus operandi*, and in all things determined that they would function and present themselves as a "team." No longer would there be a "pastor," an "associate pastor" and a "staff," but, rather, all of the full-time Newman ministers would function as "co-pastors." They took turns facilitating staff meetings and organizing agendas, they rotated the writing of bulletin articles, divided up parish administrative responsibilities equally and granted to one another full authority and autonomy in mutually agreed upon areas. It was confusing at first to the bishop, remembers Vos, who wanted to know

The Newman Pastoral Team in 1988. From left to right, they are Nic Dressen, Brenda Meemkin Graber, Jacqui Landry, Marlene Meierhofer, Frances Nosbisch, Gary Mead, and Gale Maxwell.

Members of the Newman Pastoral Team in 1991: Linda Wall, Marlene Meierhofer, Brenda Graber, MaryJo Bot, Nic Dressen, and LeRoy Zabel.

Brenda Graber at work in the front office at Newman. With seventeen years seniority, she has served the community longer than any other Newman minister ever has.

who, exactly, he should talk to when he called. "That depends," Bill persisted in telling him in reply, "upon what you want to talk about." Remarkably, that team approach to ministerial authority has weathered twenty-eight years of proud and constant use and and persists to this day among Newman staff members. While some newcomers to the community still need to be reminded occasionally that it is not always to the "priest" that their inquiries and concerns should be addressed, Newman members actively embrace and wholeheartedly support this collegial model of leadership. As long-time staff member Brenda Graber explained it while being interviewed for the *St. Cloud Times* in the fall of 1997, "We work as a team. We're each responsible for special duties. We think of our team as represented by a wheel with spokes, and each of us is an integral part of that wheel. At different times, someone with particular expertise or knowledge will be in the middle or the hub of the wheel, but the hub is always changing, and no one person is more important than any other."

Within a very short time, a desire to adhere to Burghardt's six criteria and to make an unshakeable commitment to shared responsibility spread beyond the staff and began to flourish within the community as a whole as well. As former staff member Sam Jadin recalls, the "priests" and pastoral team members were not put on a pedestal at Newman; the staff made themselves a part of the community in every way possible and encouraged leadership development in others. As early as 1968, a community-wide "Suggest-In" was sponsored by the Newman Council at which parishioners offered constructive suggestions about such matters as the envelope system and finances in general, liturgy and music, the usher system, freshman orientation, and publicity on and off campus. After its construction in 1964, the Newman Center had been established by Bishop Peter Bartholome as a "semi-public oratory" whose membership was limited to students enrolled at St. Cloud State College, faculty and staff of the college, and minor members of their families. The community grew considerably throughout the decades of the 1960s, however, and the pews of the chapel were filled weekly by students and other parishioners who sometimes met, but often failed to meet, the original criteria for membership. By the fall of 1971, Bill Vos, Adrian Ledermann, and Katherine Kraft found it necessary to call an all-parish meeting in order to discuss with members of the ever-growing community how leadership and direction ought to be determined for the future. At an October 28 brainstorming session, a decision was made to replace the "Newman Council" with a formal Parish Pastoral Council, a post-Vatican II possibility only beginning in those early years to be embraced within the Church at large. The St. Cloud Diocese, in fact, did not issue official guidelines for the formation of parish councils until two

At a party given in his honor, Sam Jodin sits on a "throne" wearing red and regal church garb, waiting to be served. Other than in jest, throne-sitting has never been a posture assumed by Newman ministers.

years later, in the fall of 1973. A steering committee composed of Newman members Sonia Eveslage, Mike Noonan, Chuck Ernst, Mary Ann Passe, Isabel Schmidt, and Mary Heinen was appointed to develop a constitution and set of operating procedures for the new council. Ade Ledermann remembers with amusement the many long and delightful discussions he, Mike Noonan, and Sonia Eveslage had over the details of the constitution's wording. "We each had our own unique perspective," Ade recalls. "Sonia wanted to get straight to the point, Mike wanted to make sure the proper 'legalese' was included, and I was trying to interject a little theological verbiage."

By January 17, 1972, Newman's first constitution had been written and ratified; it called for the election of a parish council composed of twelve members, five representing the non-student registered members at Newman and seven representing St. Cloud State students who were formally registered. On February 27, 1972, the first election was held and the first Newman Pastoral Council was selected. Its members included non-students Bette Bartos, Pat Ernst, Art Grachek, Mike Noonan, and Jim O'Neill, as well as St. Cloud State students Dave Gruber, Mary Heinen, Bob Heydman, Mary Hughes, Barb Miller, Sharon Montgomery, and Greg Sopko. The pastoral team in this emerging era of lay leadership and co-responsibility knew that they needed to give these parish leaders real "teeth" if they were to feel authentically empowered to direct the community. Hiring and firing power became one of the first forms in which those teeth were provided. Bishop George Speltz more or less accommodated the council's authority with respect to personnel and, in the years that ensued, whenever ordained ministers would show interest in a posted position at the Newman Center, the parish council conducted all candidate interviews. The council's final decision was then communicated to Speltz at the Chancery, who would make the formal appointment. Thus it was

Paul Johnson, who was a member of the Newman Pastoral Team between 1976 and 1978. His creative efforts in liturgy, in theology instruction, in developing the peer ministry program, and in building up the Newman library will long be remembered.

The Newman Liturgy Committee at work today. Chair Carla Lagerstedt sits at the head of the table.

that Paul Johnson, OP, Sam Jadin, O. Praem., and Bill Dorn all came to serve the Newman community. Non-clerics were also interviewed and selected by the parish council working in consultation with the parish personnel committee. Through these very tangible experiences of shared responsibility, community members and staff members alike attest that they became "opened up" to the viewpoints of others and began to understand more fully what it meant to lead, and to follow, in a spirit of humility, selflessness, and authentic openness to the voice of Spirit speaking in and through all people. The process of galvanizing and institutionalizing that constant openness and mutual responsibility culminated in the 1992 revision of the Pastoral Council Constitution of Christ Church Newman Center, which still guides the community today and which speaks eloquently of how the Pastoral Council, "with the pastor as presider, form one body and are co-responsible for the pastoral care of the parish." Collegiality, collaboration and consensus, not "Robert's Rules," are explicitly affirmed as decision-making methods by the constitution, and ten standing committees are established to carry out necessary leadership functions in a wide variety of areas comprising the community's life. In contrast to and distinct from the hierarchical, top-down approach to governance still operative in so many facets of the life of the institutional Church today, the Newman Constitution avows clearly that when either the Council itself or one of its established committees sets out to make a decision,

The Documents of Christ Church Newman Center

St. Cloud, Minnesota

The booklet containing Christ Church Newman Center's Mission Statement, Pastoral Council Constitution, and operating by-laws is distributed to all new members of the community.

> ample time must be provided and maximum input encouraged for consideration of all matters. Members must listen with an open ear and encourage active participation from all, which at times may require subordination of one's personal feelings and desires. Collaborative problem-solving will involve producing creative ideas, gathering factual data, making a choice among alternative options, implementing and evaluating the choice. There is to be a common decision at each stage of the process

which commits each member to the decision in such a way that they are solidly behind it and willing to accept all consequences of the decision.

In 1987, under the guidance of Robert Burke from the Office of Pastoral Planning for the Archdiocese of St. Paul/ Minneapolis, Christ Church Newman Center became one of the first parishes in the St. Cloud diocese to implement a comprehensive, long-range planning process. Student and permanent community members were invited to join an ad hoc, Long Range Planning Committee which worked to draft both a Mission Statement, later approved by the parish council, and a long-range planning questionnaire administered to members of the parish at large. Designed to assess the perceptions, needs, values, and concerns of community members themselves, the data thereby accumulated was studied and analyzed by the Long Range Planning Committee and used to determine the appropriate content of a few broad goals. Once these goals were established, additional members of the parish were invit-

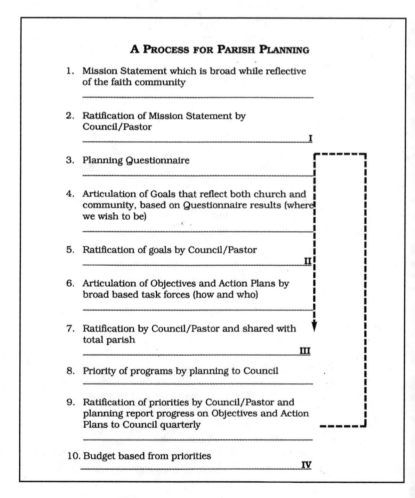

A PROCESS FOR PARISH PLANNING

1. Mission Statement which is broad while reflective of the faith community

2. Ratification of Mission Statement by Council/Pastor
   I

3. Planning Questionnaire

4. Articulation of Goals that reflect both church and community, based on Questionnaire results (where we wish to be)

5. Ratification of goals by Council/Pastor
   II

6. Articulation of Objectives and Action Plans by broad based task forces (how and who)

7. Ratification by Council/Pastor and shared with total parish
   III

8. Priority of programs by planning to Council

9. Ratification of priorities by Council/Pastor and planning report progress on Objectives and Action Plans to Council quarterly

10. Budget based from priorities
    IV

Outline of the Long-Range Planning process utilized by the Newman community since 1987.

ed into the process and given the opportunity to join the "task forces" created around each goal whose job it was to delineate specific objectives and action plans which would insure the implementation of the goal. The end-result of this inclusive process was the publication of a three-year plan designed to direct the community that had been crafted from the bottom up, not imposed arbitrarily according to the whims, desires or peculiar agendas of those sitting at the top. This collaborative planning process has been repeated faithfully every three years since its inception, and has served effectively to focus and direct the energies of the Newman ministerial staff, the parish council, and the parish committees.

LONG-RANGE PLAN 1998-2001

Christ Church Newman Center
approved May 9, 1998

INTERGENERATIONAL

Goal: *We will work to affirm the validity of each member's spiritual journey by encouraging opportunities for intergenerational conversation and interaction in order to expand the community's experience of prayer and service. This affirmation will be evaluated by the Parish Pastoral Council.*

Objective:
1. To continue offering high quality education opportunities which allow Newman members from different generations to learn with one another and from one another.

Action Plan:
a. The Pastoral Team will continue to plan "Made Not Born" and "Salsa" sessions. An additional effort will be put forth to encourage students to attend "Made Not Born" sessions. Two to three times per semester, permanent community members will be issued a special invitation to participate in a "Salsa" session.

b. The Peace and Social Justice Committee will continue to plan a spring educational event relevant to all parish members.

c. The Education Committee and the Pastoral Team will continue its commitment to a religious education program for grades P3-12 which emphasizes family involvement and parental responsibility. Special efforts will be made to encourage college students and other adults to participate in the learning experiences.

Because of such palpable efforts made to foster co-responsibility, members of the Newman community have grown accustomed to assuming leadership in unhesitating ways over the decades. Marlene Meierhofer, OSB, recalls, for example, how the "pastor" wasn't even present when she was interviewed by Chair Dave Williams and other members of the Newman Education Committee for the job of Director of Religious Education in 1987. "They were a vital group of people," Marlene still marvels, "very willing and able to do many things, and they were used to running the show." Twenty years after his tenure as a member of the pastoral team at Newman between 1976 and 1978, Paul Johnson, too, still adheres to those principles of collegial leadership that came to life so forcefully at the Newman Center. "One of my dreams for the

Newman member Wendy Altobell proclaims the Word with authority and grace.

Art Grachek offers a blessing to a young member of the Newman Community during the communion rite.

future of the church," Johnson muses today, "is that we might figure out a way to do some radical decentralizing, freeing and strengthening the authority of the College of Bishops." Katherine Kraft also maintains to this day that her encounters at the crossroads with that vital and involved faith community at Newman transformed her mightily, and taught her in indelible ways to have a deep respect for the people, the laity, who are the Church. "Church ministers really don't have authority which they come to 'give' to the people," Kraft professes. "They need to listen to the authority within the people. To listen—how important that is."

Exercising the Priesthood of the Laity

By the summer of 1971, the Newman bulletin was able to report with satisfaction that "Sister Katherine (Kraft) and a number of lay members of the Newman parish" had been granted permission by the bishop to assist with the distribution of Holy Communion. From that point on, both male and female parishioners were summoned forth, trained, commissioned and scheduled regularly to serve as lectors, hospitality ministers, and Eucharistic ministers during Sunday liturgies, enhancing and facilitating the prayer of the community through the use of their skills, talents, and

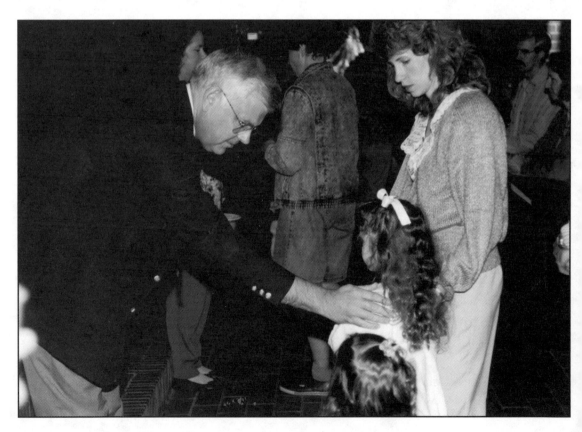

generosity. Such lay participation and leadership in the liturgical life of the community have taken many forms over the years, and more than one Newman minister will admit that at times the boundaries were stretched—just a bit, and never irresponsibly—in order to recapture and regenerate the laity's priesthood, which had been so sorely neglected and disrespected over the course of the centuries. A Liturgy Committee was established for the parish that entered enthusiastically into the planning of meaningful worship experiences by participating in on-going scripture reflection sessions with the staff and providing input on possible homily content, music selections and special seasonal activities. Gale Maxwell recalls with pride and delight how many St. Cloud State students who started out on the committee wanting merely to promote songs that were "fun to sing" at Mass, came to develop a fairly sophisticated sense of liturgy as they progressed through their years at Newman. The knowledge, experience, and confidence those students gained became invaluable to them and enabled many of them to become leaders and stimulators of quality liturgy in other Catholic Christian communities. Sam Jadin, furthermore, remembers how affected he was as a staff member by the active role the liturgy committee and the community as a whole took in challenging preachers on the pastoral team to make their homilies intellectually challenging and relevant. "Their comments and high expectations," Jadin reflects, "guide me to this day as I prepare my work in other places."

Katherine Kraft, Bill Vos, Paul Johnson, and Ade Ledermann all look back on the years they spent at Newman at various times throughout the decade of the 1970s and marvel at the beauty and the power of some of the liturgical experiences that were created, not simply through their work as professionals, but through

Newman members listen intently to a homily during a Sunday liturgy.

I am your god

you are my people

Lent 1979
St. Cloud Newman Center

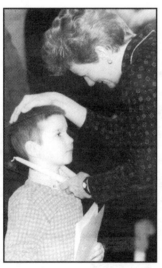

Blessing throats on the Feast of St. Blaise.

the efforts, expertise, and talents of the entire community laboring together. Both compelling meaning and contagious joy began to pervade the praying life of the community. Newman became one of the first parishes in the diocese to experiment with dramatizations of the gospel, "discussion homilies," and communal penance services. Bill Vos, Kathryn Kraft and Paul Johnson recall with wonder one particular communal penance service held at Newman during Lent at which families were invited to speak together about their sinfulness, and about those things for which each family member felt the need to ask forgiveness from the others. During another Lenten season, a creative series of four prayer services were proffered at which various individuals stood before the community and demonstrated a particular skill they had developed, while offering their reflections at the same time on how the exercise of that skill had become a spiritual experience, influencing, shaping and informing their relationship to God. Mil Voelker gave a prayerful presentation on cooking; Gale Maxwell put together an organ and trumpet recital; Tom and Jan Keaveny expounded on the spiritual dimensions of parenting, and Jerry Korte demonstrated his passion for painting and the unique path to God it opened up for him. A few years later, the now long-standing St. Blaise tradition began at Newman. The traditional blessing of throats is offered each February on the Sunday closest to the Feast of St. Blaise, but joining the pastoral team as the ministers of the blessing are community members involved in healing professions. The priesthood of the laity—be they physicians, nurses, counselors, surgeons or social workers—is thereby exercised visibly and emphatically. When in March of 1975 layman John Dwyer appeared as a guest preacher one weekend at all the liturgies, the parish bulletin noted aptly that "his contribution beautifully illustrates the importance of members of the community coming forward to enrich others with whatever gifts God has given. The work of God's Spirit is operative in all of us."

As the community grew in knowledge of, and sensitivity to, those things that made for prayerful, joyful, inclusive and dignified liturgy, the pastoral team, the Liturgy Committee and the parish council together took responsibility for initiating, studying, recommending and, when and if the time came, for approving various changes and developments. Some wonderful ritual and sacramental customs, which have since become the norm at Newman, were begun in this era dedicated to supporting the emerging priesthood of the laity. Having all worshipers share from the one cup in the wine poured out, as well as from the one loaf, blessed and broken, for example, began to be a regular part of the communion rite. It wasn't long before real bread baked each week by community members themselves came to replace the sanitized white wafers in common usage at the time which did not at all respect the admo-

nition of the *General Instruction of the Roman Missal* that "the nature of the sign demands that the material for the Eucharistic celebration truly have the appearance of food."[28] It was in this era, too, that the children present at liturgy were first invited by Bill Vos to come and stand around the altar during the Lord's Prayer, that the assembly as whole began to stand throughout the duration of the Eucharistic prayer, that "face-to-face" confessions as well as communal penance services were introduced, that communal celebrations of the anointing of the sick were integrated into the experience of Sunday Eucharist, that preparation for the the sacrament of reconciliation was moved to fifth grade and was removed as a requirement for the celebration of First Eucharist, that baptism by

Above, the children of the community gather around the altar during the Lord's Prayer, a weekly tradition at Newman.

Bill Voss (right) sits with a parishioner in the reconciliation room at Newman. In 1977, "face to face" confession was still a new and unfamiliar option.

immersion became an option and that the baptismal initiation of the Church's youngest members into the life of the community began to be celebrated, as a norm, within the context of Sunday liturgies when the whole community was present. Lay members of

In the context of a regular Sunday liturgy (left), Adrian Ledermann baptizes a child in the name of the community.

Presider Kevin Anderson (below) listens to the Proclamation of the Word with the assembly. An overhead projector (bottom), not missalettes, facilitates the participation of the Newman community during liturgy.

the community, furthermore, began to take responsibility for facilitating baptism preparation "classes" for new parents and for assisting with the marriage preparation process as sponsor couples. Presider's began to sit in the front pew with the rest of the assembly in the early 1970s and the overhead projector came into use, allowing music to be projected on one side of the wall behind the sanctuary area so that missalettes and music sheets could be abandoned, and the people at prayer would be encouraged to listen to the Word proclaimed and keep their heads up when singing together, becoming attentive to ritual cues rather than reading them from

With no missalettes in which to bury their heads, Dennis and Anne Fields and other members of the assembly (above) join together in singing an opening song. The Easter Candle at Newman (below) made from more than thirty years by the Bartos family

May the
Morning Star
which
never sets
find
this flame
still burning.
—Exsultet

a book. In 1968, Vern and Bette Bartos and their children began their long-standing family tradition of making the Paschal Candle lit anew each year during the Easter Vigil service. The Newman community to this day waits with bated breath each Easter Eve for the unveiling of the venerable beeswax candle, knowing that each new candle contains within it wax from all the others which have preceded it. It is a graceful testimony to the continuity of the tradition of community ownership for the quality of prayer which issues forth from the members of Christ's Body who gather in the Christ Church Newman chapel.

Newman staff and parish members alike were deeply concerned from the start about making all members of the praying assembly feel welcomed, respected and included; long before such steps were taken in other Catholic Christian communities, the Newman community was making deliberate efforts to strengthen the visibility of women in the sanctuary, even if that meant, at first, only that there would be female, as well as male, altar servers at work each week. The decision to foster inclusivity of language in scripture, song and prayer texts used in the context of liturgy was another significant step forward that the lay people living and worshiping at the crossroads took on their own. A group of concerned women in the parish brought the issue of language inclusivity to the attention of the Liturgy Committee, whose members listened respectfully and carefully. Gale Maxwell admits that initially, even for herself, it was not a comfortable issue to confront, and she experienced some internal resistance, especially when she realized that she might have to give up "Sons of God" as a part of her song repertoire. As always, though, Gale goes on to reflect, "that community stretched me and taught me how important it is for all of us to listen to each other, hear each other and then adjust how we do business accordingly, even if for no other reason than that the feelings are important to someone, and as a sister or brother in community I ought to be ready and willing to accommodate that. All people possess some piece of the truth and some piece of the spirit, and that's what a community in action ought to be like." Maxwell even found herself able, eventually, to help students who were resistant begin to understand their obligation to be open to transformed understandings. "When they would tell me," Maxwell says, "that when they came to college everything began to change in their lives and they wanted their church to be a comfortable haven where things didn't change, I would tell them that they were certainly being unfair to their Church and to their God if they became open to growth in every other arena but their faith lives. That seemed to make them think."

From those first conversations with the Liturgy Committee and Newman Parish Council of which Maxwell was a part, an "Inclusive Language Committee" was born which went to work studying, making suggestions and experimenting. Their work on lectionary passages, prayer language, and song texts grew in sophistication and quality as time went on, and the committee did an admirable job of educating the Newman community as a whole about the need for inclusivity in reference to both God and human individuals. All changes were introduced gently and respectfully, and as Maxwell remembers it, the permanent community was generally quite accepting because the vision had, after all, begun with members of the community themselves. As the years progressed and their level of awareness, sensitivity and understanding increased, many student and permanent members alike came to have passionate convictions about the ways in which language, especially God-language, has the power not just to include or exclude, but also to form and shape people's attitudes and outlooks in profoundly constructive, or destructive, ways.

There were times, naturally, when some of the liturgical developments embraced by the Newman community caused consternation on the part of their local bishop, but the ways in which the community opted to handle such tensions is telling. Newman parishioners, for example, even back in the days of Wil Illies and Nick Zimmer, had adopted the custom of receiving communion in the hand, an ancient, centuries-old practice that, like standing during the Eucharistic prayer, had been lost and was gradually being

Gale Maxwell, music director at Newman from 1979 to 1989.

recovered as a result of the research and reform prompted by the
Second Vatican Council. Once Christ Church Newman Center
was granted status as a full-fledged parish at which all sacraments
could be celebrated, the bishop, of course, had to be invited yearly
in order to preside over the celebration of confirmation. When the
first invitation was issued to George Speltz in 1972, however, he
refused to come unless the Newman staff agreed to see to it that
communion would be distributed on the tongue, as was still the
practice in most parishes throughout the diocese at the time. The
parish council and staff met together and deliberated over how best
to respond; their decision was to inform the bishop politely but
firmly that communion would be shared at Newman "in the same,
respectful and traditional way that it has always been shared."
Speltz then informed the community's leaders that he would come
to Newman for confirmation only if there was no communion rite.
The parish council pondered the situation carefully one more time
and concluded that they would hold fast to their convictions; a
non-eucharistic celebration of confirmation would be planned.
Fidelity to a responsible and sound liturgical principle in which they
had come to believe, and affirming their integrity as co-responsible
members of the Body of Christ, was more important to them than
acquiescing to the demands of the bishop. Katherine Kraft remembers with a grin that even the youngest members of the Newman
community seemed to imbibe early on that unflagging sense of

Confirmation at Newman,
1972. Here, Bill Vos assists
George Speltz as confir-
mands come forward.

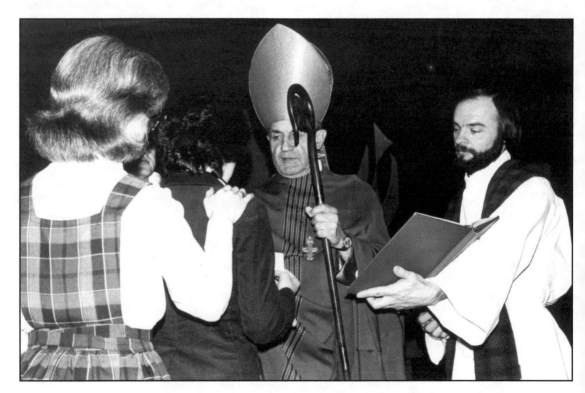

equality in dignity among all members of Christ's Body; during the non-eucharistic confirmation service that subsequently ensued, young Denise Beumer watched closely as Bishop Speltz presided and then turned to whisper to her parents: "How come that guy gets everything he wants handed to him?" No matter how unequivocally committed to its principles the Newman community has been, however, its members have rarely been irresponsible in claiming their authority, insensitive to the need for unity in matters essential to the faith, or inhospitable toward those who disagree. That first confirmation event is a case in point. After the celebration in the chapel had ended, many members of the community went out of their way to invite the bishop down to the Terrace for the reception and social that followed. Speltz was nervous, Ade Ledermann recalls, but he went down anyway and ended up having such an enjoyable time in conversation with community members that he was one of the last to leave.

Women Step Out and Up

Jacqueline Landry, who served the Newman community as a member of the pastoral team from 1985 to 1989 and is now a campus minister at Harvard University, calls herself "one of the few success stories of lay women in ministry." She has worked within Church structures for more than seventeen years now, and to this day, she credits her ability to persist in the face of many frustrations to the "formidable foundation" with which she was provided through her first job at the Newman Center in St. Cloud. "Those years at Newman grounded me because I didn't have to fight to have a role," attests Jacqui without hesitation. "I was empowered by my colleagues in ministry and didn't need to be dependent upon ecclesiastical authority for my credibility as a minister." Jacqui's memories are a tribute to the way the crossroads community that took root on the banks of the Holy Spirit's River allowed itself to be transformed through the encounters, conversations, and interactions of which it became a part on the university highway. Through an evolutionary process that was gradual, but steady and unflinching, the members of Christ Church Newman Center began to grasp how vitally important it is for women to be acknowledged as people with equal authority, talent, and credibility when it comes to the spiritual leadership of Christian communities. Katherine Kraft was the true pioneer in St. Cloud; her courage and skill paved the way for those who would follow. "I really felt called out in those years" says Kraft, "I didn't always feel ready, but I came forth and I learned." When she was first commissioned as a Eucharistic minister, Kraft remembers that this early, and at the time, unusual, venture of a woman into a more visible liturgical role caused a few men to move out of her communion line and refuse to receive at her hand. One of those men, however, later told Kraft

Newman minister Jacqueline Landry.

that he had reconsidered his position on her role as a minister of the Eucharist, and conceded that it was being jarred out of the comfort of familiarity, more than anything else, that had caused him to react as he did. "The more I see you up there," that man finally acclaimed, "the more it seems right."

As early as 1967, the Newman bulletin contained a note from a concerned young woman urging uninvolved men to offer to read at Mass. At that time, women were still not permitted to assume any ministry within the sanctuary, but bulletin quips appearing in that era hint that a wry awareness of the shortsightedness of such a policy was already alive and well in the community. On Mother's Day in 1965, for example, the parish bulletin offered the following food for thought:

> I wonder what the complete meaning of Genesis is when it says, "It is not good for man to be alone."
> I wonder if Eleanor Roosevelt was serious when she suggested that "day nurseries be provided for young children as a possible way to take full advantage of women in the nation's work force."
> I wonder whether women solve more problems at meetings than they cause by being away from home.

By April of 1974, the bulletin contained many more overt and pointed announcements like the following:

> How do you deal with such Pauline statements as, "Man is made in the image of God, and woman is made in the image of man," or "Wives be submissive to your husbands"? Is the Church structure male because of religious or political reasons? If you are interested in the area of women and the Church, come and discuss with Newman pastors, Fr. Vos, Fr. Ledermann, and Sister Katherine. Sponsored by some interested women of the parish.

Marlene Brixius, the very first Newman woman to move into the sanctuary. *Newman News* reported in 1959: "It is always men who serve Mass, men who prepare the vestments, men who light the candles for Mass. Women rarely get the opportunity to enter the sanctuary. Infringing on these privileges is Marlene Brixius, who has been in this enviable position as sacristan for a year . . ."

By 1974, too, Katherine Kraft had become an admired and respected co-pastor of Newman community and was hard at work, not just distributing communion at Sunday liturgies but assuming a wide variety of administrative tasks and functions as well as presiding regularly over Friday communion services and offering her reflections on the day's readings. In time, she came to preach occasionally at Sunday liturgies as well, and thus began a longstanding tradition at Newman. As Bill Vos points out, "In the early days we wanted women to preach because we believed it was important in principle; we wanted to introduce the possibility and to expose people to the power and potential of our women as Ministers of the Word." By the time Nic Dressen became pastor in 1983, however, having lay staff members preach had become a matter of necessity. The numbers of available ordained ministers began to decline and "associate pastors" were in short supply to provide assistance in weekly presiding and preaching duties. Whether principle or necessity was the motivating factor, in the past twenty-five years Katharyn Waldron, Regina Mooney, Edie Reagan, Francis Nosbisch, Jacqui Landry, Mary Ehle, Marlene Meierhofer, and Linda Wall have all assumed regular weekend preaching responsibilities as an ordinary part of their roles as members of the Newman Pastoral Team. The Newman community has embraced and welcomed the homiletic leadership of these women enthusiastically, and has come to value it highly.

For a long time, there have been quite a few women and men within the Newman community concerned deeply about creating space and opportunity within the Church for a more balanced representation of women in the Body of Christ at prayer. In the spring of 1986, for example, a group consisting of a number of Newman members met for some weeks to read, discuss and reflect upon the first draft of the United States' bishops' pastoral letter, *Partners in the Mystery of Redemption—A Pastoral Response to Women's Concerns for Church and Society*. Mil Voelker, Maxine Barnett Cermele, Dick Cermele, Patty Hackett, Jacqui Landry, Sandy Bot-Miller, and Chris Reicher submitted a summary of their conversation and study to the *St. Cloud Visitor*; about a year later, long-time Newman member Mil Voelker, who had been both an assistant professor of English and the Affirmative Action Officer at St. Cloud State University, was asked by the *Visitor* to comment on the latest revisions of the draft in light of that time of study. Her words are unequivocal and telling:

You may be asking for trouble when you invite an old English teacher about revisions of a first draft. Suffice it to say, the draft of the pastoral on women needs some work. . . . The bishops condemn the sin of sexism and express their intent to reject it. Yet they are partners in the ultimate act of sexism in their unswerving belief that women's full partnership in ministry through ordination is unthinkable. . . . There is also an over-emphasis on the role of wife and mother in the document. I believe marriage and motherhood to be the most important part of my own personal many-faceted life. However, there seems to be a bias toward motherhood and staying at home with the children that is at best unrealistic today and at worst demeaning to those who serve valiantly in a chosen lay single state . . .

In 1988, Voelker was invited to write another opinion article for the *St. Cloud Visitor* in which she was asked to express her concerns about the Church. In a word, Voelker declared, "my concern is survival." She went on to ask:

Presider Nic Dressen and lector Mil Voelker walk side by side into the Newman assembly.

When is the stigma of woman as unworthy going to be erased? As the world gains more insight into the unimportance of sex differences in most areas, the Church maintains the tradition of limiting the priesthood to males. The Church is a living organism. It is people, many of whom are as educated or more educated than those in power . . . but how often is an issue debated with an outcome other than the status quo? It is this intransigence that gives me pause. Will women stay with a church that welcomes their ministerial participation but will not ordain them? I have said on the pages of the *St. Cloud Visitor* before: Don't deny women the sacrament of ordination. Empower them with the gift of the Holy Spirit.

Another highly competent woman, Katharyn Waldron, came on board at Newman in the fall of 1974, the first full-time lay campus minister to be hired who was not a member of a religious congregation. She was equipped with an M.A. in Systematic Theology from Union Theological Seminary in New York City and remained a vital part of the pastoral team for two years. Katherine Kraft resigned from her position at Newman in the Spring of 1977, and felt it necessary, in a letter to parishioners, to squelch some of the rumors that had been circulating about her reasons for leaving. It simply is not true, wrote Kraft, that

> —I'm leaving to work full-time in an underground movement to make Barb Grachek the first woman pope.
> —Jimmy Carter has asked me to serve as the first woman White House chaplain.
> —Seven years at Newman would drive anyone back to the cloister.
> —Robert Redford has proposed to me.
> —I can't stand the wine we use at Mass.

Kraft was replaced by Trudy Schommer, OSF, who served the community well for two years. She paved the way for the arrival in 1979 of both Frances Nosbisch, OSF, who had a graduate degree in theology and years of invaluable experience in education, spirituality, and faith formation, and Regina Mooney, who, like Katharyn Waldron before her, was a professional lay minister who did not belong to a religious community. When the twenty-seven-year-old "Gigi" finished her schooling at Yale University and began her position at Newman, the *St. Cloud State Chronicle* did a story on her arrival whose headline read: "Woman Pastor Works for Newman Center." Mooney had seminary training; she was the first non-cleric on staff to have completed a Master of Divinity degree. Mooney reflected openly on how difficult it had been for her to watch all of her classmates be ordained, knowing that she had identical training and expertise, yet because of her gender was not permitted to be officially sanctioned by the Church as the ordained spiritual leader of a community. In that *Chronicle* interview, Mooney also insisted that it is, indeed, possible to be both a Christian and a feminist, and affirmed her trust in women who feel they have been called to the priesthood, regardless of what the pope continues to avow about the impossibility of recognizing such a call as legitimate. She spoke simply but clearly of the leadership model that continued to guide ministry at Newman: "We see ourselves as enablers, not dictators. It's the idea of being a shepherd, a caretaker of the faith . . . the congregation at Christ Church Chapel also ministers to the Newman Center pastors, helping to eliminate the

Gigi Mooney in 1981.

lines of hierarchy even further." The September after Gigi's arrival, Adrian Ledermann wrote the following letter to St. Cloud's diocesan paper, *The Visitor*, gently chiding its editorial staff for shortsightedness in acknowledging only clerical additions to the Newman staff. Wrote Ledermann:

> Dear Editor,
> We were delighted with the article on Rev. Sam Jadin who has joined the pastoral team at the Newman Center to do campus ministry. The article, however, made no mention of the other two members who have also joined the Newman team. They are Gigi Mooney and Sister Frances Nosbisch, OSF.
>
> I believe that the team model of parish ministry is a valid model and has been in effect at Newman Center for the past several years. People sometimes wonder who is pastor and who makes the decisions. Our team concept of pastoral ministry has the team making major decisions with individual members of the team being responsible for particular areas of the ministry as decided by the team. Allow me, therefore, to put a plug in for the total Newman Center Pastoral Team.

Edie Reagen and Bill Dorn in 1985.

Frances Nosbisch stayed on as a member of the Newman Pastoral Team for eleven years, sharing her considerable talents with the Newman community until she headed east to Boston University in 1990; she pursued and ultimately completed both a Master of Divinity and a Doctorate of Ministry degree there. Gigi Mooney left in 1982 and was replaced by Edie Reagan, who had a Divinity degree from Weston School of Theology. Edie's successor in 1985 was Jacqueline Landry, who was equipped with a Master of Divinity degree from Wesley Seminary, and when Linda Wall joined the Newman ministry team in 1990 after finishing graduate school at the

A predominantly female pastoral team in 1987: Frances Nosbisch, Nic Dressen, and Jacqui Landry.

Newman minister Linda Wall in 1999.

University of Notre Dame, she, too, came credentialed with a Divinity degree. These women brought years of academic theological study and supervised pastoral training to their ministry at the Newman Center; they were as skilled and qualified as any of their clerical colleagues, and, aside from presiding over Eucharistic liturgies, their pastoral duties excluded nothing. Marriage preparation, teaching on a wide variety of topics, counseling, baptismal preparation, liturgy planning, small-group facilitation, presiding over wake services and other communal prayer experiences, serving on diocesan committees, writing proposals, giving talks and presentations both on campus and at other parishes, serving as staff liaisons to any and all parish committees and assuming a wide variety of financial and administrative responsibilities are just a few of the many tasks these competent and talented lay women have performed. Every bit as much as the ordained men with whom they worked over the years, they became trusted spiritual leaders within the community, and were supported and esteemed by the Newman parish membership. Their constant and credible presence in visible roles within and outside of the sanctuary has contributed immensely to the advancement of a broader vision of how professional ministry ought to be defined, regulated and understood within the Church; it has demonstrated, furthermore, that women can, in fact, serve as powerful icons of Christian servanthood and leadership, and can stand at the head of an assembled community with grace and power, presiding over its work, its prayer, and its play as priests, prophets and shepherds.

In their 1985 *Pastoral Letter on Campus Ministry, Empowered by the Spirit*, the National Conference of Catholic Bishops wrote: "It is of historical significance that women 'who in the past have not always been allowed to take their proper role in the Church's ministry,' find greater opportunities on campus to exercise their leadership abilities."[28] But the campus is a crossroads,

The people of God who have grown up—in more ways than one—alongside the banks of the Holy Spirit's river.

and a crossroads is a place where all things are met and all things become possible. From its earliest days, the crossroads community that rooted itself in St. Cloud allowed women and all members of the laity—the whole People of God—to find greater opportunities to exercise their leadership abilities, and to discover and take that proper role in the Church's ministry that had been denied them for so long. Theologian Leonard Doohan once declared that non-clergy have to be willing to move up, clergy have to be willing to move over and all of God's people have to be willing to move out into the world in service of Christ through justice and compassion.[29] John Henry Newman no doubt would agree, and in essence meant precisely that when he counseled with far-reaching wisdom a century ago that the Catholic cause all over the world would benefit mightily if the university could become a true middle station at which laity and clergy could meet, "so as to understand and to yield to each other." That kind of understanding and yielding comes only to converted hearts, steeped in holy humility; that kind of understanding and yielding also requires an unflinching trust in the presence and work of God's Spirit in all of God's people without exception. Lay and clerical members of the Newman community in St. Cloud have endeavored to trust, to understand, and to yield to one another nobly and persistently over the decades. Perhaps it is not too much to believe that the Holy Spirit is pleased with the People of God who for the past seventy-five years have grown up—in more ways than one—alongside the waters of her river.

Notes

1 Leonard Doohan, "Laity," *Encyclopedia of Catholicism*, ed. Richard McBrien (San Francisco: Harper Collins, 1995), p. 746.

2 Doohan, p. 746.

3 Jean Guitton, *The Church and the Laity: From Newman to Vatican II* (Staten Island: Alba House, 1964), p. 14.

4 Sheridan Gilley, *Newman and His Age* (Westminster : Christian Classics, Inc., 1990), p. 348.

5 Quoted by Jean Guitton, pp. 47-48.

6 Quoted by Guitton on p. 159.

7 "Meeting Modern Man," William Durkin, *ERA*, Spring 1963, p. 15.

8 Evans, p. 122.

9 Evans, pp. 13-14.

10 Evans, pp. 60-61.

11 Evans, p. 61.

12 Jacqueline McMullan, "The People of God are Called to be Accountable," *St. Cloud Visitor*, 30 April 1987, p. 7.

13 "Newman Clubs Are Vital," *Catholic World*, March, 1950.

14 Evans, pp. 43-44, 54.

15 Evans, pp. 22, 54.

16 Evans, pp. 102-103.

17 Evans, p. 103.

18 Evans, pp. 115-116.

19 Evans, pp. 127-128.

20 Joan Schmid, "TC Graduate States Value of Local Club," *Newman News*, c. 1956.

21 Catholic High School Quarterly Bulletin, Vol. XIX, no. 1, April 1961, p. 7.

22 James P. Shannon, as quoted in Jude Johnson, OP, *Newman Leadership: An Introduction and Suggested Course Manual* (Huntington: Our Sunday Visitor, 1963), p. 22.

23 Sally Thompson, "Peer Ministers' Aid Other Students," *St. Cloud Times*, 12 January 1979.

24 "Dwyer Personified Role of Catholic Layman," *St. Cloud Times*, December 23, 1986.

25 Evans, pp. 131-132.

26 Evans, pp. 131-132.

27 "Says Nuns Can Carry Out Newman Work," *St. Cloud Visitor*, September 19, 1965, p. 5.

28 *General Instruction of the Roman Missal*, fourth edition, March, 1975, no. 283. From *The Liturgy Documents, A Parish Resource*, revised edition, (Chicago: Liturgy Training Publications, 1985).

29 "Empowered by the Spirit: Campus Ministry Faces the Future," no. 25.

30 Leonard Doohan, as quoted in Jacqueline Landry, "The People of God are Called to be Accountable," *St. Cloud Visitor*, April 30, 1987, p. 7.

Chapter 7

Pilgrim Prophets and Highway Healers

"There is a peace which the world can give, and which we need, in order to go on living. It is ordered by the Law, which, if it is good Law, provides a formation which is as far as possible according to the needs of loving. But no Law can fully satisfy the need to love, and the restless Spirit seeking a way to transform. . . . Prophets . . . in a sense, are the power which transcend and transform the Law."
— Rosemary Haughton

"Campus Ministry is much like living in the middle of a highway. . . . Into this world steps the campus minister as a prophet, a poet, a preacher, a social critic, a patriot, a moralist, a reconciler, a counselor, a witness."
— Frances Nosbisch and Nic Dressen

Transformation is integral to the living of a truly Christian life. As we have seen, however, in order for transformation to occur, the structures of formation sometimes have to break down, and periods of darkness have to be endured before the inbreaking of the Spirit produces new light, and deeper love. Often, the release of the Spirit's transforming power occurs only when people are drawn into the perplexing "wilderness" of an in-between state where comfort and familiarity are no longer present, and assumptions, which before seemed self-evident, begin to crumble.[1] The prolific intersections taking place daily on a university campus produce such wilderness experiences more readily than do the circumstances of day-to-day life elsewhere. Those who choose to traverse the campus highway in order to study, work or pray are thus often drawn into transformed understandings and enlarged horizons before others, and become pioneers and prophets in the sometimes painful, but always holy, process that creates converted hearts and lives.

217

What kind of people are prophets, exactly? Biblical scholar Carroll Stuhlmueller purports that, while prophets did not constitute the "line of survival" for our Hebrew ancestors in faith, their presence did insure that the line remained worthy of survival. Their challenges did not constitute necessary daily "food," but they were the spice that made the food worth eating.[2] The most essential task of the prophet is to bring the hidden presence of God visibly to the surface, to point out what others overlook and to proclaim, "Behold! There is our God!" The prophet, in other words, highlights holiness in neglected places and draws into the center of awareness an insight or a sensitivity that was before only peripheral, so that it can be incorporated into the structures that order a community's life.[3] In so doing, prophets enable all people of faith to live out more fully not only what God desires for us as individuals and as a human community, but also what love requires of us as individuals and as a human community.

Campus ministers, John Whitney Evans contends, stand between the town and the gown, the pulpit and the lectern, the sacred and the profane. As Newman leaders moved into the volatile decade of the 1970s, they began to understand as they never had before that they could not avoid the prophetic role being thrust upon them by virtue of their growing presence on the university highway:

> The theologian was not by that fact a liturgist, but the campus minister was. The professor of ethics was not a moralist, the campus minister had to be. The instructor in social doctrine or sociology need not be an activist, but the campus minister could scarcely ignore the idealism of students or the needs of the times . . . the campus minister was emerging as a principal catalyst for testing the assumptions and values of higher learning and fusing knowledge with life.[4]

The commerce done on the campus highway, in other words, and the resultant conversing, colluding and colliding of visions and values that takes place there, seems inevitably to catalyze prophetic insight. As a group of Christian women and men settled in at the crossroads called St. Cloud State, the Newman community has, however unwittingly, found itself thrust into the assumption of a prophetic role on more than one occasion. As a result, it has prompted the two institutions of which it is a part—the Church and the university—to legitimize and centralize some important awarenesses that had been consigned for too long to the periphery. We have seen already how that prophetic mission played itself out with respect to the meeting of faith and intellect, the practice of liturgy and worship, and the emergence of lay integrity, identity, and leadership within the Church. The story of how the prophetic task was realized in the community's embrace of peace, justice, and charity on the banks of the Mississippi is no less fascinating.

Moving Social Responsibility to the Center

Giving alms to the poor and practicing charity as a virtue have long been considered central in the Christian tradition. The social encyclicals issuing forth from the Holy See since the late nineteenth century, however, as well as the documents of the Second Vatican Council, began to emphasize the social dimensions of charity more markedly than ever before. Tending to the needs and the sufferings of others was presented with increasing frequency not only as something to be practiced in one's private life and relationships, but also as the very essence of that redemption which the Church is called to bring into the world.[5] Not long after the new Newman facility had risen up on the banks of the Mississippi in the early 1960s, Monsignor George Higgins was invited to the center to present a lecture. Higgins was the director of the Social Action Department of the National Catholic Welfare Conference in Washington, D.C., and at the time was a member of the Preparatory Commission on the Lay Apostolate for the Second Vatican Council, as well as one of the Council's official consultants. He was also among the select handful of Christian leaders with whom President Lyndon Johnson had consulted before making his address to the nation on civil rights and voter registration. On the evening Higgins appeared before the crowd gathered at the St. Cloud Newman Center, he delivered a stirring and provocative message. "If we sufficiently understood that the all-out struggle against injustice is the responsibility of every Christian," he avowed, "our Christianity would be different. It would be so different that the world would no longer be faced with the paradox and scandal, so common in modern times, of Christians who pass through the midst of the gravest social injustices almost without seeing them and without considering their deep causes." Higgins' message anticipated by several years the strong statement made by the document arising out of the 1971 World Synod of Bishops, *Justice in the World*. That document proclaimed unequivocally that action on behalf of peace and justice is a constitutive dimension of the preaching of the gospel and cannot be downplayed or ignored by anyone who dares to claim the name "Christian."

A recognition of charity's broader dimensions came early to the St. Cloud Newman movement. Service to those in need was a part of Newman Club activity from the very beginning. Over time, however, that commitment to serve was drawn more and more into the center of Newman's self-understanding and sense of mission and gradually became a constitutive dimension of the crossroads community's life. Throughout the 1930s, 1940s, and 1950s, as we have seen, Newman Club members volunteered regularly at the "St. Cloud Orphanage," and the club took up countless collections to help support the efforts of world missions projects and various local service agencies. By 1965, however, the Newman bulletin was regularly printing excerpts from articles and books meant to prod community members toward a sharper sense of the inescapably obligatory nature of charitable giving, and of the concrete action on behalf of justice to which it ought to lead. On January 3, 1965, for example, the bulletin contained the following quote from an article in *Ave Maria* magazine:

> True Christian renewal will not be accomplished until Christ shines forth without blemish in His church, until Christ is completely fed in the poor, until Christ the farm laborer is given human working conditions and a decent wage, until Christ the refugee is given welcome in lands of plenty. It is the love of Christ that we share at the altar that must drive us on.

To feed Christ in the poor was one responsibility which student and permanent members of the Newman community assumed without question. They took to heart the challenge behind Gandhi's poignant reminder that "to the millions who have to go without two meals a day, the only acceptable form in which God dare appear is food." For many years, the parish has taken up a second collection in brown-paper shopping bags on the first Sunday of every month in order to support the needs of the St. Cloud Food Shelf, and the children involved in Newman's religious education program deliver donated food to the agency regularly. Renew groups, groups of peer ministers, junior and senior high school students and numerous other individuals from the parish have consistently volunteered to serve food at local homeless shelters and soup kitchens. The community also provides drivers at designated times each year for the local "Meals on Wheels" pro-

The familiar label affixed to the brown-paper shopping bags used for the Newman Center's monthly Food Shelf collection.

gram, which brings hot lunches to shut-ins in the St. Cloud area, and in 1995 began working in cooperation with University Lutheran Church of the Epiphany to serve a free Saturday afternoon meal once a month to those in need. The sacred tradition of the Holy Thursday "Give and Take" collection, furthermore, has persisted in the Newman community for more than two decades. The collection baskets are passed as usual during Holy Thursday liturgies, but on this one occasion each year the monies collected are not used to help finance parish needs. Instead, all present are told simply to "give" if they feel able as the basket comes around, or to "take" from it if they consider themselves to be in need. No limits are placed on the amount that can be taken from the basket, and no questions are ever asked. Initially, some feared that the practice would "foster theft" and that many drop-in attendees would take undue advantage of the easy availability of so much money. In actuality, however, far more people contribute to the bounty of the basket than take from it, and those who do remove money have nearly always honored the trust that is placed in them. The "Give and Take" collection has summoned Newman members of all ages and backgrounds to practice what they preach about the virtues of giving with no strings attached.

In the mid-1970s, the Newman crossroads community ventured boldly into prophetic waters by suggesting out loud that concern for those in need does, in fact, operate at the periphery of life for many people and is not always permitted to dwell in the center where it can affect and transform the structures of their lives and the institutions of which they are a part. Attempts to encourage such a shift among Newman members took root and began to grow, and 1973 witnessed the introduction of a significant Newman tradition designed to alter habits and augment awarenesses. The publication of "Advent Alternatives" continues to this day and was designed from the start to encourage the Christian community on the banks of the Holy Spirit's river to conjure up novel ways to celebrate the coming of Christmas that would expand the Santa tradition and make the focus of the season less exclusively materialistic. During that inaugural 1973 Advent season, some remarkably creative home rituals were suggested, like the construction of an alternative Advent Wreath made with a center candle symbolizing Christ and five additional candles representing the races of humankind, one black, one brown, one red, one yellow, and one white. "Have your children light one candle each week," the Newman bulletin counseled, "and then spend some time talking as a family in positive ways about the contributions of that particular race." The dimension of the "Advent Alternative" tradition that has persisted most unflagging, however, is the publication of local opportunities for giving that can be embraced as a way of extending the generous spirit of the season beyond the parameters of one's own home, nuclear family, and loved ones.

221

Initially, the needs advertised by the Newman bulletin were very personal and very specific: "Family of 4 needs help with past-due electric bill of $164.16. A shut-off of gas and electricity has been threatened." "In need of maternity clothing, size 12, and gifts for girl 4 and boy 3." "Husband has special medical problems and consequently less income; has special unpaid bill of $50 and needs help by first part of year." "Family of 10 struggling through on food stamps; food basket for Christmas would be greatly appreciated." In more recent years, though, the Newman Peace and and Social Justice Committee has assumed responsibility for publishing the Advent Alternative's list and has chosen to focus on the needs of local service agencies like the Salvation Army and the St. Cloud Women's Guild, who in their turn work to serve the very personal needs of large numbers of people.

ADVENT ALTERNATIVES

The following is a listing of a few area agencies and their special needs this holiday season. In keeping with our yearly custom, this list is provided as an opportunity for individuals and families in the Newman community to respond to the needs of children and adults in the community at-large in preparation for the Feast of Christmas. Thank you for your generosity and support!

The Salvation Army needs volunteer "Bell-Ringers" to stand at its various Christmas Kettle locations between November 25 and December 18. Also needed are volunteers to sit at the Sharing Tree site at Crossroads Mall to receive gifts and donations. Contact Mary at 252-4552 if you can donate some of your time to help out. Volunteers (especially male volunteers) are also needed to help lift, carry and transport food baskets and toys. Contact Christy or Vanessa by the first week of December at 252-4552.

Women's Guild is in need of toys for children through age 14, and mittens for children. Please place donations of toys or mittens in the boxes provided in the Newman Lobby by December 16.

"Advent Alternatives" possibilities are published each year in the Newman Sunday bulletin.

Newman also became involved for the first time in the 1970s with OXFAM, a non-profit international agency funding disaster relief and self-help development projects in Africa, Asia, and Latin America. That involvement began with the sponsorship of day-long fasts designed to encourage parish members to come face-to-face with hunger, an experience confronted daily by many millions around the world. All money not spent on food by individuals participating in the days of fast were then donated to OXFAM in support of its development efforts. Later, such fasts became more sophisticated in nature and involved the university's food service. The Newman Center, along with it ecumenical colleagues in campus ministry, would together advertise and promote fast days among St. Cloud State students and arrange with the administrators of the campus food service to have the money participating students did not spend on meals during the day donated to OXFAM. Often, ecumenical prayer services followed the experience of fasting. Several "Hunger Meals" were also staged throughout the 1970s and the 1980s; the last such meal, in fact, was offered by the Newman Peace and Social Justice Committee in 1990. Hunger Meals were fascinating educational efforts designed to illustrate the inequities of food distribution around the world. Those participating would draw a number which would determine the quality of the meal they would receive, an arbitrary practice indicative of the random nature of life's circumstances, and of how little control people have, really, over where they are born and what resources will be available to them as they grow up in the world. The vast majority of the people who arrived for the event would be fed no more than a cup of broth. A very small number would receive a bowl of rice, and a smaller number still would be served a full meal replete with meat, potatoes, fruits, breads, and vegetables. The Hunger Meal was an exercise in experiential learning, designed to move a peripheral awareness closer to the center by pointing out as palpably as possible the unjust disparities that exist between the majority of the world's people who live daily with great want, and the privileged few in the developed world who live with plentiful resources and luxuries abounding. Over time, the Newman community used a wide variety of educational techniques like this one in order to encourage its members to draw concern for those in need into the center of their individual decision-making processes and lifestyle choices, and to see more clearly the connection between their waste and other's want. As a 1975 bulletin piece exhorted:

EVALUATE YOUR LIFE
do not leave lights burning when they are not needed.
rethink your use of paper, plastic and metal foil wraps.
grow some of your own food and bring your children "closer
   to the earth."

223

return grocery sacks and ask that your order be placed in them.
don't throw away something that can be fixed.
avoid engine idling . . .
do not scatter paper, cans, bottles or unwanted material over
the countryside.
do not overhunt and kill for profit.
plant trees.
quit smoking.
trade that motorboat for a canoe or sailboat . . . see nature,
improve your health and reduce a serious source of
pollution.

Concrete, small-scale suggestions like these and educational events like the Hunger Meal were regularly connected to a broader vision and a theological framework for Newman members through the efforts of the pastoral team and other qualified individuals within the community. During the 1974 Lenten season, for example, the Newman staff introduced the scriptural theme of "Liberation" by affirming: "Lent and Liberation belong together, for liberation is at the heart of Christ's redemptive work. As one listens to the scripture readings for this season, God's voice, down the echoes of history, rings out a resounding, 'Let my people go!' Let them go out of slavery in Egypt, idolatry in Canaan, exile in Babylon! Let them go out of their sins of injustice, of oppressing the poor, of self-indulgence, hardheartedness, unconcern, of thinking they can love Me without loving men [sic]. Then let them come and worship me and I will hear them and be their God!" In keeping with the spirit of that proclamation, a variety of people were invited to preach at weekend masses during the six weeks of Lent on some aspect of the Christian responsibility to work for liberation, and to seek that internal freedom of which we all are in need in order to become authentically committed to the freedom of others. The congregation that gathered each week during that Lent of 1974 were treated to the following homiletic challenges:

> Ken Irrgang, campus pastor at the College of St. Benedict, on "Liberation theology as applied to the poor among us, especially the Mexican-American."

> Helen Gilbert, Instructor of Folklore at St. Cloud State University and the College of St. Benedict, on "The Church enters the struggle for women's liberation and equal rights."

> Robert Kiefer, associate pastor at St. Peter's Parish, on "The Church enters the struggle for justice in the Third World."

> Dr. John Helgeland, St. John's University Theology Department, on "The Church enters the political world to develop structures for peace."

> Bill Vos and Ade Ledermann, well-rested after a month of preaching reprieve, on "The Victory of Liberation? When?"

224

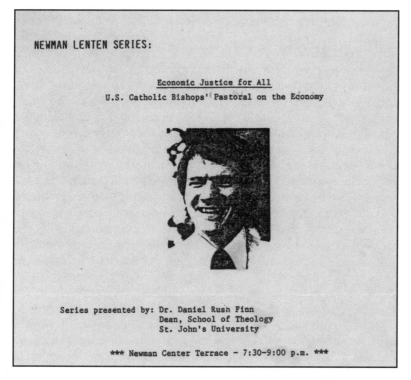

NEWMAN LENTEN SERIES:

Economic Justice for All
U.S. Catholic Bishops' Pastoral on the Economy

Series presented by: Dr. Daniel Rush Finn
Dean, School of Theology
St. John's University

*** Newman Center Terrace - 7:30-9:00 p.m. ***

Newman parishioner Dan Finn enriches the 1987 Lenten season for all community members.

In keeping with the spirit of that 1974 effort, during a Lenten season thirteen years later, Daniel Rush Finn, a faculty member at St. John's University in Collegeville and a long-time Newman parishioner, proffered a series of talks on the United States Bishop's provocative pastoral letter, *Economic Justice For All.* His three lectures, held in the Newman Terrace, explored the spiritual and theological roots of concern over the distribution, stewardship, and use of the world's wealth, then examined concrete policy proposals and issued a final, more personal challenge entitled "How Do I Respond?"

Making a Corporate Commitment

These examinations in theory of the more demanding institutional implications of the Christian commitment to social responsibility came to fruition in one small but important way within Newman parish structures when, in the late 1980s, a budget category was established by the Finance Committee designated as "Assistance to the Needy." Through the foundation of that category, the parish created a concrete, structural mechanism to insure that not all of its financial resources would be expended internally, and that a portion of the community's wealth would always be earmarked to move beyond the confines of Newman's walls and be put to work assisting people within the broader St. Cloud community and beyond. When Mansuetus Setonga, an East African priest from Tanzania arrived to do graduate study at St. Cloud State in 1993,

Newman Pastoral Team member Nic Dressen (left) shares a moment of friendship with Tanzanian Mansuetus Setonga on the day of Setonga's graduation from St. Cloud State University.

for example, the community extended itself in financial support of Setonga, and of the good people of his home diocese of Same, Tanzania.

It is never easy to do more than pay lip service to the demands of charity; it is never easy to do more than relegate concern for those in need to the periphery to await attention if and when time and money allow. By 1987, the Newman community had crafted a Mission Statement that proclaimed, "We are a hopeful community that welcomes the stranger and hears the cry of the oppressed." But about a decade before articulating that mandate so beautifully on paper, the community was issued a very specific and demanding summons to live it out. In 1975, after the fall of South Vietnam produced 135,000 refugees with no place to call home, social service agencies and directors of charities throughout the nation were asked by the United States government to offer help. The United States Catholic Conference became one of eight non-profit agencies that agreed to work cooperatively with the Office of Immigration on efforts to resettle Vietnamese families in the United States. No group of refugees could be granted legal admittance to the United States, however, without "sponsorship" by an individual, group, or organization willing to assume some responsibility for seeking out housing, community assistance, and support for them upon their arrival. The United States Catholic Conference and its non-profit colleagues went to work seeking sponsors, and thus it was that a refugee resettlement program coordinated by Catholic Charities of the Diocese of St. Cloud was established in Central Minnesota. Between 1975 and 1982, Minnesota became a new place to call home for some 25,000 people from Southeast Asia through the efforts of this program. In June of 1975 the Newman community agreed to venture into the responsibility of sponsorship; twenty-two people showed up at an initial meeting held to measure interest and commitment. As one couple present at that first meeting put it: "We were so concerned about the war in Vietnam for such a long time and felt unable to do anything; this seemed like such a good way to show that concern." Two Newman parishioners offered to open their homes to refugee families until they were ready and able to find housing for themselves, while numerous others pledged support by way of providing food, clothing, regular monetary contributions, and assistance in job retraining and employment searches. On July 10, 1975, the Nguyen Van Ban family of six arrived at the home of Ed and Margaret Wilson; the Pham Van Huan family of five settled in at the home of Dave and Kathy Huberty on July 22. Both of these delightful families remained with their hosts until late fall of that year and then moved to apartments of their own in St. Cloud. In 1979, Newman parishioners helped with the support of five more families who arrived in St. Cloud area, and Ed and Margaret Wilson welcomed yet another family, the Sinaraths, into their home for a short-term stay. In July of 1990, the Newman

The Phan family at Newman in 1991.

community agreed to serve as a co-sponsor, with Ecumenical Refugee Services of St. Cloud, of the Hong Vien Phan family. Once again, a committee of Newmanites came together and procured an apartment, solicited used furniture, purchased kitchen and laundry supplies and brought together food and clothing so that when the Phans arrived at the airport in Minneapolis on September 10th, they could be taken to a well-stocked and welcoming home. The community continued to offer support and assistance as the Phans settled in and set about building a highly successful new life in St. Cloud. Today, Vien and Hue Phan and their four talented children, Van, Tu, Thu, and The, remain loyal members of Christ Church Newman Center and enrich the community with their presence, their generosity, and their graciousness.

Venturing forth from Home to Serve and to Learn

"Praxis" is the Greek word for performing or doing, and the term is used commonly today to refer to that aspect of Christian discipleship expressed through actions and choices. Christians at their best have long understood that mature faith is characterized not merely by acts of worship, or by intellectual assent to a body of truth claims, or by the making of charitable monetary contributions. Mature faith also leads inevitably to passionate participation in endeavors aimed at transforming human lives and communities.[6] Taking to heart the challenge to practice the things preached and prayed about at Sunday liturgies has long been a characteristic of

The highly popular volunteer opportunities booklet published annually by Newman's Peace and Social Justice Committee.

the Newman community. Today, when the Peace and Social Justice Committee publishes its annual booklet listing volunteer service opportunities of many kinds within the greater St. Cloud area, several hundred copies of the booklet are gone in a flash and second and third "printings" are nearly always necessary. It was in the early 1960s, however, that the Christian call to take praxis seriously first began to impel some members of the crossroads community into life-transforming adventures a little farther away from home. A pioneer in this regard was Newmanite Bette Daniels, who graduated in 1961 and joined "The Grail," an international lay apostolate for women. Daniels journeyed with the apostolate to LaFayette, Louisiana to teach English and Speech to students of Cajun descent in a small parochial high school. The experience broadened her horizons, her sensitivity to injustice, and her commitment to Christian servanthood. Daniels later wrote an article for *ERA* in which she reflected on her time in Lousiana and took the Church to task for failing to challenge the deep-rooted segregation of the South:

> One of my greatest disappointments was the failure (so it seems to me) on the part of the Church to deal with segregation. Not only are the parochial schools in this area segregated, but so are the Churches. Small towns which could do perfectly well with one Church, have two—one for white Catholics and one for colored Catholics. . . .Yet in spite of this problem, it is very often people within the Church who are leaders against segregation.[7]

It wasn't long before other Newman students began to look for opportunities to serve beyond the city limits of St. Cloud. Early in 1963, the priest-director of the Extension Lay Volunteers, whose home base was in Chicago, came to speak to Newman students about possibilities for service in "home mission" regions in the southern United States where Catholics in general, and Catholic

St. Cloud Newman member Judy Sausen (fourth from left in the top row) signed up to serve with the Extension Volunteer Program.

professional personnel in particular, were in short supply. A young lay missionary named Connie Scott, who was also part of that visit to St. Cloud, wrote later to Wil Illies of how impressed she had been by the St. Cloud Newman students. "Their enthusiasm and vitality are unmatched," she avowed. "The interest and intelligent, searching questions they asked the evening we were there showed more than a normal reaction. They are a credit to you." Less than one month later, twenty-five Newmanites gathered for the inaugural meeting of a lay missioner training course held at Newman Hall. The six-week course endeavored to foster in students a sense of apostolic zeal and spirituality. Newman Club member Judy Sausen later signed up and served for a time with the Extension Volunteer program.

These early pioneering attempts to travel to new environs, which broadened horizons and offered novel opportunities to be of service, came to fruition in the mid-1970s when "service learning trips" over academic-break weeks were developed by the ecumenical campus ministry group working together on the banks of the Mississippi. Students were drawn through these trips into six- or seven-day experiences of service and reflection and were exposed to a wide variety of conditions and concerns in places like New Orleans, New York, Washington, D.C., and Chicago, where hearing Reverend Jesse Jackson address the Saturday morning PUSH (People United To Serve Humanity) meeting was always a favored highlight. UMHE (United Ministries in Higher Education) minis-

Numerous Newman service trip participants have had the privilege of hearing Jesse Jackson address the members of operation PUSH in Chicago.

St. Cloud State students Barb Diercke and Sharon Schmiesing (in front) work at the Olive Branch Shelter during a Volunteer Ministry trip to Chicago in the mid-1980s. Schmiesing, her husband, and their three children are dedicated members of the Newman Community today.

Five SCS students visit homeless in Chicago

by Bob McClintick
Staff Writer

While most students were relaxing during fall quarter break, several SCS students experienced the life of the Chicago, Ill. homeless.

Under the guidance of Sister Frances of Newman Center, five SCS students and parish member Margaret Wilson departed Nov. 29 on a week-long journey to the streets of Chicago.

"I went to get the experience of working among the poor—to see how those people really live," said Sharon Schmiesing, SCS student. "The more I can help someone, the better I feel."

It is a good experience for white, middle-class people to go to a big city and work among the diversity of homeless people, Sister Frances said.

"Most students don't go with real specific expectations," she said. "They are caring and want to make a contribution. They know it will be a good experience."

Chicago Food Depository. Work on the line consisted of sorting, repackaging and cleaning unsalable food from four major Chicago food outlets to be sold to local food shelves for 7 cents a pound.

On a tight schedule, the group paired off to assist workers at several homeless shelters in the area. Some spent their first night at the Wellington Avenue United Church of Christ Shelter, while the others were taken to the Sousa or Olive Branch shelters in Chicago.

What people do not realize is that most middle-class people, especially college kids, are using up their paychecks as they come, Sister Frances said.

"Actually, they are only two paychecks away from living on the streets themselves," she said. "Once on the street, it does not take long for creativity and resourcefulness to drain away and be replaced by the will to survive."

Courtesy Photo

SCS students Barb Diercks and Sharon Schmiesing hand out evening snacks to the homeless at Olive Branch Shelter during their recent trip to Chicago during winter quarter break. Diercks and Schmiesing were two of five other SCS students who went to Chicago to help the homeless and better understand their situation.

Although some of the homeless are able to break out of the cycle, many more do not, Sister Frances said.

ter Marv Rapinski was a true leader in this regard; he once spear-headed a twelve-day marathon trip for sixty students to three major cities with the assistance of Newman minister Adrian Ledermann, who remembers being impressed but utterly exhausted by the noble adventure. In 1984, under the leadership of Nic Dressen and Edie Reagen, Newman began an independent tradition of "Volunteer Ministry Trips" designed to give Catholic college students extended experiences of service, prayer, and community. In order to provide exposure to the realities of urban poverty, a week-long trip to inner-city Chicago for up to eleven students was sponsored each year during the university's fall break in late November, and the

Newman student Mary Kempenich reads to children in a day care center in rural Kentucky.

conditions of life in rural Appalachia were experienced during a yearly spring-break trip in early March. But, urban or rural, the breakthroughs in insight and perspective that occurred for students as a result of these pilgrimages were very real, and very powerful. As 1997 participant Carrie Phillips felt compelled to recommend after her week-long stay in the Appalachian mountain region, "I hope students at St. Cloud State will look beyond our little world on campus. Sometimes we can get so wrapped up in our own daily routine of college life and classes. There are a lot of things happening in the world around us. We simply must become aware of them." The Newman approach to such trips, however, has always been an unpretentious one. In preparatory meetings held prior to the start of each experience, students are encouraged to understand that they are not venturing forth on a "missionary" trip and are not going to "spread the faith" or to offer their talents and time to people whose lives will be profoundly changed by their service. What they are capable of giving in a week's time is really very limited; what they receive and learn is immeasurable. A *St. Cloud Visitor* article chronicling one of the trips announced quite accurately that "Volunteers Changed Selves, Not Culture," and Newman minister Jacqui Landry aptly told the newspaper that, "we didn't rescue them, they rescued us." In 1986, junior Jenine Bertsch described well the honest and authentic attitude the Newman community has always looked for in the students sent forth on its volunteer service experiences. "I went," Bertsch avows, "because I did not want to go. I did not want to see those people—I wanted nothing to do with them, and I was scared of them. So, I decided I better go. I live a perfect, little, middle-class life and am happy with it. These people do not have a nice life—so I thought it was about time I saw the other side."

Serving and learning are two integral dimensions of the Newman Volunteer Ministry Experience. Building community among student participants and teaching them the value of taking time out

Participants in the spring 1999 service trip to LaFayette Louisiana, headed by Newman Pastoral Team member Kevin Anderson and Molly Dose, Newman's 1999 ministry intern.

The long road trips which have become a part of the Volunteer Ministry Experience help to build bonds of community and friendship.

to do theological reflection and to make faith connections in the context of prayer were also built in from the start as critical components of the process. Student Jean Ann Moraski, who graduated in 1992, described one such experience of prayerful pondering at the end of her time in Kentucky: "We had a beautiful reflection gathering with our small group. With three lit candles, Jacqui told us that one monk said, 'You can't have action without reflection.' We each planted in dirt a seed of hope and told what we hoped for. I hoped for more beautiful people such as Sister Gemma and Albinia to come after they have passed away to take care of the elderly and not to let them be forgotten. It was a very emotional time of reflection."

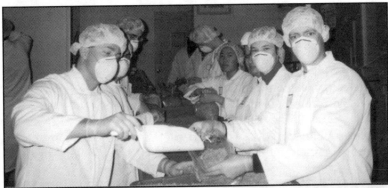

Newman volunteers at work packaging cereals at the Greater Chicago Food Depository in 1995.

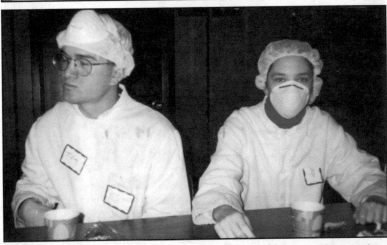

Matt Caduff and Trace Landowski take a break from the work.

Whether produced for the journals they were required to keep, or for the "mini-homilies" they have often been asked to give for the benefit of the Newman congregation during weekend liturgies upon their return, the personal reflections of St. Cloud State students who have been a part of the Volunteer Ministry Program over the past fifteen years are trenchant and telling. Consider the following excerpts from student Stacia Fink's journal chronicling her 1989 experience in Chicago:

6:00 P.M., Sunday, November 27. Chicago. How exciting to leave my tiny corner of the world! Our first stop is at the Metropolitan Community Church, whose members are primarily gay or lesbian. At the service we soon understand the purpose of our trip is to meet people who are, as a whole, oppressed. Its amazing how ignorance is the largest barrier to understanding people. My goal for the week is to increase my awareness of homelessness, poverty and oppression.

6:00 A.M., Monday, November 28. Corpus Christ Convent, Chicago. I wake to the clicking of the ancient radiator and the sound of the elevated train rushing by a block away. We will be staying with four sisters at the convent, an old, three-story structure located in the dangerous south side. It is surrounded by decaying apartment buildings: crumbling wooden staircases, boarded windows, overflowing trash and weeds. The convent's doors remain locked day and night.

We spent our first morning at the Greater Chicago Food Depository in the gleaning lines washing and packing canned and dry goods. GCFD collects expired and surplus food from distributors and redistributes more than two million pounds of food to Chicago shelters and agencies monthly. The marketing director says there are 32 million people below the poverty level in the U.S.—600,000 in Chicago. I am appalled at the numbers.

I work for two hours on the line with Ethel, an older, black woman, and we become friends. I realize that we whites are the minority, salt speckles among the pepper.

8:00 P.M., Sousa Shelter. Sister Frances brings Lisa and me to our first overnight shelter. I am curious and terrified. About 45 women and 70 men are let in, allowed to eat a small meal, and shower and sleep until 7 am. A desk worker said fights are not unusual among the guests. Fights with knives. Lisa and I distribute nightgowns and towels to the tattered women as they enter . . .

Stacia Fink (right), meeting new people from different backgrounds.

1 pm, Wednesday, November 30. Irene's Day Drop-In Shelter. After serving lunch to 25 women, I sit down at a table where people are painting and making clay sculptures. Jean, the art therapist, visits periodically to teach the women creative forms of expression. I meet two very special people: Barbara and Mavil. Barbara, a black woman with no teeth, makes such beautiful sculptures, I ask if she will help me make one. I also become friends with Mavil, a brilliant painter and sculptor. Although she is deaf and cannot speak, we communicate through smiles and touching.[8]

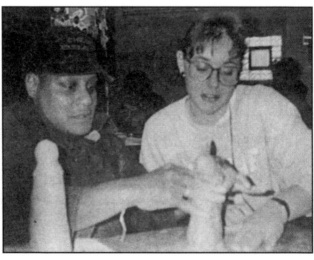

On the volunteer group's day off, St. Cloud State student Brent Augustinek (above) learns to skate at a rink atop Navy Pier in Chicago.

Above right: talking, sawing and learning in southeastern Kentucky.

The Newman students who choose each year to forego the sandy beaches and sunshine usually associated with spring break adventures and head off instead to rural Appalachia on a service trip experience things like painting, planting, building, repairing, tutoring, doing day care, selling used clothes, visiting, listening, and learning. These trips to the mountains have produced reflections every bit as penetrating as those inspired by the complexities and contradictions of inner-city Chicago. Reprinted below are pieces of a moving presentation made during weekend liturgies to the Newman community by the students who participated in the 1995 spring break experience:

Dave Giesen

God's power was made visible when Jesus raised Lazarus from the dead. Many who had come to visit Mary and Martha and had seen what Jesus did, put their faith in him. "*Seeing is believing.*" I know that in another place in the Gospel of John, Jesus says, "*Blessed are those who have not seen and have still believed.*" But for me seeing, hearing and doing sure made it easier to believe.

I really don't think that I expected a week in Appalachia to have a major impact on my life. But during that eight-day adventure, I gained some memories, lessons, and insights that will last me a lifetime. I've found that it is difficult to communicate to people the full impact of my experience in the mountains. When people ask me what I did on my spring break, I tell them that I chopped down a tree, and I put up a fence. I went to church on Sunday, and I prayed every night. I played catch, I played cards, and I played tapes. I tried to climb a mountain—but failed. And I tried to teach a couple of West Virginians how to chew sunflower seeds—but failed at that, too.

234

West Virginian "Eudie" (at left), has become a favorite friend and mentor of St. Cloud State students who venture to Malden each year.

Even as you listen to these ramblings of mine, you probably wonder how such simple occurrences could have had such a profound impact upon me . . . I guess you just had to be there. By being there and by seeing, hearing and doing what I did, I came to believe more than anything else that it is only by giving of ourselves that we can ever learn the true meaning of life.

Megan Curran

This year spring break occurred during the first week of Lent, and because of that, I know that I will never forget the Lent of 1995. Now I don't want you to think that I decided to go on Newman's Volunteer Ministry Experience because I wanted to offer up my spring break for Lent or anything like that. It's just that I like to travel, meet people, and do service projects now and then, and this sounded like a really cool opportunity.

On my spring break, I did travel over 2,300 miles, I did meet some wonderful people, and I had a really cool time. But I also learned something about my Christian faith . . . I learned something about what it means to believe in Jesus. Believing in Jesus is a pretty fuzzy concept, but because of what happened on our trip, I came to realize that "believing in Jesus" also means believing in each other and believing in acts of service and kindness. In West Virginia, I saw how a few people can still make a real difference.

Let me tell you about our painting project that was intended to make one wonderful woman feel better about herself. That woman was Hope Osborne, a coal mining widow who takes care of her mentally challenged son and her 84-year-old mother, Miss Bessie. Hope is also a VISTA volunteer and a very gifted quilt designer. For a couple of years, she worked in a dingy, drab, and dull space that was certainly not worthy of an artist of her ability. But thanks to some pink and purple and green and blue paint and our creativity and hard work, her work space came alive with a classic . . . and classy "flying geese" pattern. We all wish that we could have been there when Hope saw her resurrected work space for the first time, but we are confident that our little acts of service and kindness brought some new life to Hope Osborne.

A house in Wallins Creek, Kentucky, the spring destination of the Newman Volunteer Ministry group for many years.

A Volunteer Ministry group poses with two Sisters of the Assumption, who supervised their work in Wallins Creek, Kentucky.

For many years, Newman service learning groups traveled to eastern Kentucky to link up with "CAP," the Christian Appalachian Project, which has put both short and long-term volunteers to work in the region for many years. Later, students began working with a group of Little Sisters of the Assumption in the tiny town of Wallins Creek, Kentucky, just outside of Harlan. After 1994, the Newman group made Malden, West Virginia, its destination and has since enjoyed the privilege of working with James Thibeault and the quilting cooperative he helped to establish among the talented natives of the town. James and the good people of Malden have been gracious and generous hosts each time the crew from St. Cloud, Minnesota, shows up, and have even constructed a special quilt symbolizing the bond of friendship which has grown between St. Cloud and Malden. Each member of each new group arriving in the hills of West Virginia signs her or his name on one of the several blank squares sewn into the quilt's overall design; the friendship quilt then hangs throughout the remainder of the year in the Newman Center building.

The Cabin Creek logo.

Whether in Malden or in Wallins Creek or in some place else altogether, however, Newman volunteers have always been both changed and deeply touched by the poverty and the isolation, the generosity and hospitality, the simple values of family and home, and the absolutely unique culture that characterizes the people of Appalachia. As non-traditional student and longtime Newman member Bonnie Stachowski put it after her 1987 experience: "My stereotypical thinking was changed. [The trip] was another way to change that, to actually learn what was real instead of some images I had learned without having experienced these people . . . I had to dig deeper and look beyond that to not make those judgments." Kristi Kluntz, who went to Appalachia in the Spring of 1999 wrote simply, "Sometimes we need to step back from the life we're used to living and find out why we're living it. . . . Life in Malden is simple but the love is abundant."

Students spend break helping flood victims

Eight student members of Christ Church Newman Center went to West Virginia to battle floods

By Muhammad Karim
NEWS EDITOR

During spring break, eight SCSU students, all volunteers at Christ Church Newman Center, traveled to the hills and mountains of the south in an effort to assist a quilting co-op business. They ended up spending one day helping a victim of flood waters evacuate her damaged residence, according to junior Carrie Philips.

This is the fourth year Christ Church Newman Center has sponsored a delegation for the purpose of assisting a group of dedicated quilters with their co-op business in Malden, West Virginia. The business has had such clients as the late Jacquelyn Kennedy-Onassis, according to Philips.

"We went to Malden to help the co-op with its renovation efforts," Philips said. "We were assisting them in creating a visiting center. In the beginning, all of us engaged in simply trying to do what was needed of us."

Philips said they helped by painting, wall papering, and gardening and doing yard work. During this period, a flood raged through Malden forcing it to be declared a disaster area. Philips said

Shane A. Opatz/ASSISTANT PHOTO EDITOR
Eight student members of Christ Church Newman Center went from freezing Minnesota temperatures to southern water savaged soil over spring break. Volunteers (left to right) Tammy Dodge, Sarah Wintheiser, Carly Antus, Monica Zilka, Hannah Gurno, Kelly Serfling, Ann Armstrong and (not pictured) Carrie Phillips, spent their time away from classes aiding a resident of West Virginia whose home was the target of flood damage.

Above, a State Cloud *Chronicle* article describing the 1997 Volunteer Ministry trip to Malden, West Virginia.

At right, members of the 1999 group hard at work peeling vegetables in LaFayette, Louisiana.

Space to Explore a Cultural Revolution

Service adventures far from home were not the only experiences fostered by the Newman community that developed and deepened students' commitment to work as prophets and healers in the world. When Bill Vos looks back at the start of his ten-year tenure at the Newman Center, he recalls that his only apprehension about assuming the job in 1969 was his awareness of the turbulence of the times—the "cultural revolution" going on in society, in politics and in the church was at once stimulating and tension-

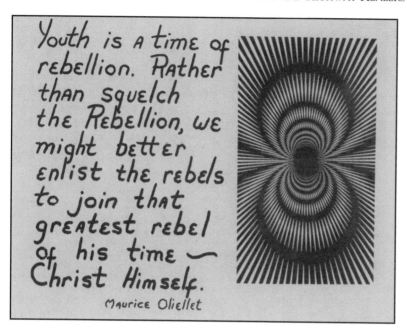

Youth is a time of rebellion. Rather than squelch the Rebellion, we might better enlist the rebels to join that greatest rebel of his time — Christ Himself.

Maurice Oliellet

The front of a Newman brochure first published in the late 1960s.

filled. Not surprisingly, as the 1960s and the 1970s progressed, the Newman Center dwelling at the crossroads where all things are met came to function as a real locus of activism, thoughtful discussion, and experimentation. Students caught the contagious sense of social responsibility that was afoot in those years; for a while they were admirably turned outward and perhaps a bit more willing to got out on a limb for the convictions they were coming to cultivate than those who came before, or after, them. At least throughout the 1970s, Vos affirms today, they also still trusted the Church and maintained a high level of participation in the Catholic Christian community, even when they curtailed or rejected participation in other institutions. Their participation, furthermore, was characterized by search and exploration in ways it never had been before. Both Catholic and other campus ministers at St. Cloud State in those years worked hard to promote theological reflection on the probing ventures into social responsibility and political activism so prevalent at the time, prompting students to make make faith connections that would ground their activity in the richness of the gospel tradition.

The Newman Pastoral Team did some of that prompting by creating opportunity and space within the Newman Center facility where searching students could spend time in thought, conversation and dialogue with one another, and with other searching people of faith. The Newman Terrace, for example, was used regularly on Sunday nights to show thought-provoking films on current social issues, which were followed by guided discussion. For a while in the late 1960s, the Newman Terrace was called "McCarthy's" in

The entrance to the Newman Terrace today, a gathering space for members of the Newman community. The sign above the doors was painted in 1993 by student Stacey Bakula.

OPEN EVERY EVENING
FOR FAST DELIVERY
CALL **253-2131**
LARGE DINING ROOM
•*PIZZA*
•*SUBMARINES*
•*SANDWICHES*
•*HAMBURGERS*
396 1st Av S Newman Center Downstairs

The famous orange match books designed to advertise the Newman Terrace pizza operation.

honor of DFL Senator Eugene McCarthy and was set up as a snack bar where students could purchase inexpensive food and hang out. An order of french fries and a hot dog would often be on special for twenty-five cents, and cheeseburgers and fishburgers were ever-popular favorites. In the fall of 1969, however, "McCarthy's" closed and the Newman Terrace Pizza operation began. A large pizza oven was installed, and the Terrace began to offer a wide variety of stadium-type pizzas as well as submarine sandwiches, chicken, and shrimp between 11:00 A.M. and midnight, Monday thru Friday, and 4:30 P.M. until midnight on Sundays. Deliveries were even made in the campus area. For a while, in order to provide a break from the more serious films being presented on Sunday evenings each week, a Monday night special was run: $1.00 for any small pizza and free showings of W.C. Fields and Laurel and Hardy movies, as well as old episodes of the Three Stooges and the L'il Rascals. Other evenings featured performances by local musicians who came to sing and play "coffee shop" style. In time, paid managers were hired to run the Terrace pizza operation. They concocted enticing invitations like, "Bring your Sunday bulletin down; it's worth one free taco." That particular invitation went on to assure students: "You do not have to relinquish this valuable document; it will be returned."

The Terrace wasn't the only space made available within the Newman Center's walls in order to encourage crossroad conversation and horizon-broadening explorations. Pottery sales, art, and photography displays in the Newman lobby and elsewhere became a regular part of the scenery, and in November of 1971 the "Creative Art Shoppe," also called "Adiaphora," opened next door to the Newman Library. Adiaphora was a community endeavor fully staffed by volunteers designed to provide a place for creative spirits, craft dabblers, and local artists of all sorts to sell their wares at no expense to themselves. The November 7, 1971, bulletin, furthermore, announced the arrival of the "Organic Food Cooperative of St. Cloud," which set itself up for business in the small room to the left of the stage in the Terrace, which is today the nursery. The business was described as "a cooperative effort to purchase food and non-food items that have been grown in a natural environment," and was promoted as "a non-profit buying club that will stress an alternative approach to our relationship with our environment and our fellow human beings." The presence of such an intentional enterprise, with an intentionally developed social conscience, was a delightful addition to the Newman facility, and it wasn't long before the Co-op started serving "sumptuous and wholesome" lunches to students and others every Wednesday and Friday at noon. The cost of the meal was simply "whatever you think it's worth." Bread baked by Co-op members in the Newman kitchen first became available in July of 1972; by October of 1978 the bak-

Jeffra Flaitz (left) and Kristin Willette put their freshly baked bread out to cool in the Newman Terrace.

ery had been incorporated as a separate entity, owned jointly by four people. Jeffra Flaitz, Kristin Willette, Connie Pepin, and Monica Bowman together ran this alternative business not focused on making a profit but on providing a service. The four bakers arrived each morning at around 5:00 A.M. to put their whole wheat, soy, pumpernickel, Four Grain River, and Swedish rye breads into the oven and then start to work on the granola, cookies, and whole wheat egg muffins that were also offered daily. The *St. Cloud Daily Times* published a feature article on the community bakery that year and described how radio personality Garrison Keillor showed up one day to join in the fun; he later dedicated the Judy Collins song, "Cook With Honey" to Jeffra Flaitz and Kristin Willette. The bakery's products were sold out of the Terrace in the mornings, at The Eclectic Kitchen and Hunstigers in town, and at the Co-op, which eventually moved to its own location on East St. Germain Street in St. Cloud. "The bread we bring you is more than just bread," Flaitz said in the *St. Cloud Daily Times*, and stressed that the bakery existed for economic, social and political, as well as nutritious, reasons. None of the bakery's products contained additives, and "love" was always listed as an ingredient on every package. As Flaitz described it, "quality must always be recognized as the number one priority . . . the bakery operation is a reflection of our respect for the value and integrity of the grain. It is a symbol for the one-thousand-year-old history of bread baking and the tradition of the art passed from generation to generation, involving a broad range of culture backgrounds. . . . The typical American buys bread from a shelf in a grocery store and has no idea how it got there; we like to put people in touch with all that . . ."

The Dark Side of the Revolution

The campus highway environment often catalyzed the inbreaking of the Spirit and helped to draw the Christian community settled there into new awarenesses and sensitivities that were growthful and necessary. The tremendous social, religious and political upheaval experienced by the nation in the late 1960s and 1970s, however, was magnified in the environs of the university and had a dark side which was neither helpful nor holy. In that era, feelings of confusion, anxiety, and restlessness arose in many individuals, who, at times behaved destructively. Members of the campus ministry staff in those turbulent years found themselves doing considerable amounts of counseling and engaging daily in intense, one-on-one conversations. The need for guidance and direction seemed so urgent that in 1971 the Newman Pastoral Team established "Mountain," a phone information service organized and operated by trained students, which for a while focused primarily on drug emergency referrals. The crisis and referral line began by offering services seven nights a week from the early evening until two o'clock in the morning. Later, those hours were expanded and "Mountain" operated effectively for several years, despite attempts made to shut the service down by a few individuals in the St. Cloud area who were convinced, wrongly, that abortion referrals were being given to those who called in about unwanted pregnancy situations. Clandestine callers even endeavored to procure "evidence" by attempting to press and trap student counselors into providing abortion information. Such information was never given, but the Newman staff found it necessary to engage in numerous conversations over the matter with Bishop George Speltz, who was concerned that the phone operators not even provide referrals to agencies that might then themselves make available information about abortion services. Those conversations, Bill Vos, Katherine Kraft, and Adrian Ledermann recall, were for the most part characterized by healthy, respectful exchange and dialogue; as painful for the pastoral team in the 1970s as it had been for Wil Illies and Nic Zimmer in the 1960s, however, was the all-too familiar stress of having people regard Newman ministry with suspicion, failing to give credit or credence to the competence, prudence, skill, and truly Catholic concern of the professionals who guided it. When called in to discuss liturgical, doctrinal or other matters with the bishop, Bill Vos recalls that he frequently found himself saying, "With all due respect, Bishop, we're doing something important here and we're doing it responsibly. This is a specialized ministry in a special setting, and it requires a somewhat different approach than is required elsewhere. Please trust us." And for the most part, Speltz would let things be. Kraft, Ledermann, and Vos all remember with amusement one conversation in particular they had with the bishop at the Newman rectory; Speltz was speaking at great length about a matter of particular concern for him when Herman, Ledermann's and Vos' pet mynah bird, suddenly squawked "Oh be quiet!" The laughter that ensued eased the tension considerably.

A far more serious kind of tension, however, and a truly dark moment, arrived for the Newman community in the fall of 1980. On Sunday night, October 27, at the end of that year's Homecoming festivities, a shocking tragedy struck at the Newman Center. Catherine John, described as "a likable SCS senior with a warm, contagious grin," was stabbed to death at the Terrace Pizza Restaurant. Another St. Cloud State student, who served as one of the restaurant's assistant managers, was found guilty of her murder eighteen months later and was sentenced to life in prison. As Ade Ledermann put it in a letter to parents written about two weeks after John's death, "I wish we could blot out the events of the past two weeks. We can't. . . . Throughout these tragic events we have been called to do special ministry, to calm fears, reestablish trust and support grieving relatives and friends. God's love and blessing bring hope during tragic times." Francis Nosbisch took a van load of students to the funeral, and a special memorial service was also held at Newman for those who could not make the trip to John's hometown. Catherine John's death filled the Newman staff and community with deep sadness and profound pain. One of the achingly difficult dimensions of the whole experience, too, was that the perpetrator of the crime was a student as well, and the staff was also in close contact with him, and with his family, throughout the ordeal. As Francis Nosbisch explained it in an interview for the St. Cloud State *Chronicle* five years later, the responsibility, and the desire, of Newman as a Christian community was to try to be concerned for both the victim and the perpetrator. "We had to find ways to deal with shock, anger, and grief, to try to understand and also find some kind of forgiveness." Fear became a very palpable experience for many after that, especially for women who came to use the center's facilities, and a certain uneasiness and mistrust crept into the environment that was difficult to shake. The Newman Terrace had to be reclaimed again and reestablished as a safe and holy space. The violent and senseless loss of a vibrant and caring young woman within the confines of a place meant to promote love and life above all else produced a wound in the fabric of the community's life together that did not quickly heal. As Ledermann muses today, "I still feel the pain of it; it stays with me and probably always will. I hated those homecoming weekends after that."

Troubling Activity for the Guardians of the Center

A 1965 bulletin counseled Newman students and parishioners: "May your conscience keep you disturbed." Members of the Newman community took that advice to heart, so seriously, in fact, that their disturbed consciences sometimes moved them to speak and act in ways that disturbed if not the consciences, then certainly the comfort, of others. Moving sensitivities and awarenesses from the periphery and into the center, as prophets do, has a way of doing that, especially for those who believe that certain awarenesses belong at the periphery and are not worthy of institutionalized respect. In its younger years, the Newman movement nationwide often had its wings clipped and the scope of its concern limited by national leaders who viewed most forms of campus activism as no more than a peripheral rebellion against parental authority, piety, the Church, or Christian sexual norms that was hardly worthy of legitimation. Their response, for example, at the 1933 Atlantic City convention of the National Federation of College Catholic Clubs to Hitler's emerging persecution of liberals, intellectuals, and Jews typified the aloof position they adopted on nearly all campus political issues in the early decades of the movement. The delegates were told by their president that censure of Nazism was "not . . . pertinent to the function of our organization" and voted a "hands-off policy."[9] For similar reasons, Newman leaders across the country initially refused to affiliate with the Vatican-approved international student peace movement, *Pax Romana*. The national chaplain general claimed it was a "political" organization and that it might even be tinged with socialism, a sin nearly as noxious, and as fervently to be avoided, as being "tainted with communism."[10] Fortunately, after 1950 the National Newman Federation became more internationalized in its awareness and gradually began to break out of its isolationism, especially following Pius XII's 1951 call for a world order "in harmony with the principles of social and political justice so firmly funded and sustained by the Church."[11] The movement started to involve itself with legislative efforts being made on behalf of displaced persons and immigrants and showed renewed concern for foreign students. Yet the national federation as a whole remained reluctant to become directly involved in political action, and even when the civil rights movement began to make headway in the nation, most southern clubs, and the Federation's Executive Committee, still urged "caution."[12] With a determination characteristic of people imbued with a truly prophetic spirit, however, the Newman movement in St. Cloud did not often err on the side of caution and did not readily compromise its convictions.

Fortunately, the St. Cloud Newman community's embrace of the civil rights movement did not ruffle nearly as many feathers among the guardians of the center as other efforts would in ensuing years. In the fall of 1964, several Newman leaders on the banks of the Mississippi, including Wil Illies, Dan Taufen, and Alice Wick, were involved in the sending of a giant telegram to the White House that bore the names of 1,335 persons and contained 3,953 words in support of Lyndon Johnson's civil rights bill. Later that year, the campus religious organizations and the Student Headquarters for Action and Responsibility (SHARE) sponsored a campus address by Mrs. Spetima Clark on the political aspects of the civil rights movement and the non-violent approach to social change. On June 26, 1966, the Newman bulletin declared:

> Possibly more young people were impelled to imitate Christ by the actions of those persons who bore witness in the streets of Selma, Alabama, generously identified with the uncomfortable Body of Christ than one might have dreamed as even possible. . . . We must be relevant to the needs of Christ in this our time. Now. We must now "walk in a manner worthy of our calling," then others will imitate our lives. Then they will be inspired to love one another as Christ loved us.
>
> We might consider this admonition given by Dante and so admired by the late President Kennedy, "The hottest places in hell are reserved for those who in the time of great moral crisis, maintain their neutrality . . ."

The assassination of civil rights activist Dr. Martin Luther King, Jr., on April 4, 1968, stunned the St. Cloud community and, of course, the entire nation. On April 6, a special Mass was held at Christ Church Newman Center in memory of Dr. King; Wil Illies announced the service with the following words: "The death of Dr. Martin Luther King . . . is a time of reflection for the great needs in our country, the need for justice and charity, the need for respect and brotherhood, the need for honesty and peace. It is also

"A King Remembered"
1929 - 1968

A prayer service held at
Newman in honor of a wise
and courageous prophet.

a time for prayer. It is in this spirit that a special Mass will be celebrated at Christ Church at the St. Cloud Newman Center at 12:00 noon on Friday, for the cause of justice, charity, and peace, and in the name of Reverend Martin Luther King." A few days following that special Mass, the St. Cloud State academic community paid its respects to Dr. King at a special memorial service held in Stewart Hall on campus. Both students and faculty members participated in the program, which included poetry readings, eulogies, songs, and prayers. Wil Illies read an editorial from the *National Catholic Reporter* during the service entitled "Death of a Prophet."

Martin Luther King, Jr., opened himself to criticism from supporters and foes alike toward the end of his lifetime when he began to speak out against the escalation of the American war effort in Vietnam. Those in St. Cloud who entertained sentiments similar to King's also were subjected to mixed responses. As Ade Ledermann remembers, preaching about the war was always a vexing challenge, because whatever was said usually made somebody unhappy. On the one hand, there were those who believed that spiritual leaders never said enough and failed to issue condemnations sufficiently scathing of the sins of American involvement in Vietnam. On the other hand, there were those who thought the Church should keep its nose out of the affair all together and were made uncomfortable by even the most cautious call to moral critique that was proffered from the pulpit. Despite the challenges, however, Newman ministers and their ecumenical colleagues actively supported endeavors to raise moral questions about the conduct of the war. It wasn't long, in fact, before the "St. Cloud Citizens Concerned About the War in Vietnam" began to meet at the Newman Center. Chair Dr. John Phillips described the group as "an organ for those who want good discussion and who are interested in doing something about the war in Vietnam." In 1967, the group sponsored a full-page ad replete with signatures in support of the "Negotiate Now!" statement first endorsed by Bishop James Shannon of the Archdiocese of St. Paul. A number of local priests and nuns, including Newman chaplains Wil Illies and Nick Zimmer, as well as Newman librarian Sister Loyola and future Newman chaplain Adrian Ledermann, signed the statement. Among the names appearing in the long list of negotiation advocates were also several other present and future members of the Newman congregation, including Lyle VanPelt, Ed Pluth, Frank Roehl, Fred and Rosemary Petters, Art Grachek, Mary Humphrey, Jim Pehler, Gerald Mertens, and John and Marjorie Coyle. On August 13, 1967, the Newman bulletin reprinted a commentary offered by Bishop Sheen on the nationally advertised "Day of Prayer for Reconciliation":

> Is there not something amiss in our government when the President asks us to pray and the Supreme Court tells us where we may not pray—namely in our schools? Furthermore, is this reconciliation to be limited only to our citizens? Could we not also be reconciled with our brothers [sic] in Vietnam? May we plead only for a reconciliation between blacks and whites, and not between blacks and yellows?

The Newman community also advertised and participated in a city-wide candlelight march in support of a Vietnam moratorium. Indicative of the kind of health and balance the community always tried to maintain even in its most prophetic moments, it printed the following litany in a 1968 bulletin:

Killing seems to have become a way of life for many people . . .
Hatred is the mother of murder, and how many people in our
day are filled with hatred . . .
We can be dishonest and steal and destroy, yet self-righteous-
ly complain about the war in Vietnam . . .
We can get so taken up in our own small world that we ignore
the Vietnam situation . . .
Some of the worst evils in the world have been justified in the
name of God and country . . .
Some of the remarks of hatred by "good" Catholics and
"good" Christians are enough to make one weep . . .
Prophets are never welcome among their own people, and are
often burned by their own people . . .
Is war ever moral . . . ?
Strange, isn't it, that selfishness infects all of us to some
extent, and many to a large extent?
Strange, isn't it, that war smells of selfishness and selfishness
smells of war . . . ?

Interwoven with the Vietnam war issue, of course, was the
question of the draft and of how the Christian community at the
crossroads should guide young people who believed that their
Christian identities made it impossible for them to participate in
the killing of other human beings. The bulletin regularly supplied
thoughts from the United States bishops about the integrity of conscientious objection and advertised the availability of draft counseling in St. Cloud, even going so far as to hire, in conjunction with
the other members of Christians in Cooperation, a full-time draft
counselor for one year who worked out of the Newman building. A
"Draft Information Center" was set up for a while on the first floor
of the Newman Center, and in 1973, the Newman Pastoral Team
risked speaking out openly in favor of unconditional amnesty for all
those who had been placed in conscience conflicts as a result of the
Vietnam war and had chosen not to participate. They called
amnesty the Christian response to the gospel message and declared
that "through it we respect an individual's right to dissent, bring
healing to a nation and try to eliminate hatred and vindictiveness."

The Newman community's concern with the ways violence
desecrated of the spirit of the gospel did not end, of course, with
the coming of the cease fire in Southeast Asia. The community's
leadership continued to provide education and information on the
content of Church teaching with respect to the immorality of war,
of the creation of nuclear arsenals and stockpiles, and of the pro-
longation of the arms race. A 1973 bulletin, for example, quoted a
compelling 1968 document of the United States bishops entitled
"Human Life in Our Day":

We call upon American Catholics to evaluate war with that
"entirely new attitude" for which the II Vatican Council
appealed and which may rightly be expected of all who, calling

themselves Christians, proclaim their identity with the Prince of Peace. We share with all men [sic] of good will the conviction that a more humane society will not come "unless each person devotes himself [sic] with renewed determination to the cause of peace." We appeal to policy makers and statesmen to reflect soberly on the Council teaching concerning peace and war, and vigorously to pursue the search for means by which at all times to limit and eventually to outlaw the destructiveness of war.

North American military involvement and the clandestine support of civil factions and guerrilla groups in Central America became a controversial political issue in the 1980s, and many Church leaders insisted that it be brought to the forefront as a religious issue as well. The Newman community was generally open to explorations of the gospel implications of the issue, and sponsored several educational events designed to prompt reflection and broader understanding. In 1989, for example, Newman leaders welcomed a visit from a Peace Brigades International worker who enthralled and enlightened the listening crowd as she discussed her work as a volunteer providing international accompaniment for threatened human rights officers and nonviolent activists in El Salvador and Guatemala. Newman Pastoral Team member Bill Dorn and his campus ministry colleague Peg Chemberlin of UMHE were particularly impassioned about the immorality and illegality of

Campus minister Peg Chemberlin of UMHE addresses a group of protestors in St. Cloud opposed to United States aid to the Contras in Nicaragua.

Protesters let off due to lack of evidence

The Rev. Peg Cammack-Chemberlin led the singing Tuesday morning before a group of about 75. The gathering was a show of support for the four protesters who faced trial that day.

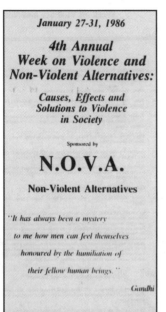

A NOVA flyer (top) and a student paper advertisement (above) encouraging CAASA involvement. Both NOVA and CAASA came to life in part because of the bellwether efforts of campus ministries at St. Cloud State.

United States government involvement in Central America. Together, they made very deliberate attempts to move conversation about the issue away from the periphery and into the center of concern for the Christian community of faith. When in the summer of 1986, Minnesota Representative Arlan Stangeland voted in the United States Congress to support a $100-million-aid bill for the Contras who were attempting to overthrow the government of Nicaragua, more than one hundred people, including Dorn and Chemberlin, gathered at Stangeland's office in protest. Dorn, Chemberlin, and three others refused to leave and staged a "sit in," an act which eventually led to their arrest. They were later tried, convicted of trespassing and sentenced to serve one day in jail. Said Dorn: "I did what I did because of the poor being oppressed and innocent people dying by terroristic attacks funded by our government." Chemberlin added: "Growing up I saw pictures and names of some of the people and have known of the (Moravian) church in Nicaragua since I was young. They are my brothers and sisters in Christ, and I feel a personal responsibility to be involved."

In 1979, the N.O.V.A. (Non-Violent Alternatives) group was founded on campus, a St. Cloud State student organization formed for the purpose of providing a forum to study and discuss violence and its alternatives. The Newman community was supportive of NOVA's efforts from the beginning, and on more than one occasion Newman staff people have been invited to speak at one of the many workshops provided as part of NOVA's annual "Week on Violence." In more recent years, UMHE campus ministers like Linda Geisling and Michael Sharp have served as the group's official advisors and have provided active campus ministry leadership around issues of violence on campus and elsewhere. Former pastoral team member Jacqui Landry played a very active role, furthermore, in bringing violence against women to the forefront of consciousness for the campus community. During her three years of commerce on the university highway she served, in fact, as the faculty advisor and "chaplain" for students involved in CAASA (Campus Advocates Against Sexual Assault). CAASA inaugurated the training of volunteers who then became part of a campus-wide advocacy system for victims of sexual assault. After completing forty hours of supervised preparation, student advocates received Department of Corrections certification and made themselves available to do public speaking, crisis intervention, and drop-in counseling. Newman, UMHE, Lutheran Campus Ministries, the Housing Office, and the Women's Studies Department worked very closely together on this venture, and it was in part through their bellwether efforts that an authentic commitment to the concerns of women was moved from the periphery and into the center of policy-making awareness at St. Cloud State University, where it eventually provoked the creation of an official "Women's Center" on campus.

"Prophets Are Never Welcomed . . ."

Francis Nosbisch, who served and traveled with the crossroads community on the banks of the Mississippi for eleven years, muses today that the greatest growth for those working, praying and learning on the campus highway has always come during the hardest times. We learned to ask ourselves in those times, says Nosbisch, "not just how we should react, but what we wanted to stand for. We learned to ask ourselves, 'Who do we want to be?' in this situation, and then to make decisions about how we wanted to act based upon the answer to that question, instead of just allowing ourselves to be acted upon." One of the hardest of those hard times, and one which also prompted great growth, came in the fall of 1986, when Newman minister Bill Dorn was dismissed by Bishop George Speltz from his position of leadership within the crossroads community after writing an opinion piece for the *St. Cloud Visitor* on the Church's ministry to homosexuals.

To this day, understanding more accurately and embracing more fully the experience, sexual and otherwise, of gay and lesbian Catholic Christians is a concern that many still refuse to acknowledge as worthy of being drawn into the center of institutional consideration and legitimation. It is also a concern which, to this day, stirs up a level of feeling and emotional divisiveness unparalleled by that generated in the consideration of most other issues. For more than two decades, many Christian leaders have borne the brunt of scathing attacks and cutting condemnations for attempting to do little more than promote dialogue and discussion about homosexuality. School Sister of Notre Dame Jeannine Gramick and Salvatorian priest Robert Nugent experienced the effects of that emotional divisiveness when they came to St. Cloud in 1985 to present an educational seminar entitled, "Tearing Down the Walls: Learning to Dialogue with Lesbian and Gay Christians." Only a week before their scheduled appearance at Christ Church Newman Center, Bishop George Speltz informed the organizers of the event that he could not permit the seminar to be held at a Catholic facility because, based on what he had heard and read about the speakers, he was uncertain that the Church's teaching on the moral wrongfulness of sexual union between homosexual persons would be upheld and that the "right kind of spiritual support would be offered to those who needed it." The Lutheran campus ministry center subsequently agreed to host the event and, since the hospitality of the Lutherans would allow the seminar to go on as planned, the Newman staff decided not to do battle with the bishop over the incident. The entire ecumenical campus ministry team at St. Cloud State, however, was baffled and profoundly concerned by the bishop's response to an educational, not a political, event designed not to advocate or advance any particular moral viewpoint, but simply to promote understanding and discussion. That baffled concern, as it turned out, was a telling portent of things to come.

Bill Dorn, a priest of the Diocese of Crookston, Minnesota, was interviewed by the Newman community and hired as a full-time member of the pastoral team in the fall of 1984. He quickly earned a reputation as an eloquent homilist, an effective teacher, an ardent advocate of the oppressed, a compassionate counselor, and a skilled administrator. During his two-year tenure with the community, in fact, he was instrumental in developing a steward-ship program that helped greatly in putting the parish on solid ground financially, and in establishing responsible procedures for budget processing and planning. He even managed, almost single-handedly, to arrange for a visit by the Reverend Jesse Jackson to the St. Cloud State campus. The flurry of controversy that came to sur-round Dorn in the fall of 1986 unduly and narrowly focused atten-tion on what was but one dimension of his ministry at Newman. The fact remains, however, that it was Dorn's work with lesbian and gay students on campus, as well as his concern for the well-being of all homosexual members of the Catholic Christian com-munity, that today stand out most clearly in the memory of those who dwelled with him on the banks of the Holy Spirit's river, and who traveled there with him through a troubling but transforming highway experience.

When gay and lesbian students at St. Cloud State, who had organized themselves into an unofficial support group, first request-ed official recognition, status, and sponsorship as a university or-ganization, Bill Dorn was asked if he would be willing to serve as the group's advisor. Dorn was pleased, as he had long desired to see such a group move from the periphery and become more integrat-ed into the structural center of the university system. He talked the matter over with his Catholic colleagues on the Newman staff and with his non-Catholic colleagues on the ecumenical campus min-istry team; both groups agreed that such an explicit commitment to the concerns of gay and lesbian students made by a representative of the Christian community was worthy of their unqualified sup-port. The Newman Pastoral Team then consulted with the parish council in order to solicit their approval. It was readily given, despite the fact that council and staff members alike were aware that Dorn's involvement with the group was bound to be contro-versial in some corners. It was at about this time, Dorn recalls, that Speltz began calling him over to the chancery about every six weeks in order to ask him about his activity with the support group and to remind him that he should be encouraging all gay and lesbian students to choose a lifetime commitment to celibacy. In this arena, as in several others, the Newman community differed with Speltz in outlook and approach and, while the conversations that took place between Newman parish leaders and their local ordinary were often tense, as a general rule they were also quite respectful, and an uneasy but genuine truce would settle in between them. Whatever truce existed with respect to the Newman community's concern for the gay and lesbian members of Christ's Body was broken, however, when Bill Dorn penned a brief article for the diocesan paper's September 18 opinion page in response to the question: "How should the Church minister to homosexuals?"

at issue

A weekly opinion page presenting viewpoints from around the diocese on current Church issues

September 18, 1986/ Saint Cloud Visitor/Page 7

How should Church minister to homosexuals?

"Accept them as equals in faith"

FATHER WILLIAM DORN

(Father William Dorn, a priest of the Crookston Diocese, is on the pastoral staff of Christ Church Newman Center at St. Cloud State University.)

Homosexuals, growing up in a religious atmosphere which says, "your experience of your nature is unnatural, distorted, evil," internalize that they are evil, learn to distrust their experience and become self-doubting and guilt-ridden individuals. Told by the Church that their sexual orientation is unnatural, they internalize that they are sick. Told they cannot love, they internalize that they are unloveable people because they know that people who do not or cannot love are not easy to love either.

The Church needs to begin by recognizing that it is not enough to minister to homosexuals. It must minister among them and with them.

We have a responsibility to develop a theology of sexuality that sees sexuality as blessing and understands homosexuality to be part of the gift. We need to develop a spirituality that trusts and embraces the embodied experience of homosexual people. And such a process leading

Concerning Sexual Ethics (1976) acknowledges the futility of such a division between sexuality and person. "According to contemporary scientific research the human person is so profoundly affected by sexuality that it must be considered as one of the factors which give to each individual's life the principal traits that distinguish it."

The Church needs to recognize that its condemnation of homosex-

"Combat stereotype through education"

EMMA ESKELSON OSB

(Sister Emma, a member of St. Benedict's Convent, St. Joseph, is a former elementary school teacher and currently a chemical dependency counselor.)

There is a stress today on the religious dimensions of ordinary, everyday experiences. This cultivates an awareness of the reality of God, that permeates all of our human events. We don't do away with human experience to touch the reality of God — but, it is in and through these experiences that God's unconditional love is present and active in our lives.

Personal sexuality orientation, whether that be heterosexual, bisexual or homosexual, is a gift from a loving Creator. It needs to be affirmed as such and integrated wholistically into one's faith life. Sexuality is our being, not merely the function of certain organs. It pervades every act of our body selves. Homosexuality, finding one's psychological, affectional, emotional and physical affinity with persons of the same sex is using one's sexuality not for procreation but for creative energy.

As Catholic Christians who believe in and live the Gospel of Jesus, we are challenged by that Gospel and the social justice teachings of our Church to reach out to alienated sexual minorities whose unique problems and needs make it difficult to participate in the life of the Church. Stereotypic thinking needs to be confronted by education.

Persons who struggle for personal integrity have unique gifts to bring to

The article, as Dorn himself and numerous others pointed out later, was written at the request of the *Visitor* and was clearly marked as one of two opinion pieces offering speculation about possible future directions. It was neither a false representation of Church teaching nor a direct attack on the teaching authority of the Church. The Benedictine sister, in fact, whose opinion piece was printed side-by-side with Dorn's, expressed concerns nearly identical to his own about the Catholic reluctance to understand homosexual orientation as a gift from God that needed to be integrated into the life of faith in precisely the same way as heterosexual orientation. It was against Dorn, however, that the wrath of the bishop would be most potently directed.

The opinion page that triggered the controversy in 1986.

Dorn's carefully written article suggested that the process of developing a Christian theology, spirituality, and ethic around issues of sexuality should be dialogical in nature and should involve lesbian and gay individuals as equal partners with other members of the Church in that dialogue. He went on to write:

> No Church ministry will succeed as long as it continues to insist that homosexual orientation unlike heterosexual orientation can be totally and universally separated from lifestyle. The Vatican's own *Declaration of Certain Questions Concerning Sexual Ethics* (1976) acknowledges the futility of such a division between sexuality and person. "According to contemporary scientific research the human person is so profoundly affected by sexuality that it must be considered as one of the factors which gives to each individual's life the principal traits that distinguish it."
>
> The Church needs to recognize that its condemnation of homosexuality is based on a questionable use of uncertain Scripture passages (a method it would not tolerate in any other circumstance) and on a slavish adherence to an overly biological understanding of natural law.

Dorn believes to this day that the opinions he expressed in that article were threatening precisely because they were well-reasoned and written with both knowledge and care. They did not go beyond the bounds of past statements he, or countless others in the Church, had made in the past. "If I had been less careful," Dorn asserts, "I don't think I would have been as threatening. I was trying to propose a new methodology for coming to conclusions about matters of sexuality in the Church—a responsible way of approaching scripture and tradition that would open up the possibility of different answers. That's what was so threatening."

On September 30, 1986, less than two weeks after the article appeared, George Speltz dismissed Dorn from his position at the Newman Center. Speltz adamantly avowed in several newspaper interviews that ensued that he had deep compassion for lesbian and gay individuals, but that the Church's sanctions against homosexual "misdeeds" were among a set of divinely sanctioned truths in which the Church could never waver and, as the bishop saw it, Christian compassion is not meant to come at the expense of those truths.[13] Dorn did not, in his *Visitor* article or anywhere else in the course of his time at the Newman Center, ever publicly sanction genital sex between gay men and lesbians. Rather, he called consistently for the Church to acknowledge sexuality as something much broader and richer than genital sex, to acknowledge the need for emotional and spiritual intimacy between same-sex partners, and to recognize that sexual orientation cannot be separated from lifestyle. But Speltz insisted that, as he and other people read it, Dorn had, in fact, condoned homosexual genital acts. "Gay people resent it very deeply," Speltz said in an interview for the *St. Paul Pioneer Press and Dispatch*, "when you say that genital sex between homosexuals is unnatural and cannot be condoned. But the Church does say it. And the Church says it because St. Paul says it. That's divine revelation . . . it's a question of whether we're helping them in a healthy way and in a Catholic way unless we take a stand about the wrongfulness of their acts." At another point in the interview, Speltz, referring to a scripture passage, said, "God says they will receive 'due penalty for their errors.'" The bishop then went on to speculate on a manner that shocked many that "it would not be stretching things to say that one of the ways nature reaches out here is through AIDS."[14]

Nick Coleman, a columnist for the *St. Paul Pioneer Press* noted wryly about a week after Dorn's dismissal that, "Bishop Speltz controls the *Visitor* and it was his editor who asked Dorn to express his views on homosexuals. In essence, the bishop's newspaper asked Dorn to express his opinion on a controversial issue. Then the bishop fired him because, well, because he expressed his opinion on a controversial issue."[15] Others, of course, knew that while the article was the public reason provided by Speltz for his action, firing Dorn was the culmination of a long period of uneasy tension between an outspoken priest and a cautious bishop made increasingly uncomfortable by the priest's provocative presence in the diocese, his boldness, and the stands he took that "pushed at the edges." Amazement and consternation followed in the wake of Speltz's abrupt decision to dismiss Dorn. The bishop, both Dorn and Nic Dressen affirm today, had hoped that Dorn would disappear quietly, but the Newman community was not about to allow the prelate to avoid accountability for his action. Dorn called a press conference, and the Newman lobby was filled with reporters. Dorn's dismissal made front-page headlines in the *St. Cloud Daily Times*, and the incident was also reported and debated in the *New York Times*, the *San Francisco Examiner*, a newspaper in Ireland, and countless national Catholic publications. About a hundred and fifty people from the St. Cloud community gathered on the steps of the diocesan cathedral following the press conference to sing, pray and protest the bishop's actions, and their experiences of "church oppression" in general. The Newman staff and most members of the Newman community were hurt and outraged, not only because they were being forcefully deprived of a respected leader, but also because the decision to dismiss him was made, as pastor Nic Dressen put it, in a "closed and authoritarian manner." Speltz insisted on making the dramatic move instantly, and refused even to consider the far less disruptive option of allowing Dorn to finish out his contract and leave at the end of the academic year. More important, his decision to dismiss Dorn was made without ever asking Dorn to clarify what he wrote, without any discussion with the

A priest at the center of controversy

One of the many headlines that appeared in both local and national newspapers at the time of Dorn's dismissal.

Newman parish community, and without any consultation with any group of people representing the laity or clergy in the diocese of St. Cloud. In a formal statement, Mary Jo Bot, president of the Newman Pastoral Council at the time, declared that council members found the bishop's action "frustrating, saddening and stifling."

In the week immediately following the publication of Dorn's brief opinion article, he received much supportive mail, but also a series of nasty letters in which he was accused of leading people astray and was called a "faggot," a "queer lover," a "bastard," and a "communist." As Dorn himself describes it, "several times I was assured that I would go to hell . . . all by people espousing their faithfulness to the gospel." It was the "leading people astray" accusation, at least overtly, that carried the greatest weight with Bishop Speltz. In a letter to Nic Dressen informing him of Dorn's dismissal, Speltz wrote: "Over the past year Father Dorn has made it clear in a number of public statements . . . that he is in strong disagreement with the Church's teaching on homosexuality to the extent of questioning the Church's use of scriptural passages. . . . From many letters, telephone calls, and conversations over the past year a wide sector of the Catholic community in this area has made it clear to me that they understood Father Dorn's statements on homosexu-

256

ality as clearly in disagreement with the Church; and they are deeply disturbed by this." It mattered less to Speltz, apparently, that another wide sector of the Catholic community in the area was not at all disturbed by Dorn's statements and saw in them a well-reasoned, prophetic and compassionate call to see members of the gay and lesbian community as equals in faith and partners in discipleship. Even some who disagreed with Dorn's opinions resented the bishop's patronizing presumption that their faith and understanding needed to be protected by action from above, and that they were completely without the ability to form discerning and responsible moral decisions on their own once exposed to varying or contradictory viewpoints. As Newman member Greg Johnson told the *St. Cloud Times* after the incident, "the frustrating part is the bishop is presuming to know what's good for me and my ability to sort out the good from the bad." Dorn, the Newman Parish Council, and many others expressed apprehension in the event's tumultuous aftermath that Catholic Christians were losing their right to respectful and mature dialogue within the Church. Dialogue, they affirmed, should be a valid function in the Church, and adult Christians should be able to carry on public conversations about particular concerns, even complex concerns, without having the boundaries of that conversation defined for them by others, and without fear of reprisal or reprimand. The Newman Parish Council provided several opportunities for student and permanent members of their faith community to discuss their feelings and concerns in both small and larger group settings, and also invited Speltz to come and meet with the people of Newman in order to dialogue with them about the issues that had surfaced as a result of Dorn's dismissal. As Mary Jo Bot put it in her letter of invitation to the bishop, "our community is struggling to turn this 'dying' experience into one of 'resurrection.' We are asking for your assistance in this process." Speltz at first agreed to a November 4 meeting, then later canceled out because he lent credence to secretive, malicious whisperings and unfounded rumors and thus believed, erroneously, that Dorn was still staying at the Newman rectory. Dorn had, in fact, moved out shortly after his dismissal and was staying with a friend in the Twin Cities.

An article which appeared in the December issue of the nationally respected Catholic periodical *Commonweal*, summed up well all that was most disheartening about the affair to both student and permanent members of the Christ Church Newman Center community. A faculty member at St. John's University in Collegeville, Robert Spaeth, authored the article that lamented the fact that before the public reaction to Dorn's article and subsequent dismissal had a chance to get rolling, the *Visitor*'s editor called a halt to the debate and decided to print none of the "largest stack of letters, newspaper clippings, and statements" that he had ever gathered. Spaeth averred that such an early, unilateral closing down of a growing dialogue on authority, the treatment of homosexuals, and the Catholic press seriously damaged the credibility of the *St. Cloud Visitor* and also had destructive ramifications that spread much farther. Two primary causes can be discerned, declared Spaeth, for the whole sorry train of events which followed the publication of Dorn's article—imprudence and a lack of courage:

> The charge of imprudence must be laid at the door of Bishop Speltz, who saw a problem and tried to solve it with power. Prudence would have suggested that Father Dorn's sympathy with the homosexual people in his care be understood as natural and inevitable; that the replacement of Dorn, if necessary, be achieved through negotiations, not discipline; that even if Dorn had to be removed, the act not be done in response to a public statement solicited by the bishop's own newspaper . . .
>
> The *Visitor*'s decision abruptly to turn off the spigot of public opinion must, in my view, be judged as a departure from courage —the courage to print opinions opposed to the bishop's decision and the courage to trust the Catholic community.
>
> The case of the bishop versus the priest in St. Cloud can be summarized as a massive failure of public dialogue in the local church—failure of dialogue in the Catholic press, with homosexuals, and between bishop and priest. The failure in all three of its manifestations was preventable, if only prudence and courage had been ranked higher.[16]

In a letter to the editor of the *St. Cloud Daily Times* penned in a similar spirit, Merle Nolde, OSB, reminded the St. Cloud community of the story in the fifth chapter of the Acts of the Apostles about the Pharisee who prevented the first community of disciples from being silenced forever by his fellow keepers of the Law. Nolde mused that perhaps it would be well if there were a Gamaliel alive today to say to present Church authority: "Be patient, do not interfere. If the dissent is inauthentic, not grounded on truth, it will vanish of itself. If it is of God—if there is a grain of truth in it which we have lacked in the past—it will ultimately prevail and you will not want to have opposed God's prophets."

For the most part, the Newman community was extremely supportive of their beleaguered spiritual leader throughout the ordeal. There were a few dissenting voices, of course, who believed that Dorn had gotten what he deserved and were glad to be free of what one St. Cloud woman called his "inappropriately political" use of the pulpit, and of what one parishioner described as his exclusive interest in "the divorced, the homosexuals, and the downtrodden" to the detriment of his ability to be concerned about anyone else.

The Newman Parish Council, however, issued a strong statement to the press in support of Dorn and his ministry and, during the weekend liturgies at which Dorn announced his dismissal to the student and permanent community members gathered before him, the congregation reacted with shock, anger, sadness, and deep hurt. Frances Nosbisch remembers that at one liturgy someone yelled out, "We love you, Father Bill!" and the whole congregation stood up and began to applaud. Women, and, in particular, women religious, Dorn recalls, were especially supportive, perhaps because their own experiences of oppression and diminishment at the hands of "clear and definite" Church teachings allowed them to empathize in poignant and personal ways. The St. Cloud State University community also rallied to Dorn's support, and the staff at the university counseling center sent him a letter affirming his compassionate service, and attesting that his "willingness to support the human needs of gay men and lesbian women in our community has made our service more responsive to this population." On the weekend of October 4 and 5, during the time that the Church celebrates the feast of that saintly peacemaker and friend of the outcast, Francis of Assisi, Bill Dorn celebrated Eucharistic liturgy for the last time with the Newman community. At those liturgies, Dorn issued a final summons to the congregation seated before him, a community that had endeavored once again to face the challenges of the crossroads squarely, and allow itself to be touched by the transforming power of the Spirit:

> Last week I bowed before this altar at the end of the 9:00 Mass knowing that I would not ever do that again. As I did so we were singing, "We are justice for the poor, we are rage against the night, we are hope for peaceful people, we are light." I plead with you to continue to be justice for those who are poor economically or by reason of their membership in outcast groups. Rage against the night of hatred and oppression. Be hope in a world too full of fear to be embracing of gay and lesbian people, to full of despair to be open to the future. Be light in a world full of the darkness of ignorance and prejudice. Bring the knowledge of the human person you gain from your academic disciplines and the hopefulness you gain from your study of the Gospel together in a common search for the truth that makes us more human, more whole, more like the God in whose image all of us have been created.

On November 6, Dorn returned for a farewell party in the Newman Terrace given in his honor, a bittersweet occasion that nonetheless unified the community and brought laughter and healing to a time of great pain. On December 9, members of the parish council finally met with Speltz and two other chancery officials; a meeting between the full parish community and the bishop never happened. Speltz indicated in a follow-up letter that he felt the

A much-needed moment of laughter shared by Newman leaders at Bill Dorn's farewell party.

meeting "went off in a Christian spirit of reconciliation, although your delegation and those of us at the Chancery recognize that significant differences will make reconciliation impossible. I regret the hurts this whole matter caused the Newman community."

The hurts the whole matter caused the Newman community were far-reaching, and not easily shaken. Nic Dressen affirms to this day that never in his life, either before or after the incident, does he remember being so very angry for such a very long time. "It was the first time," Dressen attests, "that I ever felt victimized, the first real experience I ever had of being oppressed, of having something unjust 'done to me' that I couldn't control." The former Newman pastor also acknowledges that he was confronted in the fall of 1986 with the dysfunctional side of the Church system in a way he never had been before, and realized that there really were times when bishops "do what they want to do and then find reasons to justify it." He goes on to muse sadly: "There was nothing compassionate, and nothing pastoral in what Bishop Speltz did to Bill Dorn and to the Newman community. He acted as an autocrat and as a dictator. It was a power play far more than it was anything else and it really made me wonder for a long while whether or not I could continue to be a part of a system that allowed for that." For Jacqui Landry, too, the experience was eye-opening and illusion-shattering, and made her question her desire to remain in ministry. She received hate mail and even death threats, and for her, "it was my first shake-up, the first time I saw the dark and sinful side of the Church face-face." As a result of a chain of events which were set in motion by the St. Cloud experience, Bill Dorn later left the Church and was suspended permanently from the priesthood. He suffered much pain and personal consequences which were far-reaching and hurtful. Today, some peace and perspective have come, but he has reflected deeply on the whole affair over the course of the last twelve years. He now observes astutely, and not without sadness: "For a long time I thought we were talking about sexuality. Then I realized that we weren't. We were talking about power . . . I realized, later, that as long as I remained guilty, ashamed and vulnerable, I was acceptable. Once I had integrated all aspects of my life fully and acquired real internal authority, things were different. The reason I was no longer fit to be a priest was that I was no longer guilty and ashamed—and that made me a threat."

To its eternal credit, and in spite of all the anguish, the crossroads community clinging doggedly to the banks of the Holy Spirit's river moved through that 1986 crisis with care and grace, not just reacting but making thoughtful decisions along the way about how it wanted to speak and what it wanted to stand for. Community members worried, first and foremost, that lesbian and gay members of Christ's Body who had become more hopeful as a result of their contact with Dorn and with other open and accepting members of the Catholic Christian community would become disheartened and disillusioned once again and feel themselves to be the victims of yet one more rejection. The Newman parish thus worked hard to persist in communicating welcome, and, about six weeks following Dorn's dismissal, the staff received a letter from the St. Cloud State Gay and Lesbian Support Group thanking them for the hospitality they had been shown, and expressing appreciation for the support they had received in the wake of Dorn's removal. "You have truly gone the extra mile for us in these difficult times," the letter acknowledged gratefully. Jacqui Landry reflects today that it seemed the community became even more tenacious about social justice issues afterwards, and more determined than ever in its outreach to all who felt marginalized. Newman members also became resolute in their fidelity to open and healthy ways of communicating about matters of importance, and in their dedication to establishing procedures that would insure that kind of openness in all arenas of parish life. The Dorn tragedy, Landry affirms today, really galvanized the community, and even those who vehemently disagreed with Dorn's stands and his style were angry and unsettled because of the closed, patronizing and dysfunctional manner in which the situation had been handled at the top. They were determined to model something different at the local level. As Frances Nosbisch marvels today, even in the toughest of times at Newman, student and permanent members of the community alike have managed to discern the difference between health and unhealth; the best in them has always emerged and stood fast in the face of adversity. "Time and time again," she professes with real pride, "the community has risen to the occasion, and newness and hope have come."

In an October 12, 1986, interview with Jacqui Banaszynski of the *St. Paul Pioneer Press Dispatch*, Bill Dorn reflected: "Jesus said the greatest commandment was to love your neighbor as yourself. He was quoting Deuteronomy. He was reminding a real entrenched, institutionalized religion what its roots were. The heart and core of Judaism was love, and they developed all these laws to ensure that people were loving. But the law began to take on a life of its own. And I think that's what's happening again." Part of the prophetic task, as we have seen, has long been to highlight the presence and concern of God in places where people do not always imagine it to be present, and to draw important sensitivities that are only peripheral into the center of a community's life. Another piece of the prophetic task has also long been to denounce institutional policies and practices that begin to function for their own sake, losing sight of their original purpose, and of the wise and loving values they were designed to express.[17] Living and learning at the crossroads over the past seventy-five years has often propelled the Newman community into the assumption of both of these prophetic tasks—in the areas of liturgy, theological education, justice, charity, leadership, social responsibility, and attentiveness to the voices of those who are without voice. To do so, to be "spice for the food" in this way, has sometimes been painful, and has sometimes meant suffering misunderstanding and rejection at the hands of others. As Jesus knew all too well, prophets are not always welcomed in their own countries. But transformation, and an enlarged capacity to love, have often been the results, for Newman community members, for campus community members, and for the broader Church as well. Perhaps Bill Vos said it best of all when he looked back, twenty years later, on the powerful, personal legacy left to him as a result of the years he spent facing the crossroads challenges of life at Newman:

> The whole experience stretched me a lot. I could see issues more openly and more deeply than I could before. Even rubbing elbows with the faculty in a bowling league was a broadening experience, because we'd get into discussion on all kinds of issues. Those years made me much more understanding of things like sexual orientation, feminism, and the nuances of serious moral questions; it was a terrific preparation for church work in other places, for church work in general. That's the greatest contribution that Newman ministry makes to whole Church, I think. The university campus and what happens to the Church there can be a stretching experience for the whole church, a challenge to move beyond the homogeneity of mind set and experience, and get out of narrow parameters and thinking.

Notes

1 Haughton, pp. 134-135.

2 Class notes of Linda Wall from 1 October 1985, taken in *Early Prophecy*, a graduate course taught by Carroll Stuhlmueller at the Catholic Theological Union in Chicago, Illinois.

3 Stuhlmueller, from class notes 1 October 1985, and Joseph Blinkinsopp, *A History of Prophecy in Israel* (Philadelphia: Westminster Press, 1983), pp. 15, 17, 74.

4 Evans, pp. 169-170.

5 Monika Hellwig, "Charity," *The Modern Encyclopedia of Catholicism*, ed. Monika Hellwig, p. 161.

6 "Praxis," *Encyclopedia of Catholicism*, ed. Richard McBrien, p. 1036.

7 Bette Daniels, "The Apostolate Can Open Eyes," *ERA*, Spring 1962, p. 3.

8 Stacia Fink, "The homeless: dealing with mixed feelings," *SCSU Outlook*, Spring, 1989, p.11.

9 Evans, p. 88.

10 Evans, pp. 88, 105-106.

11 Evans, p. 105.

12 Evans, p. 107.

13 Jacqui Banaszynski, "Harsh criticism hurts, bishop says," *St. Paul Pioneer Press and Dispatch*, 12 October 1986, p. 10A.

14 Banaszynski, p. 10A.

15 Nick Coleman, "Some sins can't win at church," *St. Paul Pioneer Press and Dispatch*, 9 October 1986, p. 8B.

16 Robert L. Spaeth, "Cloud over St. Cloud," *Commonweal.* 5 December 1986, p. 648.

17 Stuhlmueller, from class notes, 1 October 1985, and Blinkinsopp, p. 74.

Chapter 8

No Place to Park

"Out of shadows and images and into the truth."
—Inscription on John Henry Newman's tombstone

Because Christ Church Newman Center was built to serve St. Cloud State students, and because most St. Cloud State students in the early 1960s lived on campus, the complete absence of anything even remotely resembling a parking lot adjacent to the facility was not considered a serious drawback. In time, however, the student population grew, changed and became less exclusively residential, and more and more people who were not connected to the campus began to arrive at the Newman Center each Sunday for liturgies, and at other times during the week as well. The lack of convenient parking began to cause consternation and grumbling. Street parking was available, and several lots on campus were open for public use over the weekends, but there were many who did not enjoy the lengthy, Sunday morning jaunts from locked car to church doors that were necessary, especially in the dead of a Minnesota winter. In 1977, Adrian Ledermann composed a tongue-in-cheek bulletin message, complete with a clearly marked diagram of all parking area possibilities, in order to offer a little perspective and encouragement:

A familiar sight at Newman.

I'm sure glad I live next door to the Newman Center, because if I had to park way out there and walk. . . . Then I recalled the time I was upset because I could not find a parking spot near the hospital, and not because of an emergency. I only wanted to meet Fr. Stangl so we could run five miles. Maybe you are not as inconsistent as I. . . . The following parking areas are available within a four to five block area (five-minute walk). Taking the extra time can help to make the whole Sunday experience more of an event: walk off the long sermon, meet others in the same fix, avoid hassle with parking tickets—Newman needs the money more than the City.

One of the three lots situated directly across from the Newman Center that were purchased in order to make the construction of a parking lot possible. This particular house was preserved and converted into the new Newman Rectory.

Twenty years later, Newman's long-lived parking problem was finally solved. Kevin Anderson, priest of the Diocese of St. Cloud and native of Elk River, Minnesota, barely had had time to get his feet wet as the newest member of the Newman Pastoral Team when, in the fall of 1995, Ardis and Armand Falk, owners of the three houses situated directly across from Newman on First Avenue South, approached the Newman community with an offer to sell. The community immediately began a discernment process involving the pastoral team, several parish council committees, the Newman Pastoral Council itself, the city of St. Cloud, and the diocese. An all-parish meeting was held to enable members to voice their opinions regarding the $275,000 expenditure that would be necessary to acquire the property. The community finally decided to take advantage of the unexpected opportunity, which would not likely repeat itself, and at the same time to launch into new and unchartered territory in another way. The women and men who were part of the community implanted at the intersection of the Church and the university had never before needed to raise a large sum of money for a building project, and the thought made many uneasy. A professional consulting firm was hired to guide the parish through a capital campaign, the goal of which was to raise $500,000

WALKING NEW GROUND

Christ Church Newman Center
396 First Avenue South
St. Cloud, MN 56301

~ Our Goal ~

Almost seventy-five years ago, a Newman Club was established on the campus of St. Cloud State. The Newman Club was committed to walking new ground as it sought to meet the spiritual, intellectual and social needs of students.

in order to fund the purchase of the Falk properties, the subsequent construction of a parking lot, and other major repair and renovation projects the Building Committee had long been itching to address in order to improve the condition and accessibility of the thirty-five-year-old Newman facility. Long-time Newman members Art and Barb Grachek graciously agreed to chair the effort, dubbed the "Walking New Ground" campaign, and volunteers were solicited to visit and/or talk with every individual and family in the community in order to solicit financial commitments to the $500,000 goal that could be paid off over a five-year period. The campaign, in short, was a success; pledges well in excess of the goal were acquired, a spacious parking lot materialized on the west side of the Newman Center building, and, today, the frustrated refrain, "There's no place to park!" echoes far less frequently down the sidewalks and through the hallways. The Holy Spirit, however, does not encourage any community of disciples to stay parked for

Newman's first capital campaign, aptly christened the "Walking New Ground" effort.

Ads appearing in the St. Cloud State *Chronicle* featuring the infamous tennis shoe logos.

too long in any one spot. Complacency, after all, has long been the greatest obstacle to transformation in the Christian life. Perhaps the community would do well, then, not to savor the pleasures of its new parking area with too much relish and to keep remembering anew with each passing day how to lace up its sneakers, and keep on moving.

In the early 1990s, Nic Dressen, with the support of his colleagues on the pastoral team and on the Public Relations Committee, devised a new symbol for Newman ministry at the crossroads. It was the classic, "Chuck Taylor" canvas high-top tennis shoe made by Converse that was popular with basketball players in the 1950s and 1960s. An artist on campus was hired to work up several usable sketches of the shoes, and to this day those sketches serve as a recognizable logo, and an enduring symbol, of Newman ministry at its best in the crossroads environment which is St. Cloud State University. When the shoes sketches were first introduced, Dressen's explanatory article affirmed that they were meant to suggest a Christian endeavor that "is friendly, comfortable, relaxed, contemporary, simple traditional, inclusive, practical and enjoyable—just like Chuck Taylor high-tops." He went on to point out that not just the visual image, but also the words "canvas Converse," say much about what goes on at Newman. The word "canvas," for example, usually refers to the course cloth made of hemp or flax that is used for tents and sails of ships. The word, "canvass," furthermore, means to sift or examine by way of discussion. The word "converse" is generally used to describe the act of talking and exchanging thoughts and opinions in a mutual manner,

Newman community members of all ages (top and at left) practice the art of conversation—and face the challenge of conversion—together.

A picture of Nic Dressen (below) that appeared in the campus newspaper one month after his arrival at Newman in 1983.

and the word "conversion," of course, refers to the goal of all Christian discipleship—a transformation or change of heart succeeded by a reformation of life. Like our ancestors in faith, Dressen concluded, we are pilgrim people of God. "We are wondering and wandering, discussing and discerning, challenging and changing. As each new year begins, we are joined once again by members of the St. Cloud State student community who keep us alive and growing, learning and changing, conversing and laughing. We lace up our sneakers together and set out on our Christian pilgrimage of faith. If the shoe fits, keep on wearing it."

A Final Homily That Says It All

In the fall of 1983, Nic Dressen arrived to begin his pilgrimage as "pastor," or ordained member of the pastoral team at Christ Church Newman Center. Twelve years later, on June 18, 1995, he laced up his Chuck Taylor's for the last time and deliv-

Scenes from Nic Dressen's farewell dinner in June 1995. Lyle and Elizabeth Van Pelt and Mil and Fran Voelker (bottom right) chat with Dressen; Wil Illies (middle right) commends Dressen and the Newman community for carrying on the tradition so well, and Dressen (above) and Bob Wick (top right) take a turn at sharing their thoughts while holding the community's "talking stick."

ered a final homily before the Newman community he had come to love. His moving words sum up well the spirit which came to rest, and settle, over the community during those twelve years, a spirit which continues to define and shape it to this day. The late 1980s and the decade of the 1990s emerged as a real period of maturation and anchoring for the crossroads community on the banks of the Holy Spirit's river, a time when leaders and congregation members

270

alike came to a united sense of who they were and of how they wanted to travel together into the future as a family of disciples choosing to do loving commerce on the bustling university highway. The seven objects which Dressen chose to place in his shoebox time capsule during that concluding homily are fitting representations of the major encounters and intersections that have been a part of the community's life during the past three-quarters of a century; they are, in other words, sacramental signs and symbols of the breakthroughs in insight and understanding that have happened, and which invariably happen, whenever and wherever women and men of faith make themselves open both to transforming others, and being transformed by others. Dressen's crowning summation of that faith-filled adventure as it has taken on life at at Newman is reprinted in full below:

> Last week I revealed to you my fifty favorite movies. Well, today I'll reveal my favorite TV program of all time. It was M*A*S*H. Even the reruns are good. The original episodes of M*A*S*H ended in May of 1983, just before I arrived at the Newman Center. So I thought it might be good to take a clue from M*A*S*H as I, twelve years later, come to the end of my stay in this community.
>
> In the final episode of M*A*S*H, as you recall, Margaret Houlihan got her footlocker. And she turned that into a time capsule. She asked all of the people of the M*A*S*H unit to come forward and place something in that time capsule, a memory of their stay in Korea.
>
> Well, I don't have a footlocker, but I thought a large shoe box would do.
>
> When I was a child, shoe boxes were wonderful things. Shoe boxes were the places I kept all of my treasures—a few coins from lawn mowing, maybe a pretty rock I found at the beach and, of course, my baseball cards. So I found this large shoe box and decided to make this my, and our, time capsule of the last twelve years.
>
> I decided to put into the time capsule seven things. Not because I could only think of seven things, but because seven is a holy number. I thought about choosing seventy things, but I knew that would be too many and would keep us here way too long.
>
> So here come the seven things for the time capsule:
>
> The top of a bishop's staff. Bishops are leaders, and pastors are supposed to be leaders as well. I learned long ago, though, that this is not really a bishop's staff. It is a large question mark that bishops always carry around. Ed Hays said that question marks are really exclamation points who bow their heads in humility. So I offer this as a symbol and sign of our students over the years who always ask questions—who raise good questions about God, about the Catholic Church, about life and relationships and families. Those students who come

COME EXPERIENCE
G.L.A.D.
(GAY/LESBIAN AWARENESS DAY)

FEBRUARY 18, 1987

G.L.A.D.

ST. CLOUD, MN

ATWOOD MEMORIAL CENTER,
SCSU, ST. CLOUD, MN
10:00 AM-10:00 PM

A flyer from a 1987 G.L.A.D. celebration on campus.

Newman member Dave Huberty and his three children, Kelly, Chris, and Michael, at the World Healing Day at St. Scholastica Convent in 1987.

here year after year with their questions have kept us alive, have kept us on our quest. As part of this community I have come to believe, too, that questioning—that virtue or that gift—is a sign of faith. When people stop asking questions, they ought to be getting worried about their faith being alive. I trust that you will keep your quest alive, and that students will keep coming year after year with their questions.

The next thing I offer is a button with a purple triangle. It was from a 1991 GLAD celebration, Gay-Lesbian Awareness Day. Going back to the beginning of the Newman Center, this community has had a reputation for being prophetic, for speaking out against oppression, for celebrating, in one way or another, peace and social justice issues of all kinds. Well, that tradition has continued during the 12 years I've been here. And there have been different issues in the social justice area that we have talked about and dialogued about and struggled with—nuclear arms, women's equality, racism, violence, war and homosexuality. This button from 1991 says this was the five-year anniversary of GLAD Day.

Well, what pleases me very much is that Bill Dorn and this community had much to do with the beginning of GLAD Day and with raising the consciousness of the campus, the St. Cloud community, and, I think, the whole Church about the importance of gay and lesbian people. We all came to realize that we really are sisters and brothers in Christ, that they are us and we are them. In a bulletin article some years ago, I wrote these words. Let me read them to you as I place this button in our time capsule:

> There is a simple and profound truth. We are the Body of Christ. Part of that body is gay and lesbian. The homosexual members of the Body of Christ are not them. They are us. They are our siblings, and our children, our friends, and our fellow parishioners. They are persons like us striving to live generous lives of maturing faith. When they suffer, the whole body suffers.

The third thing in my shoe box is a little counter that I found in my desk when I arrived here. It goes back to the days of Father Wil Illies. It goes back to the days before there was this Newman Center and this large chapel. There was simply a large frame house on this site that contained offices and a small chapel where students could celebrate Eucharist. And where they could go to confession.

In those days, students were either more pious or they had more sins. People went to confession with some frequency, and the priest had to keep this in the confessional and count each confession. (Click, click, click). Remember that sound when you were a kid? I always wondered what it was. . . . This little counting device was what it was.

Well, I've been told by a reliable source that when a certain group of students would be cleaning the house and cleaning the chapel, they would put a couple of extra clicks on the clicker when they would go into the confessional to dust. They knew that if they could prove to the bishop that there were lots of students coming to the Newman House—lots of students who were thinking great things—then he would build a great big center with a great big chapel that would grow into a great big parish some day. So they wanted to get a high count. And they got it, and we have this wonderful facility. We know better now. We know that numbers don't mean all that much. Who is counting anyway?

Well, I decided to go back to count anyway. . . .

In the last twelve years, we've had 369 weddings here at the Newman Center chapel. We now have 550 households. Our budget has doubled in twelve years, to about $320,000. And as you are probably well aware from the noise, coming and going week after week, we've had 564 baptisms in those twelve years. Somehow we'll keep growing—and we're not counting—but we do appreciate the growth physically and spiritually that happens here.

When I was ordained a priest in 1979, I decided that I wanted a glass chalice. The fourth thing in this time capsule is the remains of my glass chalice. I wanted a glass chalice because once upon a time some kid said to me, "Is there anything in that gold cup? I can't see." Somehow, I think glass makes Christ more visible when you can see in. But I should have realized too—when I started using a glass chalice—that glass is quite fragile, and that glass at some point is bound to break. Well, I think that it was after about thirteen years of using this chalice that one day I heard this crash in the sacristy. And I just smiled. I did not cry.

As I looked at this glass fragment on my desk not long ago, I stumbled across an article written by Henri Nouwen, and he quoted Leonard Bernstein in his famous musical drama, *The Mass*. Near the end of the drama, Bernstein has the priest lifted up by the people holding a glass chalice. He is wearing beautiful, ornate vestments. And all of a sudden the people come crashing down. So does the priest. You hear this loud crash from the glass chalice. Then suddenly the priest comes up again wearing only a T-shirt and blue jeans and bare feet. He reaches out and picks up the glass chalice. Stares at it. Pauses, and finally says, "I never realized that broken glass could shine so brightly."

Well, I offer this for our time capsule because of the brokenness that we've all experienced in one way or another over the past twelve years. All of us, I trust—I know including myself—have made mistakes and caused some pain. In lots of ways we have experienced brokenness. But somehow this community has made me realize what that priest realized in *The Mass*—that broken glass shines brightly.

I thank you very much for bearing with me—but more than that—I thank you for forgiving the mistakes that I made and the pain that I have caused during twelve years. And I am quite excited to be able to leave here with no bitterness, no

273

regrets, not just because of your gift of forgiveness, but also because of our community's gift of forgiveness.

The next thing in the box is this tie. This is my favorite tie, in many ways. Actually, when I first came to Newman I did wear a Roman collar on weekends. But then, the first Easter of my first year here I said, "That's enough." And since then the Roman collar has disappeared in the back of the closet somewhere.

This tie was purchased just before Bishop Jerome Hanus was ordained and installed as our bishop in St. Cloud eight years ago. I wore it to his ordination. It became for me a symbol of reconciliation with Bishop Speltz and a sign of the welcome and renewed hope that Jerome Hanus brought to me and to St. Cloud. I believe that Jerome became a great leader, a wonderful bishop, a great model of church leadership.

I put this tie on and wore it to his ordination at the Abbey Church (at St. John's University). During the vesting of the priests, I got a couple of unusual and troublesome looks from some bishops and one particular cardinal. This led me to conclude that they were envious and they liked the tie. But I also think I learned over the years from and with this community that uniforms can be divisive, and that uniforms can exclude, and that uniforms can be oppressive. In many ways, that's the nature of uniforms, and that's their purpose. I'm quite convinced, too, that the Roman collar has become a uniform that is divisive, that is exclusive, and that sometimes is oppressive.

We've had enough clericalism in our church over the centuries, and we need to do all that we can do to get rid of the sin of clericalism. I'm not sure that the tie does it, but at least it says something about wanting to do that. Last week I went out and bought a new tie for John Kinney's installation, too. So I hope he and the bishops and the cardinal will look with envy on my new tie as well.

The Bartos family and the Newman Easter candle—their labor of love becomes each year the community's symbol of faith and hope.

274

Next, I present a stub of our Easter candle from a few years ago. As some of you know, Vern and Bette Bartos, parishioners of ours, have been making our Easter candle every year for almost thirty years now. And they take the old candle, the candle stubs from our worship, melt them down, buy some new beeswax and make a new candle for us every year.

The beautiful texture that is put into this candle is put in by the blunt end of a pliers, lots of denting and poking makes a beautiful texture—a reminder to us all, I think, that it's through some struggle and through some pain and through much effort that we really are reborn. That way of creating an Easter candle says much about what Easter candles stand for and symbolize in our Christian community.

The Easter candle also serves as a reminder of life overcoming death. It reminds us that in death life is changed, but not ended. Well, here in this community I looked back in the books to see that we have had over twenty funerals in the past twelve years. Some of them had been for people who came here because they had no other place to go for a funeral. But thirteen of the funerals have been for parish members. Those of you who experienced one of those will never forget them. Many of us don't know who these people were or haven't been here long enough to be aware of all the funerals we've had. Well, these names can't be forgotten because we believe as Christian people that the living and the dead celebrate together every time we celebrate Eucharist. Every time we gather, we gather with those who are present here on the earth, and those who have gone before us in faith.

Here are the names of those who died in these twelve years: Mark Blanch, Judy Garrity, Donald Faith, John Dwyer, Sr., Jeannine Sjogren, Sandra Polesak, Agnes Justin, Daniel Kelash, Luke Lenzmeier, Mary Humphrey, John Dwyer, Jr., Michael Hlebain, and Mikey Schroeder.

And then one last thing. The Easter shoes. The story behind them is that seven or eight years ago—I forget how long—I purchased these to wear one Easter. I wanted to celebrate rejoicing and leaping and jumping and coming alive in spring. I wanted to get some kind of visual image of what it means to be an Easter person. I wanted us to be able to jump out of our ruts and start to do something new and exciting about the life of God within us. Somehow these seemed to say something about that.

These were meant to be a one-time experience, but as the next Easter approached, a number of people said, "Are you going to wear those shoes again?" And I thought I'd better wear them again, and again, and again each Easter for those seven or eight years.

Over time they became not my shoes, but our community's shoes. They've come to symbolize something that is precious, something that is practical and simple. They've come to symbolize something that is contemporary but traditional. Some-

The pink Easter shoes.

275

thing that is fun-loving and doesn't take itself too seriously. Because they're Converse shoes they speak of our conversation. They speak of our conversions.

Well, I'm not taking these with me. These belong here. They've come to be a sign and symbolize our spirit, this community's spirit, that was here before I came and that will be here after I go. So I'll take the spirit with me to keep in my heart and soul because I don't ever want to forget the spirit of the Newman Center. It is very, very important. So I take it with me. Forever.

We have a History/Archives Committee now. So I'm leaving with them this time capsule.

Someone once gave me this wonderful book, knowing that I was a M*A*S*H fan, *The Last Days of M*A*S*H*. I picked it up a week or two ago thinking maybe in here would be something that I could use as I tape my last episode as presider. In this book was an essay written by a church pastor in 1983. And he was talking about how he thought the Church was like the M*A*S*H family. Not just because this is my final episode, but because this is the feast of the Body of Christ, Corpus Christi, this seems to say much:

> In essence, M*A*S*H is more of a church than a hospital. The characters were human. They cared and cared. They had clay feet and compassionate hearts. They had smart mouths and sensitive souls. They were a family. Sometimes more, sometimes less, just like the family of God. To me they were a symbol of hope in the midst of tragedy. Caring in the midst of the ultimate injustice, life in the midst of death.

Goodbye. Farewell. Amen.

Dressen's words are ones on which it is difficult to improve. There is not much more of worth that can be said about the compelling spirit that continues to infect and inspire the Newman community after seventy-five years of living, learning and loving together at the crossroads. In the interest of recording a story that is as complete in every detail as possible, however, the following "addendum" remarks are offered as concluding commentary on the contents of the infamous shoe-box time capsule:

An Exclamation Point with Head Bowed in Humility

Openness, and the capacity to question and learn, have long been valued at Newman as virtues essential to crossroads travelers of all ages who desire to deepen their faith. As we have seen, from the moment of its birth in 1923, questions have never ceased to be present and alive within the Newman community, a community which has chosen not to avoid, but rather to encourage, interactions and intersections between faith and intellect, the sacred and the secular, Catholics and non-Catholics, women and men, clergy and laity, guardians, and prophets.

Frances Nosbisch, Bill Dorn, Jacqui Landry, Nic Dressen, and others who had a chance to wander and wonder as leaders of the crossroads community in the 1980s, remember ruefully the days when the university was smaller, and campus ministers were still invited to be a part of regular "coffee klutch" meetings with staff people from the offices of Admissions, Housing, Financial Aid, Student Life, and the Counseling Center on campus. Those informal gatherings provided a wonderful forum for both asking and listening to questions, and for entering into some very important crossroads conversations. While such klutches, unfortunately, are no longer part of the weekly routine, the Newman Pastoral Team still takes advantage of every possible opportunity to converse and to interact with students, faculty, and professional staff at the university. They agree to be a part of the training and orientation offered to student resident advisors each year, accept invitations to be present and/or to speak in residence halls, in classrooms, and at extracurricular events sponsored by other organizations, and even set up a booth each fall at the "Main Street" orientation day held for new students. More than a century ago, John Henry Newman warned his contemporaries that, in the future, there would two groups of people in the world—conscious Atheists and convinced Christians. "Atheists," Newman claimed, would be sincere unbelievers, steeped in science, technol-

St. Cloud State student Jean Trautt, an active Newman member in the late 1980s and early 1990s, was featured in this *St. Cloud Visitor* issue exploring the relationship between young, questioning adults and the Church.

ogy, and secular thought, for whom Christianity, in the way it was presented to them, would be unacceptable. Newman feared that the vast majority of humankind would one day fall into this group, an aggregate of intelligent and good women and men who would simply take for granted that Christianity was out of mode and unworthy of serious intellectual attention; a group who would not, therefore, even bother to converse with those naive enough to cling to belief.[1] As Newman knew, and as all women and men imbued with the spirit of the movement that bears his name know, "convinced Christians" can never discourage the cross-pollenization of intellect and faith and can never allow faith to restrict itself to its own nutshell. They can never hope to advance the cause of gospel truth at the crossroads unless they are willing to ask and to listen to questions, and to allow themselves to be informed and transformed as much as they seek to inform and transform others. It was for this reason that John Henry Newman considered the capacity to carry on intelligent and open conversation to be critical, and why he chose "cor ad cor loquitur" as his motto. Heart must speak to heart on the highway, if hearts are to mature in love and in Godliness, as they ought.

St. Cloud State students speaking heart to heart over pizza in the Newman Terrace.

In 1981, a student named "Bunny" wrote up a letter of welcome sent out by the Newman staff to all new students arriving on the St. Cloud State campus:

> My own involvement with Newman Center began during freshman year, when I discovered weekend Masses geared to university life, with concrete ideas and suggestions I could apply to my daily life on campus. I joined the Newman Student Group, which gave me a chance to get to know students other than from my dorm and classes, discuss beliefs and philosophies, and socialize (I'm big on socializing). Later, I

had the opportunity to try out my leadership skills as coordinator for a quarter.

My interests and activities at Newman expanded in the next couple of years. I found myself taking a couple theology classes, a member of the Parish Council, a peer minister, singing and playing guitar with the folk group at liturgies, and helping out with social action concerns. . . . Not all at the same time, of course! The amount of time and energy I've put into this community has resulted in a fabulous growth experience for me—spiritually, emotionally and intellectually. I hope your Newman experience will be as rewarding!

Check us out. Stop in and look around the Center. Visit a while with a staff member, peer minister, and/or community member. You might find someone out on the Library Terrace in a rocking chair with a book (that's my favorite place), in the Terrace Pizza place laughing over popcorn and beer with a friend, meeting with a troubled student, or sitting quietly in Chapel. In any case, seek us out! We want to get to know you!

Students (above and below) and their questioning openness remain a vital part of the Newman community today.

Encouraging Question Marks in Many Different Ways

Obviously, the growth that Bunny came to experience as a student working, learning, praying and playing at the crossroads came about because those she encountered there knew how to exercise restraint in the use of exclamation points and to create a space for search, exploration, and questioning. An informational brochure crafted by the Newman Public Relations Committee in 1991 invited students to come to Newman not to "escape" from the provocative dynamics of campus life, but rather to "inscape"—to reflect upon those dynamics prayerfully, and to practice the faith-centered art of cultivating the interior landscape where the Spirit of God rests and the capacity for growth resides. Space for that kind of cultivation has been created not just in the Newman Terrace, where so many events designed to prompt inquiry and discussion have been held over the years, but also in the Newman Library, reorganized and updated by Paul Johnson during his tenure at Newman in the mid-1970s, and since then tended with care and dedication by Newman librarian, Marie Nunn. The library, with its peaceful but commanding view of the Holy Spirit's River, has long been a haven for what one 1989 graduate described as "we misfit introverts and closet intellectuals." There was no better break from studying, that student went on to muse, than "to say a prayer upstairs followed by an hour of scanning book titles in the library."

Top, a 1991 brochure describes the Newman Center as a place where students can "inscape." Above, long-time librarian Marie Nunn (left) sits with LeRoy Zabel, Newman's Building and Maintenance Engineer since 1990. A peaceful corner (at right) in the Newman library today, overlooking the Mighty Mississippi.

Sunday night "Salsa" sessions for students, as we have seen, are meant not just to provide theological input, but also to create a safe environment for questioning without fear of being met with reprisal, reprimand, or the righteous assertion of statements ending only with exclamation points. One 1992 graduate mused, "I wonder if I would still be Catholic if it weren't for Newman." Countless other alumni and alumnae have expressed similar sentiments over

Food, drink, and open discussion are part of the Sunday night "Salsa" experience (top, left). Above, St. Cloud State students Trish Tyman and Becky Vorpe share a moment of friendship at a Newman-sponsored event.

Newman students at a retreat in 1984.

the years, grateful beyond words for the opportunity to have had their questions met with welcome, respect and accepting attentiveness. Prayer, journaling and meditation groups, bible studies, and retreat programs, furthermore, have sprung up in various forms over the years, and have appealed to some students seeking a more relaxed and relational way to search and explore. Since his arrival in 1995, Kevin Anderson has brought to the student and permanent communities at Newman his firm belief in the TEC (Together Encountering Christ) retreat program as a forming and transforming experience, and in past three years the Newman Pastoral Team has also offered "Busy Student Retreats" meant to appeal, obviously, to busy students who would otherwise be reluctant to sacrifice the time away required by most retreat experiences. The week-long Busy Student Retreat asks participants to agree to give only one-half hour each day to personal prayer time, and another half hour to a spiritual direction session in which they take advantage of the opportunity to speak "heart to heart" about their thoughts, questions, and concerns with a trained spiritual guide.

The Prayer Room on the second level of the Newman Center, another safe and quiet space for prayerful pondering.

Mary Ehle, Newman Pastoral Team member between 1989 and 1991.

The RCIA (Rite of Christian Initiation of Adults) process has also proven to be a highly effective forum for questioning students who desire to explore new dimensions of their faith. The process was designed originally for unbaptized adults and is often adapted and used as well for adults who were baptized in another Christian denomination and desire to search out what it means to become part of the Catholic Christian community. Based on a marvelous recovery of ancient Church traditions surrounding initiation, the RCIA process was implemented initially at Newman by Nic Dressen, Edie Reagen, and Jacqui Landry in the 1980s and was later developed in a more sophisticated fashion between 1989 and 1991 by pastoral team member, Mary Ehle. After Ehle left Newman, Linda Wall took over coordination of the process and oversaw its continued evolution. From the very beginning, it has functioned as an invaluable way to provide sound education and formation in faith, as well as ample space and time for the kind of questioning exploration that alone gives to the gospel its proper power to speak to a world imbued with cynicism about the relevance of religious institutions, and all too ready to dismiss doctrinaire exclamation points. During the 1998 Easter Vigil, nineteen RCIA participants, many of whom were St. Cloud State students, celebrated the sacraments of initiation at Christ Church Newman Center and were received into full communion with the Catholic Christian community in order to continue their pilgrimage of faith. We can hope that they are at work in the world today as prophets, preachers, healers, and servants who learned invaluable lessons about love while asking questions, and speaking heart to heart with others, at the crossroads.

Rite of Election draws 99 candidates

by Micheal O'Neill
Visitor Staff Writer

ST. CLOUD — "This first time I prayed it took over an hour because there was so much to say," recalled Jane Newman.

Newman, 20, is a junior at St. Cloud State University. She is one of 99 adults who participated in the Rite of Election at St. Mary's Cathedral Sunday, March 8.

Nine of the participants are "catechumens" who have not been baptized, while the "candidates" are baptized Christians seeking full communion in the Catholic Church. The sacraments of initiation — baptism, confirmation and first Communion — will be administered to those who have not yet received them at the Easter Vigil in parishes throughout the diocese.

Although Newman was baptized a Catholic, her family fell away from active practice of their faith when she was still a baby. She remembers going to church only a couple of times at Christmas.

"I always hated it," she said. "I thought it was boring."

Newman said she never had any particular feelings about church during her childhood and adolescence. "No one that I knew ever went to church or talked about God or prayers. It never crossed my mind."

ST. CLOUD — St. Cloud State University student Jane Newman is one of 99 adults from across the diocese preparing for full communion in the Catholic Church at this year's Easter Vigil. Accompanied by her sponsor, Ty Harrison, Newman participated in the Rite of Election at St. Mary's Cathedral last Sunday. (SCV Photo by Dianne Nordquist)

"I have a rapport with God."

—Jane Newman

questions at the university Newman Center. Informal questioning and introduction to the Gospel values is the first step in the Rite of Christian Initiation of Adults. It was almost a year ago that she began this process of formal admission into the church.

Newman asked about the rosary and praying to Mary. "Not that I am 'Miss Women's Lib' but I liked the fact that there was a woman in the church and not just this distant God."

She began to pray herself and said she was surprised how peaceful she felt afterwards. "Wow! It was great. I couldn't believe how good I felt. It was such a release."

Newman said her whole family has been supportive. Her father is particularly excited and has given his old Bible to her. She hopes her actions might prod the rest of them back to church, "Once they see the baby of the family can do it," Jane added.

Preparing to become a Catholic has made a difference in the way she perceives other people. "I used to be critical of everybody and speak without thinking. I could find something wrong with anyone walking down the street...I can't believe that I actually said some things."

Greater realization that she could be the person ridi-

It hasn't, however, only been matters of faith that have prompted questions and evoked conversations at the crossroads. The college years are important developmentally and represent a time when the detours and discoveries that happen on the university highway propel young women and men to name and claim their identities, to explore relationships, to make major life decisions, to sort through issues arising from both constructive and destructive family dynamics, and, for many, to search for meaning and ultimate truth. Countless campus ministers have provided attentive ears, listening hearts, compassionate counseling, prayerful insight, and gentle guidance throughout these processes. In 1989, however, the Newman community saw fit to contract with Catholic Charities in order to hire a part-time, professional counselor whose services could then be offered to St. Cloud State students free of charge. For the past decade, Kathy Woodruff has had an office on the second level of the Newman Center and has provided guidance one day a week to students whose issues and questions have required the kind of skill and expertise that only special training can provide.

St. Cloud State student Jane Newman (right) and her sponsor, Ty Harrison, participating in the RCIA process at Newman in 1992.

Let Us Walk With You

"Catholic Church on Campus"
Counseling Service
free to SCSU students

Mondays, 253-0736

Christ Church Newman Center

Saturday: 5:30 p.m.
Sunday: 9 a.m., 11:15 a.m., 8 p.m.

Mass & Events 251-3261
Office 251-3260

CATHOLIC CAMPUS MINISTRY

Christ Church Newman Center offers a counseling service to students free of charge.

The Newman Pastoral Team in the early 1990s designed many "one-page handouts" (at right) meant to assist students in sorting through issues, questions, and decisions.

Major Decisions
Don't Have to Lead to Major Depression

Studies indicate the 75% of any given college population will experience depression during an academic year. Much of this depression stems from low self-esteem related to relationships and work/career identity. It is not easy for students to sort through questions like *"Why am I here?"* and *"What should my major be?"* and *"What am I going to do with my life when I graduate?"*

Faced with severe economic pressure and academic pressure, with often intense parental pressure and peer pressure, it is becoming increasingly difficult for students to grow as individuals while they prepare for their futures. There are no simple solutions to the these complex problems, but we are convinced that students (and their parents and teachers) must *first* be concerned about healthy *human* development. For that reason, we once again offer these principles and guidelines from an old article by Fr. Jim Burtchaell:

(1) **Don't confuse education with training.** Training is specific knowledge needed for specific professional or skilled work. It is not education. Education is the opportunity, through studying a variety of subjects, to gain the information and the dexterity you need to make good use of yourmind and wit, your capacity for expression and your heart. Education prepares you to *be* someone more than to *do* something. Education is what prepares you to hear more when you listen, to reach deeper when you think, to say more when you speak.

UNDECIDED?

(2) **Never ask what you can *do* with your major.** The choice of a major is not the choice of a career. As an undergraduate, you are not making life-time decisions that will lock you in permanently. When you imagine that you are, it can be paralyzing.

(3) **Resist the temptation to figure out your career and then choose studies that lead up to it.** Pick your major on the pleasure principle, for what you most enjoy studying will direct you in finding the healthiest and liveliest way to be educated.

(4) **To select a major program of study wisely you need not figure out what other people want of you.** Remember that above all else, you go to a great school for *self-knowledge*, and to gain a greater awareness of what unique contribution you may be able to make in the world.

- The Newman Center Staff

Members of that pastoral team were (left to right) LeAnn Calhoun, Mary Jo Bot, Kathy Woodruff, Andy Grenier, Brenda Graber, Nic Dressen, Linda Wall, LeRoy Zabel, and Joyce Bach.

Good Friday march reminds walkers of modern suffering

By DEBRA OLSON
Times Staff Writer

As reporters clustered around the St. Cloud police station Friday waiting for a woman suspected of shooting her husband to emerge, a small group raised a large wooden cross in the parking lot and began to pray:

"Jesus came to give hope to the oppressed and to the sinner. Let us remember all people imprisoned within jails or within society ..."

The police department was the group's first stop on a Good Friday commemoration of Jesus' journey to Calvary. About 50 people from toddlers in strollers to grandfathers participated in St. Cloud's fourth "Living Way of the Cross" organized by Christ Church Newman Center and Bethlehem Lutheran Church, both in St. Cloud.

"The purpose of the walk is to remind people that as Christ suffered on Good Friday there are also people in our community who are suffering," said Sylvia Mertens, a member of Bethlehem's social concerns committee. "It's a reminder not to forget them."

Perhaps it is appropriate to begin the walk this year at the police department, said Cathy Huberty, one of the organizers.

"Creator God, giver of life, help us to open our arms to all your people, to work toward justice and forgiveness," the group prayed as television cameras rolled and police officers searched the shooting suspect's car.

The St. Cloud woman was arrested after her husband was shot in the Stearns County Courthouse Friday morning.

After leaving the police station, members of the gathering walked to nine other locations from St. Cloud City Hall to a shelter for the homeless, where they remembered the poor, the unemployed, victims of racism and sexism, the handicapped, children and the aged, politicians and religious leaders.

Men in suits stared and young men in cars with radios blaring waved as the group moved through town.

"I think it's a good idea," said Dave Schmitz as he watched the group disappear down the Mall Germain. Schmitz, a member of the Art Essery band playing at the Office Bar, said the pilgrim-

Cross/6A

Times photo by Mike Knaak
A group of about 50 people marched through downtown St. Cloud Friday to commemorate Jesus' journey to Calvary.

Caring for the Whole Body of Christ

As the GLAD button with the purple triangle in the time capsule indicated, the Newman community has somehow managed, through good times and bad, to continue its assumption of the prophetic task and to point out the presence of God in people and in places where it is often overlooked. In each of the four long-range planning processes which have been completed by the community since 1987, concern for the oppressed and disadvantaged, as well as a community commitment to concrete acts of service, have emerged as strong mandates. Thus it is that the Peace and Social Justice Committee has established the annual, wintertime tradition of inviting a major speaker to proffer intelligent, reflective commentary on timely issues. The community has, thereby, been continually nudged into more open-eyed encounters, and more honest confrontations, with crossroads challenges in the world at large that have definite faith implications, like feminism, criminal justice, housing and homelessness, racism, consumerism, and many others. In the past two years, furthermore, the Newman community has become a part of "GRIP" in St. Cloud, the "Great River Interfaith Partnership." GRIP is a coalition made up of thirteen local churches and agencies aspiring to sit regularly at the table with other local leaders in politics, education, and business as policies are developed and decisions are made. The coalition's goal is to speak with a cogent, collective voice for those who have no voice and to bring concerns about hurting members of the community to the forefront.

In the past decade, a wonderfully unique dimension of the crossroads community's commitment to advance the cause of God's peace and justice has emerged. Leaders and community members traveling alongside the transforming waters of the Holy Spirit's river have developed a growing awareness that the busy, fast-paced,

Expresssing concrete concern for the oppressed and disadvantaged has continued to be important to the Newman community.

285

Church group goal: Uproot oppression

Congregations, agencies launch GRIP to deal with local issues

By David Sáez
TIMES STAFF WRITER

WHAT'S NEXT

The next meeting will be core team training at Salem Lutheran Church from 7 to 9 p.m. June 2. Core teams are groups of five or more leaders in a congregation who serve as liaisons between the churches and GRIP. They meet regularly to plan actions for their congregation and GRIP activities.

To learn more about GRIP and its future activities, call coordinator John Norton at 656-9215.

Doug Clark felt his blistered palms, worn from a morning of planting trees, shrubs and flowers at the newly constructed St. John's Episcopal Church.

He looked at his raw, flush hands as he sat with 12 other local church members on the marble altar at the Cathedral Church of St. Mary Sunday afternoon.

And, as he sat there preparing to pledge his congregation's commitment to the Great River Interfaith Partnership before more than 250 people, he considered the analogy between his congregation's work on its new landscape and this ecumenical organization's groundbreaking public meeting.

"We are beginning a new gar-

powerful coalition that can sit as equals with community leaders — political, educational and business.

The community of churches seeks to be a thermostat that determines the temperature and not a thermometer that reports it, said the Rev. Katie Schneider-Bryan of the First United Methodist Church.

"We are the people we have been waiting for," Schneider-Bryan said.

"The help we need is here."

TIMES PHOTOS BY KIMM ANDERSON

Community and church leaders including (from top left) State Reps. Jim Knoblach and Joe Opatz, St. Cloud Mayor Larry Meyer and Clarence White of the NAACP, clapped and sang a song about justice Sunday after signing the Great River Interfaith Partnership covenant at St. Mary's Cathedral.

Christ Church Newman Center, as well as thirteen other local churches and agencies, have together formed the GRIP coalition.

and harried lifestyles of many women and men in late-twentieth century North America is something every bit as unconscionable, and in need of healing, as the poverty and want that characterizes life in less affluent places. As early as 1975, an excerpt from the writings of the contemporary Trappist "mystic," William McNamara, was reproduced in the Newman bulletin; as the 1980s and 1990s progressed, the themes introduced by McNamara would be repeated often by Newman ministers who were convinced that great harm is done to all of us, and to our capacity to treat one another with compassion and respect, when we work too hard and too long, forget to pause and slow our pace, and fail to cultivate in our minds and hearts the ability to recognize the incognito Christ, in both likely and unlikely places. As McNamara put it:

> We must learn to be earthy mystics, progressively fascinated by the incognito Christ. Wherever we are, whatever we are doing, we must learn to be still, to look and listen and absorb and enter into the mystery of things, the mystery of an airplane, a mountain, a lake, a poem, a blade of grass, a symphony, a cat. Our nation is more threatened from within than from without. . . . That is why in education, as in life as a whole, the things of greatest value, of greatest importance, are the useless things, the time-wasting things that don't enrich our lives materially but do make humankind worth saving, and life worth living.

Pausing long enough to recognize the incognito Christ.

We hope the Spirit will continue for many generations to touch those bustling by on the banks of her river with an increased awareness of the holy mystery present not just in lakes and mountains and symphonies, but in all members of Christ's Body who are our sisters and our brothers, whether they be black, white, gay, straight, rich, poor, liberal, conservative, male, female, abrasive or attractive. When the members of Christ Church Newman Center, and of all Christian communities throughout the world, have become "earthy mystics" able to recognize the incognito Christ in all people and in all places, then, perhaps, we will know what it means to suffer one another's hurts, and delight in one another's joys, and will refuse to rest in contentment until our ruptured Body has become whole and healed.

Who's Counting?

Numbers, as Dressen aptly noted in his final homily, really don't mean all that much. They can, however, alter the landscape considerably and can powerfully shape the contours of a community's life together. In many significant ways, the story of the last two decades of life at Christ Church Newman Center is the story of the dynamic and galvanizing influence of numbers.

By the coming of the decade of the 1970s, the "National Newman Apostolate" was undergoing vast changes. The regional, province and national structures that had long provided a forum for Newman students and chaplains from secular campuses around the country to connect with one another had become cumbersome and outmoded. There developed a noticeable decline in the number of Newman groups affiliating themselves with the National Newman Federation, in part because the shift from "club" to community or parish structures that these groups had undergone across the nation produced evolutions that rendered the national structures obsolete.[2] A special study commission confirmed that students were shifting their interests away from active participation in province and national organizations and toward immersion in activities at the local campus level revolving around meaningful worship, community-building, interfaith cooperation and direct service opportunities.[3] As a result of the commission's findings, the National Newman Apostolate was voted out of existence, the National Newman Student Federation ceased to exist, and the Newman Chaplains Association reorganized itself into the Catholic Campus Ministry Association (CCMA), an autonomous group made up of both cleric and lay professionals in which former Newman minister, Frances Nosbisch, became quite active.[4] While the United States Catholic Conference incorporated a Division of Campus Ministry into its Department of Education, campus ministry became diocesan-based above all else, and the faculty, staff, and ministers serving at local campuses became the focal point of almost all Newman activity.[5] Newman ministers in St. Cloud continue today to meet two to three times each year with their colleagues in the "MNKOTA" province covering Minnesota and North and South Dakota, but shared activities, especially involving students, are minimal.

Newman minister Frances Nosbisch was active in CCMA and was the Diocesan Director of Campus Ministry in St. Cloud. She is pictured on the flyer at right, second row from the top.

NATIONAL ASSOCIATION OF DIOCESAN DIRECTORS OF CAMPUS MINISTRY BOARD OF DIRECTORS

REGIONAL DELEGATES

Sr. Anne Russell, O.P.
25580 Campus Drive
Hayward, CA 94542
(415) 581-1970 or 538-4857
Western Delegate

Rev. Ronald Marczewski
43 Bleeker Street
Newark, NJ 67102
(201) 642-1613
Northeast Delegate

NORTHEAST

MIDWESTERN

WESTERN

SOUTHERN

Sr. Frances Nosbisch, O.S.F.
396 1st Avenue, South
St. Cloud, MN 56301
(612) 251-3260 or 253-0854
Midwest Delegate

Mr. Michael Galligan-Stierle
9401 Biscayne Boulevard
Miami, Fl 33138
(305) 757-6241 or 736-1763
Southern Delegate

OFFICERS

Rev. Art Snedeker
1031 Superior Avenue
Cleveland, Oh 44114
(216) 696-6525 x325 or 245-4142
Secretary/Treasurer

Rev. George M. Schroeder
200 Josephine
Denver, CO 80206
(303) 388-4411 x196 or 722-7669
President

Ms. Carol Fowler
327 M.A.C. Avenue
East Lansing, MI 48823
(517) 337-9778 or 332-1628
Vice President

EX-OFFICIO

Mr. Donald R. McCrabb
CCMA Executive Director
300 College Park Avenue
Dayton, Ohio 45469
(513) 229-4648 or 252-7537
CCMA Representative

Staff Assistant for Higher Education
Department of Education
1312 Massachusetts Avenue, N.W.
Washington, DC 20005
(202) 659-6600
USCC Representative (vacant)

By 1979, a national survey of campus ministries reported that the local community and sacramental models of campus ministry appeared to be emerging as the most durable, the most serviceable and the most vital.[6] As we have seen, the St. Cloud Newman Center embraced those vital models early on, being not only one of the first to abandon the old club structures, but also one of the most adamant in its determination to develop a student parish paradigm for ministry at the crossroads that would incite and inspire its participants to grow "a searching, believing, loving, worshiping . . . presence of the Catholic Church in the campus community."[7] Once the new Newman facility was built in St. Cloud in 1964, it wasn't long before numbers began to work their wiles, altering the landscape on the banks of the Mississippi considerably, and tranforming it again and again so that it could rise up to meet the ever-new challenges of the crossroads.

Numbers Produce a Parish

Toward the end of 1972, Bishop George Speltz issued an official decree proclaiming that "since our times demand a renewed concept of the presence, structure, and function of the Church on the college campus, we deem it opportune at this time to erect the St. Cloud Newman Center as a personal parish." Canonically, a personal parish is simply one whose membership is not defined by territorial limits, but rather by "personal" qualities. For many years, ethnic parishes were the most widely-encountered examples of faith communities whose membership was determined not by geography, but by personal qualities held in common by parishioners. Those who possessed the personal qualities necessary for membership at Christ Church Newman Center, Speltz declared, were college students, their spouses and dependent children, and faculty, staff or members of the administration at St. Cloud State College, as well as their spouses and dependent children. Membership, in other words, was really defined no differently than it had been in Speltz's first decree of erection eight years earlier, but the shift from status as a "semi-public oratory" to that of a full-fledged parish created several new pastoral possibilities. Weddings, for example, could now take place at Newman, a great relief to the pastoral staff at St. Mary's Cathedral where Newman members had been required to go previously in order to celebrate weddings. Funerals could also be held at the Christ Church chapel, as could the sacrament of Confirmation.

Christ Church Newman Center has become the spiritual home of a wide variety of people—young, old, and somewhere in between.

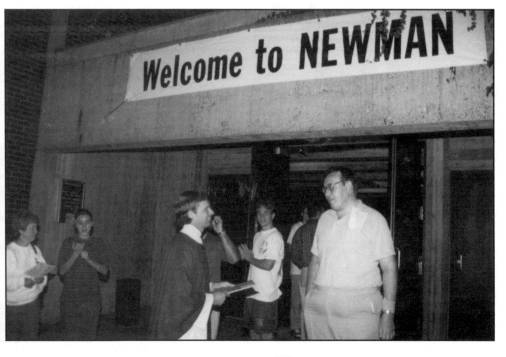

By 1976, people in the St. Cloud community at large who did not meet the specified criteria for membership in the personal parish nestled on the Mississippi's banks were coming in ever-increasing numbers to celebrate liturgy there, and many began to express a desire to make the crossroads community their official parish home. There were a few pastors in town who resented those defections and accused the Newman Pastoral Team of "stealing their sheep," but the Newman community worked very hard to monitor and control the influx of wandering "sheep" into their fold. Those who did not precisely meet the specified criteria were required to meet with the Newman Membership Committee so that they could be informed not only of the opportunities available at Newman, but also of the expectations that would be placed upon them as members, and of the responsibilities that they would be asked to assume. Sitting passively in the pew as a sheep wanting

STEWARDSHIP FORM

Does the shoe fit? How will you share of your TIME, your TALENT, and your TREASURE to help support the on-going life of the Newman Community during the 1998-99 year?

(Please complete *one* form for *each adult* in household)

Name _____   Home Phone _____

Employed at _____   Work Phone _____

Type of work _____

Time and Talent

Liturgical Ministry

Ministry
(Please ✗ only one ministry)

❏ Lector
❏ Hospitality Minister
❏ Eucharistic Minister
❏ Music Minister
  ❏ Singer (at regular weekend liturgies)
  ❏ Piano
  ❏ Organ
  ❏ Choir (occasional Feast Days only
  --Christmas, Easter, etc.)
  ❏ Other instrument _____

Mass Preference for Ministry
(✗ Mass you prefer to be scheduled/ ✓ Masses you would be willing to be scheduled at occasionally)

Saturday
❏ 5:30 pm
Sunday
❏ 9:00 am
❏ 11:15 am
❏ 8:00 pm

Membership on Parish Council Committees
(Please ✗ your interests in committee membership in appropriate boxes)

❏ Building
❏ Membership
❏ Community Life
❏ Peace and Social Justice
❏ Education
❏ Personnel
❏ Finance
❏ Public Relations
❏ Liturgy
❏ Stewardship
❏ Newman Student Association

Service Opportunities (Please ✗ your interests in appropriate boxes)

❏ Serve as sponsor for Rite of Christian Initiation of Adults (The RCIA is the process by which people prepare to become members of the Catholic Church)
❏ Youth Ministry (help with high school Confirmation and/or Mentor programs)
❏ Meals on Wheels (delivering noon lunches to area shut-ins)
❏ Help serve monthly Community Meal
❏ Help staff Caritas Food Shelf in August
❏ Bake Communion Bread (if you sign up you will be scheduled)
❏ Babysitting during 9 a.m. Liturgy (if you sign up you will be scheduled)
❏ Mass Interpreters for D/HH (deaf/hard of hearing)
❏ Help as needed with seasonal liturgical decorating
❏ Help as needed with planned activities for Newman's 75th Anniversary celebrations

Treasure

❏ I will renew my financial stewardship commitment in February during Newman's annual Stewardship Drive

The Stewardship Form that all members of the Newman Center parish are asked to fill out each year, indicating how they will share of their time and talent in order to support the on-going life of the Newman community.

only to be led and fed was never, in fact, considered an acceptable option in a community whose members were dedicated to confronting the challenges of the crossroads head on. If referred positively by the Membership Committee after that initial interview, prospective parishioners were asked to meet privately with a member of the Newman staff for further discussion, and those who were finally accepted for membership were asked to inform their territorial parishes of the decision clearly and respectfully. Even that rather lengthy and complex process, however, did not stem the tide. Shortly after Speltz's 1972 decree, one hundred and fifty family units, presumably all connected to the university, were enrolled at Newman. By 1975, that number had risen to two hundred and fifty, certainly not all of whom were connected to the university, and seven years later, in 1982, the count stood at three hundred and thirty. The Newman community finally concluded that what had, in effect, grown into an unalterable reality should be accepted and baptized. To the official description of those who could, because of their personal qualities, legitimately consider themselves members of the personal parish at 396 First Avenue South was added the line, "persons not affiliated with St. Cloud State University who choose to become permanent members of Christ Church Newman Center because of their spiritual needs." Spiritual needs have continued to arise, the counter has kept on clicking, and today the official parish roster contains some five hundred and sixty family names.

With these massive increases in numbers, of course, came increases in demands made on the pastoral team, and changes in the kinds of programming that needed to be provided. Broadening the scope of activity on the highway by the Mississippi brought great richness and increased diversity to the community, but it also brought with it some troubling challenges. Consider, for example, the following excerpt from a message penned by a member of the pastoral team appearing in a February 1974 bulletin:

> Ideally, we see the practice of having marriages here as answering several real needs. As a complete parish, giving people the opportunity to marry here was logical; all services of a parish community should be made available for those who are fully involved as members. . . . However, these ideals are not always present when people approach us to be married here at Newman. For example, frequently folks who are not committed to any parish community wish to marry here. Also, people who do not consider themselves members of the Church ask about marriage here. Still others, not seeing Newman as only a part of the whole Church, prefer to be married here or else not in the Church at all. Although we do understand the reasons and respect the convictions of those who are not actively involved in the community of faith, or have difficulties relating to their "home parish," their requests

> do pose a problem. Just to "have a wedding" regardless of
> where the couple is at in terms of commitment to the Church
> raises a question of our integrity . . .

Those same questions of integrity are still raised regularly today,
and pastoral team members every few years have to reestablish the
community's convictions and guidelines regarding requests for marriages and other sacramental celebrations, like baptism. Today, the
parish averages about fifty baptisms, and between thirty and forty
weddings, each year, and members of the pastoral team handle
many more marriage preparations than that as a service to those
student couples who live in St. Cloud during the school year but
are being married at their home parishes outside of the St. Cloud
area. Wedding and baptism requests, however, are not the only
new challenges that have arisen as a result of rising numbers along
the river's banks.

Coming to Count on Religious Education

A little more than one month after the Christ Church
Newman facility opened, the very first religious education classes
were held for children whose parents were faculty or staff members
of the university and thus were enrolled as parishioners. At first,
these "CCD" sessions, taught by St. Cloud State students Judy Buck
and Pat Hayft, were relatively simple and small in scope; they were

On this page and the next: Parents and children learn and grow together in Newman's religious education program.

held on Saturday mornings, began at 9:00 A.M., and closed at 10:30 A.M. with a Mass. It wasn't long, however, before enrollment in the nascent religious education program began to climb, and those most invested in the provision of faith formation opportunities for their children began to experiment with both the structure and the vision of the steadily growing program. By 1966, class time for the twenty-five students enrolled in religious education had been shifted to Wednesday evenings, and some junior high students began to appear for instruction; by 1969, conversation began to happen regarding "indirect" parental involvement in the program, and by 1970, parents of the sixty-four children in need of educational care were being asked for their "direct" participation. That request would become even more pointed and more explicit as time went on. Katherine Kraft and a group of very committed parents worked diligently together in that year to devise a novel approach to faith instruction; all parents were asked to take a turn at teaching once-a-week sessions, which would be held in people's homes. The movement from house to house and the relaxed and inviting atmosphere it provided

was a very positive experience for those involved and the model persisted for several years until, by 1973, the rapidly growing numbers of children enrolling annually could no longer be accommodated within the small-scale structure of weekly meetings in family living rooms. It was in the fall of that year, then, that Newman's religious education program first began to assume the rough outlines of its present shape. Four- and five-year olds met on Sunday mornings from 8:50 until 10:00 A.M.; first grade through seventh grade gathered between 8:50 A.M. and 9:30 A.M. on Sunday mornings, and eighth grade through tenth grade continued to meet on Wednesday evenings. By 1974, the first series of contemporary filmstrips on "Christian sex education" were shown at Newman for children and their parents, and high school faith formation opportunities were beginning to evolve. Tenth, eleventh and twelfth graders that year were invited to come to the rectory once a month for an evening of discussion, input, socializing and learning, and to show up weekly during the six weeks of Lent for some special, seasonal enrichment, a framework not unlike that which is operation for high school students today.

High school student participants in Newman's religious education program in the early 1990s. Pat Riley and Dana Williams are in the top photo; at left are Erin Leigh, Dustin Weis, Adam Zook, and Jason Alessio.

The incursion of individuals without any particular commitment to the parish or to the life of faith who were drawn to Newman as a place to "have a wedding" or "get a baptism done" posed one particular kind of challenge to the integrity of the community. The rapidly rising numbers of parents enrolled in the parish whose children required religious education opportunities presented a dilemma of a different sort for those most concerned with the integrity of the Newman mission. Always intertwined with the issue of religious education for the children of parish has been the question of how large a portion of the community's resources can be devoted to serving the permanent community members and their families before Newman's primary mission to the university begins to suffer detriment. Among pastoral team members for many decades the question has been kept at the forefront, and professional staff people have tried to monitor their time and energy commitments carefully in order to ensure that integration of the two different populations within the community is

More high school student religious education participants. Left to right are: Angie Birdsell, Bonnie Stock, and Alyssa Kalmoe.

furthered as much as possible, and that some balance is maintained in those efforts which require more exclusive attention to either group. Most staff members who have served the community since 1970 acknowledge readily that they worked hard to keep awareness and conversation about the balance always before them, because it is easy to begin, inadvertently, to focus predominantly on the needs of permanent community members who are more constant in their presence and more vocally invested in shaping the path of the parish. For the most part, the tension has been a healthy and a creative one, and inter-generational interactions are fostered in a wide variety of ways which are enriching and rewarding for student and permanent members alike. Even the long-standing "Coffee and Rolls" tradition, which began back in 1964, for many years took place only on those

Joe and Pat Pfannenstein chat with another parishioner during "Coffee and Rolls" down in the Newman Terrace. This Sunday morning social time is especially enjoyable for parents whose children are attending REP classes in between morning liturgies.

Sundays when college students were present because its original intent was to provide student and permanent members with the chance to socialize together following Sunday morning liturgies. To this day, those who join the parish are asked to attend a "New Members Night" at which the message about Newman's primary mission to the university is explained, emphasized and proffered as part of the package into which they must buy as parishioners of the church at the crossroads. The latest revisions in the parish Mission Statement, Constitution, and By-laws, completed between 1992 and 1993, furthermore, insure that the primacy of the community's dedication to the campus is unequivocally affirmed and establishes a parish council whose membership is constituted in such a way that those trekking daily across the university highway will always have predominant voice. Of the thirteen members of Christ Church Newman Center who make up the elected pastoral council, seven must be St. Cloud State University or St. Cloud Technical College students. Six are other registered members of the community, and one of those six is required to be a current or retired member of the faculty or staff at St. Cloud State.

Laura Krueger (left) and Loretta Lowagie (right) were both actively involved in the Newman Pastoral Council as students.

As the parish roster continued to grow, the pastoral team continued for some time to perceive the religious education of youngsters at the primary and secondary level as a concern of undeniable importance, but one still peripheral to the overall life of a community created to focus on the faith formation of students at the post-secondary level and to facilitate transforming encounters between Church and the university. Staff members Katherine Kraft, Trudy Schommer, Gigi Mooney, Francis Nosbisch, and Jacqui Landry all in their turn assumed responsibility for helping to manage the parish religious education program, but they each did so for no more than ten to fifteen hours a week, in addition to their numerous other pastoral and administrative duties. When the Education Committee directed the hiring of Marlene Meierhofer in

Marlene Meierhofer, who was the first member of the Newman Pastoral Team asked to focus primary energy on the development of the parish religious education program.

1987, a new stage in the evolution of religious education at Newman began, which also signaled the emergence of a new level of commitment to the permanent members of the community, and to the prioritization of some of their very real needs, even when those did not conveniently overlap with the mission to the university.

Meierhofer was the first person to join the Newman staff whose primary responsibility and principle focus was to be the religious education program. Initially, her position was only a half-time one, and, she remembers, during her first year on the job she was regarded as more of an "adjunct" professional and did not even participate in regular staff meetings with the other members of the pastoral team. That situation changed quickly, however. In the five years that she served the parish, Meierhofer brought both wisdom and expertise to the development of the religious education program, and also graced the community by preaching, writing bulletin articles, doing hospital visitations and bringing her contagious vitality and love for "parties" to the life of the Education, Membership and Community Life Committees. It was Meierhofer, furthermore, who worked on articulating a solid, foundational philos-

Meierhofer (left) loved parties—especially at Christmas time.

ophy for the religious education program as a whole, as well as for some of its most innovative and edifying components, including the high level of parental ownership and responsibility which it demands. She set up the "unit system," which persists to this day, and spent a great deal of time offering herself as a resource person, doing all that she could to enable parents to feel well-prepared and comfortable as they entered into their five-week teaching commitments. In addition, she established a structure of sub-committees designed to facilitate parental involvement in service and social activities for children in the program, and worked with existing parish committees to enhance the opportunities for family-oriented, community-building activity within the parish. The annual "Winterfest" carnival, or "fun-raiser," which continues to be held each February, is but one of the enduring legacies left by Meierhofer. Always conscious herself, however, of the need to integrate

An annual "Winterfest" carnival (top and bottom, left) is held each February at Newman for the children of the community and their families. Above, John Coyle (left in photo) and Jerry Mertens entertain children at the carnival with storytelling, jokes, and magic tricks.

well the student and permanent communities, Meierhofer also worked to provide ample opportunities for St. Cloud State students to be involved in the REP program, tapping into their energies and talents by using them as teachers, mentors, and activity supervisors. After leaving Newman in 1991, Meierhofer was followed by several other very fine full-time professionals like Andy Grenier, Michael Lopez-Kaley, Timothy Rowley, and, most recently, Wendy Altobell. As Newman team members, these individuals have all assumed significant pastoral duties in a wide variety of areas, but their primary focus remains the direction of the religious education program. When Kevin Anderson joined the pastoral team in the fall of 1995, he also brought with him expertise, experience, and an abiding interest in creative faith formation efforts for senior high school students; over the past four years he has helped to enhance that dimension of religious education at Newman.

A St. Cloud State University student works with children on a Sunday morning lesson.

The question of whether or not Christ Church Newman Center should help to subsidize parochial school education for those parish members who choose it for their children has long been present as but one more of the challenging tensions arising when a campus faith community is composed of both student and permanent members. Since 1989, the "Education Policy" promulgated by the Newman Education Committee with the approval of the Newman Pastoral Council has read as follows:

> Parents who choose to enroll their children in local parochial schools are asked to pay the entire tuition cost for their children's education. Because of our commitment to religious education at the post-secondary level and because of the financial responsibility that this commitment requires, Christ Church Newman Center is not able to subsidize the educational costs of the children of permanent community members who attend local parochial elementary and secondary schools.

Since the Newman Center houses a diocesan-sponsored ministry, which is itself providing Catholic education at the post-secondary level for young adults who come from all regions of the diocese,

Newman has never been asked to pay the percentage assessment levied on other parishes for support of elementary and secondary educational efforts. For a short while in the late 1970s and early 1980s, when the personal parish community was just beginning to grow, Newman did agree to pay the "fee per student" attending parochial schools, but always asked the parents of such children to be especially generous in their support of the Newman Center because of the extra financial burden subsequently placed upon the community—in essence, these parents were asked to add to their regular Sunday contributions over the course of the year an amount matching the annual cost of the fee per student that the parish paid out. It wasn't long before it became quite clear, however, that continuing this practice for ever-increasing numbers of parochial school students was a budgetary impossibility, as well as an unjust and unwise use of the financial resources of a community whose primary mission to the campus also entailed the assumption of significant monetary obligations. The issue has, at times, been a difficult one for the community to work through, and over time, some people have felt impelled to make a painful and unwanted transfer of membership to another parish able to be supportive of Catholic school education for their children. For the most part, however, the St. Cloud Newman community has remained firmly convinced that it cannot waver in its fidelity to the mission for which it was founded, and cannot in conscience compromise its ability, financial or otherwise, to prioritize that mission above all else.

Who's Counting Money?

While numerous and sundry creative challenges have arisen as a result of the "numbers" growth that came to accompany the shift to a full parish model of ministry at St. Cloud State, over time that shift also fashioned one of the most unique and vibrant faith communities ever to arise at a campus crossroads. It has also insured the continued life of that community, and of its transforming and prophetic contributions to the Church at large. Nic Dressen speculates today that Newman's establishment as a personal parish probably allowed the Newman vision to survive and thrive in St. Cloud during several strenuous periods in the past two decades when diocesan campus ministry budgets were being cut elsewhere, both around the state and throughout the nation. The solid financial and spiritual foundation provided by the permanent parish community has allowed the group of faith-filled women and men who dared to open their windows to the Holy Spirit's river all those years ago to weather storm after storm, and to remain strong and stable, even when financial support from the diocese decreased. That trend of decreasing financial support from the diocese, however, goes back not just two decades but nearly thirty-five years, to the time when the dazzling new Newman Center was first built in 1964. Apparently believing that funding the construction of the building was a gesture generous enough to last for many years to come, by 1967 the bishop had decreased the diocesan subsidy to St. Cloud's Newman Center from $24,000 per year to $18,000 per year. "The building," he said at the time, "by now should be fairly well furnished, and today's affluent students must surely be more generous than in the past." Back in 1967, that original $24,000 supplied nearly fifty percent of Newman's operating budget of $49,286. By 1973, Speltz had again reduced the diocesan subsidy to $16,800 a year, a figure representing less than twenty-eight percent of total operating expenses, and by 1982 the furnished subsidy was $15,000, less than nine percent of the budget. Today, the Diocese of St. Cloud still supplies only $25,000 per year in support of Newman's efforts with Catholic students on campus, a figure that has remained unchanged for well over a decade and now constitutes less than eight percent of a $332,000 operating budget. Regular contributions from the permanent community supply most of the remainder of the needed funds. In the early days, however, Newman leaders often had to work hard to supplement the budget with funds from alternative sources. The Newman "Associates" group was formed in 1966, for example, to provide an organized way for alumni, parents of students, business people, and friends to contribute fifty dollars or more annually in support of the St. Cloud Newman Center's activities. As a token of the community's appreciation, the Newman Associates were awarded with ceramic trivets embossed with the Newman Seal and Cardinal Newman's "cor ad cor" motto. Today, trivets still remaining from the original, abundant supply are distributed to high school seniors as part of the "Affirmation Rite" the community celebrates with them as they graduate and prepare to move on to a new stage in their life journeys. When the Associate program was discontinued, Newman Pastoral Team members up until the early 1990s contacted parents, alumni, and other contributors annually in order to augment the community's income, even as they continued to work on building up the level of financial commitment present among student and permanent community members.

Encouraging college students to contribute to the weekly collection basket was a challenge from the start. Nick Zimmer and Wil Illies crafted the rather pointed bulletin piece reprinted below in 1966:

> "Should Collection Envelopes Be Used?" This question has been kicked around for years by countless people. It is also kicked around by students, perhaps by yourself. Some students claim that they give regularly but simply don't wish to use envelopes. They wish to do their giving anonymously, and tell us that they give anonymously, which must express some sort of contradiction. But here as in other cases, facts speak

Passing the basket: a long-standing tradition that has helped to keep the Newman community alive and flourishing.

much louder than words. The facts are these: the vast majority of students don't use envelopes, but those that use envelopes contribute much more than those that don't use envelopes. Which is simply our way of saying, CONGRATULATIONS to that wonderful and persevering group of students who use envelopes. May your example prod the freeloaders.

It wasn't just the students who had to be prodded, however. While a significant portion of the permanent community has remained faithful and generous in their financial commitment to the health and growth of the community, it took a while for a widespread sense of shared responsibility for financial stewardship to take hold among Newman parishioners. The community also faced from the start the obstacles presented by that consumer-oriented approach to church-going that plagues many faith communities in North America. Large numbers of people have been drawn from the start to worship regularly at Newman because they like the style and spirit they are able to drink in and enjoy there, but not a few of them have failed to feel compelled to register officially, or to acknowledge that they have any responsibility to give to the community from which they receive. By 1972, the weekly bulletin was pleading with students to give at least the nominal sum of $1.00 a week, and with non-students and families, including "those who attend but retain membership in another parish in town," to try to contribute at least five dollars a week—not as a matter of charity,

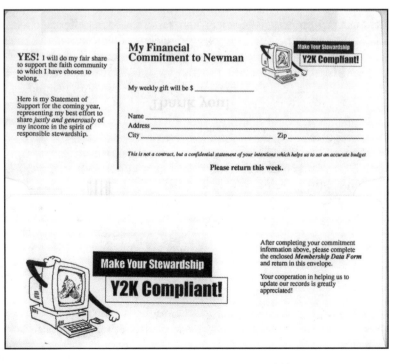

The Newman Stewardship Committee organizes and coordinates the annual effort to encourage on-going financial commitment among all members of the community.

but as a matter of justice. Quite a few financially precarious years passed, in fact, until Bill Dorn came on board in 1984 and set to work making concrete policy recommendations designed to lead the community toward more solid economic ground. A healthy sense of stewardship, and a workable stewardship program, took root and began to grow. For a while, the Newman Stewardship Committee chose to make use of prepackaged materials from successful programs utilized by other denominations; after 1990, committee members along with staff liaisons Linda Wall and Brenda Graber, decided together to craft a set of annual themes and solicitation letters that would be more suited to the spirit of Newman. These have, in general, been received as more palatable and more convincing than the prepackaged ones preceding them. Each year, the committee works hard to develop creative ways to speak meaningfully to the community as a whole about the Christian responsibility of stewardship; as in most other Catholic communities, about one-third of Newman's parishioners fail to take that responsibility seriously and refuse to respond. The remaining two-thirds respond generously and make it possible, through their regular use of commitment cards, for the Newman Finance Committee to obtain an accurate estimate of what monetary resources will be available to it each year and to plan accordingly for the construction of a responsible and accurate budget. The philosophy of financial stewardship at Newman has endeavored to be as simple and straightforward as possible. Giving, that philosophy purports with passion, is a matter of justice, not charity and, for Christian people committed to the well-being of all members of Christ's Body, the biblical practice of tithing is still a good idea: people of faith should challenge themselves to move beyond the sustenance of their own needs and wants with at least ten percent of their incomes. The Newman Stewardship Committee makes only one financial appeal each year and promises that if all community members are willing to make a just and generous annual commitment and then stick to it, no special collections, no bingo tournaments, no carwashes, no bake sales and no other bothersome fund raisers of any sort should ever be necessary. The steady growth in responsible stewardship behavior within the crossroads community has greatly enhanced the ability of the parish to operate under the guidance of an accurate budget, to prioritize the provision of just salary and benefit packages for all employees, and to plan for charitable giving to those in need. The vast majority of Christ Church Newman Center's budget today continues to be supplied by the Sunday contributions of parishioners, and the enjoyment of such financial health and independence has anchored the community in inviolate ground. It has also made it impossible for disgruntled diocesan clergy, unwilling or unable to converse openly and respectfully about their uneasiness over crossroads activities, to threaten furtively to withhold their

The Newman community at worship today—alive and generous in their commitment.

diocesan campus ministry assessments when they are displeased with happenings at Newman, as occurred both in the 1960s and in the 1980s. The loss of the $25,000 annual subsidy from the St. Cloud Diocese would be unfortunate, and would reveal a sad lack of appreciation and understanding of how very many young people from parishes all over the diocese are served daily with great dedication by the staff and people of the Newman community. It would, however, no longer pose a serious threat to Newman's survival. The spirit-fed and spirit-led community has grown up, and come into its own.

The 1998-1999 Pastoral Team at Newman. Back row, left to right: LeRoy Zabel, Brenda Graber, Kevin Carlson, Timothy Rowley; front row, kneeling: Linda Wall and Kevin Anderson.

The Legacy of the Tie

Dressen was quite right in his contention that uniforms can be divisive, exclusive and oppressive, especially when there are some uniforms that not all people are equally free to don. Richard McBrien defines "clericalism" as those attitudes and behaviors of clergy that underscore the privileged status of priests and bishops over laity, and especially over women.[8] The sin of clericalism persists in our Church today, despite the fact that it demeans the dignity of the lay Church, creates controlling patterns of behavior, produces unhelpful divisions, encourages immature and unhealthy interpersonal dynamics and, in general, sadly cripples the Body of Christ. In keeping with the legacy of those who had gone before him, a deep respect for the integrity of the lay Church, as well as a keen devotion to the principles of collaborative responsibility, grounded and guided Dressen's years of ministry at the crossroads. As Frances Nosbisch describes it, "Nic had a very special ability to encourage growth in the parish council and the committees; he understood that if you provide people with information and encouragement and then get out of the way, they can do many things." That spirit of trust in, and respect for, the authority that dwells within every member of Christ's Body, embraced so unabashedly by Dressen and by many of his predecessors, has also endured in the four years that have passed since his red tie was last seen in the hallways of Christ Church Newman Center. We hope it will endure for many years to come.

Many who have taken a turn at leading the Newman community through the perils and possibilities of the crossroads reflect in retrospect that, above all else, it is the commitment the parish has made to consensus decision-making and planning from the bottom up that has enabled it to avoid the tense divisions that so often plague and paralyze others. In both long-range planning and in the day-to-day crafting of policies and programming, there have always

Members of the Liturgy Committee work collaboratively to maintain meaningful worship practices for the community. In 1996 they were, from left to right, Kevin Anderson, Rita Moore, Carla Lagerstedt, Mary Jo Bot, Laura Krueger, and Terry Utter.

been avenues in place designed to provide people with access to decision-making conversations at many different levels, and that access prevents community members from feeling as if they need to fight to have a voice, or shout to make themselves heard. Simply voting on a policy put together at the top is nearly always quicker. No matter how cumbersome or time-consuming it may be, however, to forge a decision step-by-step from the bottom up and then work toward achieving consensus about its implementation, the process allows all involved to feel equally important and equally respected, and, in the end, yields results that are more broadly owned, unifying and long-lasting.

The Legacy of the Tie in Liturgy

Newman's liturgical celebrations also have continued to provide a meaningful arena in which the lay members of the cross-roads community are able to find their voice in freedom and in joy. Dressen sums up his experience of liturgy at Newman during his twelve-year tenure there by observing that a period of stability dawned in that time. "The era of post-Vatican II 'experimentation'

Advent: Liturgy at Newman

THE CROSS: Every Christian feast celebrates the victory of the cross. This year the large wooden cross that usually appears during Lent and Easter visits our liturgical environment during Advent and Christmas. The cross reminds us that the death of winter is necessary if we are to rejoice in the new life of spring. Furthermore the cross at Advent and Christmas reminds us that this season that is filled with us so much joy and happiness is also filled with much pain and sadness.

LIGHT: The winter solstice approaches and the nights grow longer, we light more and more candles. We are people preparing for the arrival of the Dispeller of Darkness. "Let us walk in the light of God our Savior."

COLOR: Like many communities, we see our waiting for Christ mirrored in Mary's own waiting and prefer to use blue as our Advent color. We look into the night sky with hopeful eyes that await the coming of the new Son.

MUSIC: This season is a time of joyful anticipation. Like a mother with child, we prepare with patience for the arrival of Christmas. The songs and instrumental music of Advent reflect this spirit of expectation. Unlike the media, we wait until Christmas Eve to sing our traditional caroles.

SILENCE: The times of silence will be emphasized and extended during our Advent liturgies. Given the steady noise and constant commotion of the marketplace at this time of year, we hope that you will appreciate the gentleness and peace of our Advent Eucharist.

Celebrating all seasons of the Church year well is a hallmark of Newman's high-quality liturgical life.

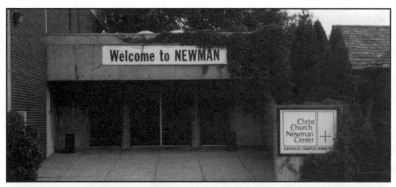

Welcome, hospitality, and shared leadership characterize the worship experience at Newman.

ended," he reflects, "and we were able to settle on a very solid way of worship together." That solid way of worship has continued to include a commitment to communicating hospitality and unhesitating welcome to all who enter the church doors, to having lay professionals, especially women, preach on a regular basis, to using gender inclusive language in prayer and song, and to encouraging large numbers of both student and permanent community members to assume leadership roles as Eucharistic ministers, lectors, hospitality ministers, and music ministers. Bill Dorn introduced the practice that persists to this day of having the presider, as well as the other Eucharistic ministers, share the bread and wine at the end of the communion rite after the rest of the assembly has finished, rather than at the beginning. The practice constitutes one more small but richly symbolic way of emphasizing that Eucharistic gathering is a community-focused, not a presider-focused, event, and of leveling out the distinctions usually made between laity and clergy when they together come to a table meant to celebrate unity and the unimportance of such distinctions above all else.

The available array of high-quality liturgical music has increased dramatically in the past decade and has enhanced the ability of the congregation as a whole at Newman to claim their rightful voice in liturgy and to pray well in song. The inspirited leadership of people like Gale Maxwell, Mary Ehle, Mary Jo Bot, and Kevin Carlson has also done so. Back in 1761, John Wesley gave the following sound advice to weekly churchgoers: "Sing lustily, and with good courage. Beware of singing as if you were half dead, or half asleep, but lift up your voice with strength. Sing all . . . sing modestly. Sing in tune. . . . Above all else, sing spiritually. Have an eye to God in every word you sing." Newman members have never sung as

A Newman student sings "lustily and with good courage."

Mary Jo Bot (above) provides musical leadership through her skill at the keyboard.

Long-time Newman member Steve Wilson (right) and his son, Paul, help to lead the congregation in song.

309

St. Cloud State University students offering musical leadership at a Sunday evening liturgy at Newman.

if they were half dead or half asleep, and the fact that they raise voices both lusty and robust each week without hesitation is but one more sign of the many ways the members of Christ's Body sojourning along the banks of the Mississippi have come a long way in reclaiming their baptismal birthrights, in liturgy as well as in countless other arenas. Mary Jo Bot began her seven-year expedition as Music Director for the crossroads community in 1991. Her extraordinary skill, coupled with a gentle but persistently encouraging style, enabled her to empower even anxious and inexperienced students with newfound belief and confidence in their own abilities. Bot's extensive background in music and her sensitivity in selecting and directing choral pieces also enabled Newman's seasonal choir to flourish, and to bring strong musical leadership to the community's celebrations of the Feast of Christ the King, Christmas, and Easter. Under Bot's deft guidance, the Newman choir was also able to present their first "concert"—a moving collection of church music from the past and the present, introduced and interspersed with selections from the writings of John Henry Newman. As all true leaders are, Bot was willing to sacrifice her need for perfection and step out of the limelight in order to allow student and permanent community members alike to develop as musicians in their own right, and to grow into a sense of themselves as true liturgical ministers whose task it is not to perform, but rather to facilitate the prayer of the community. Kevin Carlson, who took over as Newman's music director in 1998, has endeavored to preserve and advance that vision. He continues to bring his own musical skill and liturgical insight to bear as he works to enhance the richness of the worship experience at Newman, and

Heart Speaking to Heart

The Newman Choir
Mary Jo Bot, conductor

Sunday, February 21, 1999
2:00 pm
Christ Church Newman Center

As part of the 1998-1999 anniversary year celebrations at Newman, the Newman Seasonal Choir prepared a concert presentation of church music from the past and present.

augment its power to transform and challenge the gathered people of God. Some who come to those gatherings each week wear ties, and others do not. But there is nary a Roman collar to be seen.

Music Director Kevin Carlson, at left, conducts the Newman Choir during the community's Seventy-Fifth Anniversary liturgy, held on April 25, 1999.

311

Brokenness, Death, and Easter Shoes

Sadly, in the four brief years that have passed since Dressen sealed those seven objects in the shoe-box time capsule, eleven more members of the Newman crossroads community have died and so embarked upon that final pilgrimage all of us will make one day to the promised land of God's Kingdom. Their names, too, remained etched forever in the hearts of those who traveled beside them through times of joy and sorrow, insight and brokenness, triumph and struggle. Those for whom the transforming path to eternal life has been lit since 1995 by the glow of Newman's noble Easter candle are: Dennis Thayer, Robert Cumming, Elizabeth VanPelt, Lyle VanPelt, Judy Host, Diane DeHooge, John Coyle, Helen Montgomery, Donald Miller, Norma Jean Hennen, and Samuel Ellis.

Even a young and vital community filled yearly with new life cannot escape death, nor should it want to, in spite of the unwelcome pains and difficulties death nearly always brings in its wake. One of the more interesting, traditional events that has emerged at Christ Church Newman Center over the years is the gigantic Rummage Sale that takes place every October in the Terrace. Students and permanent parish members hand over their dented discards, usable hand-me-downs, and unwanted extras, and then a group of volunteers, who have been faithful above and beyond the call of duty, painstakingly sort, price and tag each item. When that fateful fall morning in October finally arrives, people actually stand in line for the privilege of perusing the long tables filled with merchandise, and then stuffing their paper bags with armfuls of salvaged cache. The Rummage Sale is a lesson in many things, including a profoundly Christian one about life being born out of death. Like the broken glass of Dressen's chalice, thrown-aside articles and damaged goods which are valueless to those who donate them are transformed into pieces which shine brightly in the hands of those who buy them. They become cast-off treasures given new purpose and new life. And so it is with the new purpose and the new life which arise out of those experiences of brokenness, pain, and death which we usually prefer to cast out of our memories. Through the power of God's Spirit, and the power of love, they are often transformed into growth, insight, wisdom, and newness of a kind we never before would have imagined possible.

Over tough roads and through construction zones, by way of detours and wrong turns, people come to grace-filled milestones on their journeys. The encounters that occur in the middle of a highway like the university, where many different people, ideas, and values cross over and sometimes collide with one another can, as we have seen, be unsettling, frightening, discouraging, and even painful. But, as we have also seen, they are fraught with as many opportunities as there are dangers, and they can be growthful, cre-

GIGANTIC

Rummage Sale

**Saturday,
October 14,
9 am - 4 pm**

Christ Church Newman Center's
Newman Terrace
396 1st Avenue South
St. Cloud
Household Goods & Cloths
Coffee & Donuts Available

The annual Rummage Sale at Newman provides a lesson in many things, including a profoundly Christian one about life being born out of death.

ative and transforming as well. When a Christian community places itself doggedly in the middle of a crossroads, as most Newman Centers do, that community has a unique opportunity, and a profound responsibility, to see to it that the conversations and crossovers happening in its environs become true events of the Spirit—occasions where the life and the power of God break through in order to prompt and prod all of us toward greater holiness, new insight, deeper freedom, and broader love as individuals, and as a human community.

In 1995, responding to a mandate given it by Christ Church Newman Center's most current Long-Range Plan, the parish council established a "History/Archives Committee." The committee was charged with organizing and preserving the many fragments of the Newman story that had been collected in countless boxes, files, and

Scenes from the grand Seventy-Fifth Anniversary Liturgy planned by the Newman History/Archives Committee and celebrated on campus April 25, 1999.

Student members of the Newman Pastoral Council stand ready to greet members of the community as they arrive.

Kevin Anderson (on the left in the photo on the right), Barb and Art Grachek chat with Bishop John Kinney before the liturgy begins.

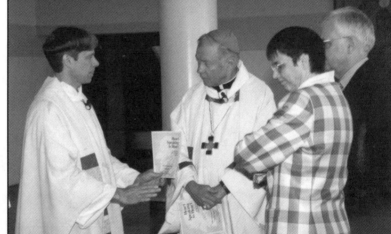

Below, the celebration begins in joy.

scrapbooks over the years, as well as with educating the community at large about the details of its own history. Also falling to the committee was the huge task of coordinating the seventy-fifth anniversary celebration, which would take place during the 1998-1999 school year. It didn't take the members of that committee long to recognize that the community's story was a good one, and that the Spirit must have flowed up over the banks of her mighty river with abundant frequency in order to grace and to guide the good-hearted group of women and men who took up residence there. The community's story seemed so good, in fact, that the Newman History/Archives Committee decided to see to it that details be put down in writing and preserved forever; this book has been the result.

Wil Illies (at right in photo at left) addresses the Newman community gathered to sing and pray together at the Seventy-Fifth Anniversary liturgy (also top photo). Illies' moving comments to the community he founded inspired a standing ovation.

During its seventy-five year history, the Christian crossroads community at St. Cloud State has witnessed the crossing-over, and sometimes the colliding, of many things: the mind and

315

At the brunch following the Seventy-Fifth Anniversay liturgy, former pastor Nic Dressen explains the symbolic importance of the broom in the history of the Newman community to the five-hundred past and present members in attendance.

the heart, the sacred and the secular, pre-Vatican II and post-Vatican II understandings of liturgy, lay leadership and clerical leadership, those who believe the Church should be seen and not heard, especially in the political arena, and those who believe the Church should speak out loudly and strongly, especially on behalf of the disrespected and the downtrodden. Young and old, certain and searching, black and white, gay and straight, believer and dissenter and many, many others have all crossed paths at Newman over the years. These pages have attempted, however imperfectly, to highlight the details and chronicle the story of some of those crossings. By now it should be clear that the meetings and the crossings have not been without tension and turmoil; it should also be quite clear that they have never failed to engender new growth, deeper understandings and transformed hearts and minds. They have come accompanied at times by laughter, and at other times by tears and, in the end, they have allowed a new dimension of the light of Christ to be proclaimed—to the Catholic Christian community gathered at the Newman Center in St. Cloud, and to the

Standing always at a cross-roads.

whole Church as well. Thus it is that as the next seventy-five years of the story begin to unfold, the Christ Church Newman community must endeavor never to remain parked for too long in any one spot. The legacy of the pink, canvas, Converse Easter shoes must not be forgotten, and whenever the temptation to settle into a particularly convenient and comfortable place becomes strong, then all Newmanites will know that the time has come once again to lace up those sneakers, jump out of those ruts, and head off with renewed life to canvass the neighborhood, converse with all those encountered along the way, and resume that holy and converting pilgrimage through the middle of the highway. Then, and only then, can young and old travelers alike rest assured that they are being true to the heart and "sole" which has animated the Newman Community perched by the waters of the Holy Spirit's river since 1923; then, and only then, will all members of the crossroads community have earned the right to close their adventure-filled days together, and pray for the last time in the words of their guide, John Henry Newman:

> May Christ support us
> all the day long,
> till the shadows lengthen and
> the evening comes,
> and the busy world is hushed,
> and the fever of life is o'er,
> and our work is done.
>
> Then in His mercy may He give us
> a safe lodging and a holy rest
> and peace at last.

For those on a Spirit-led adventure, parking for too long in any one spot is never an option.

Notes

1 Guitton, *The Church and the Laity: Newman and Vatican II.*
2 Evans, pp. 159-161.
3 Evans, p. 164.
4 Evans, pp. 164-165.
5 Evans, p. 170-171.
6 *National Survey of Campus Ministries*, conducted by The United States Catholic Conference in cooperation with The Boys Town Center for the Study of Youth Development at the Catholic University of America and Illinois Benedictine College, 1979, p. 14.
7 Evans, p. 164.
8 *Encyclopedia of Catholicism*, McBrien, ed. p. 324.

Appendix 1

John Henry Newman
1801 to 1890

J ohn Henry Newman was born in London, England, on February 21, 1801, to a family of modest but adequate means provided by his father's banking business. He was the eldest of six children and was sent away to boarding school when he was seven, although he was quite proficient at reading and arithmetic before that time. He was very bright and studious and advanced rapidly from class to class. Because he was never lacking for ideas of things to do, he was also popular with the other boys. He played the violin and loved to hear and make music.

In 1816, at the age of fifteen, Newman entered Trinity College of Oxford University as a commoner, and his association with Oxford University continued in one form or another until about 1843, just before his conversion to Catholicism. At Oxford, it did not take long for his studiousness and great intellect to be noticed. On April 12, 1822, he was elected a Fellow of Oriel College, the highest distinction in the Oxford of those days.

On June 13, 1824, Newman became a deacon and a year later was ordained a priest in the Church of England (Anglican) at Christ Church, Oxford. He was appointed curate at St. Clement's Church, a poor, run-down parish on the outskirts of Oxford. Four years later he became Vicar of St. Mary's, Oxford University, where he remained for fifteen years. His intellect and keenness of mind were much admired, and his ability as craftsman of the English language became legendary. He was a superb and renowned preacher, and during his fifteen years at St. Mary's he developed a considerable following.

In June of 1833, during a voyage home from a tour of Italy and Sicily, Newman caught typhoid and became deathly ill. It was during this time that he wrote his famous poem "The Pillar and the

Cloud" (perhaps better known as "Lead Kindly Light"). This was the third serious illness suffered by Newman. The first, experienced when he was a boy, had brought about a spiritual awakening for him and brought him to Christianity. The second, which he suffered as a young Oxford lecturer, led him to reject "liberalism" in the church. This third illness he saw as "a strange providence" and felt that God was saving him for a purpose. This purpose, he concluded, was for him to lead what became known as the Oxford Movement.

Later in 1833, Newman and others (notably Pusey, Froude and Keble) began the Oxford Movement of reform in the Church of England. These churchmen felt that a second Reformation was needed in England to shake the Anglicans from complacency and worldliness in an increasingly secular state. They published and distributed a series of religious tracts to awaken the clergy to the great truths and dogmas of traditional Christianity. In February, 1841 the *Tract 90* was published. This piece, which was written by Newman, attempted to prove that the Thirty-nine Articles of the Anglican Church could be interpreted in a "Catholic" sense, that they were opposed to the corruption of Romanism but not to Catholic dogmas as such. This caused great furor in the Church of England and led to Newman's condemnation by its bishops.

The following year, 1842, Newman moved from St. Mary's and established his residence at a small conclave called Littlemore, although he continued his responsibilities at St. Mary's. This move provided relief from the turmoil at Oxford University as well as a much less hectic environment for quiet study, contemplation, and prayer. On September 24, 1843, Newman preached his last sermon at St. Mary's ("The Parting of Friends"), and on the next day he preached his last sermon as an Anglican at Littlemore in the small church he founded. He continued to live, study, write and pray in Littlemore with other men who were similarly interested in pursuing ministry within the Roman Catholic Church.

During 1845, Newman wrote the book, *An Essay on the Development of Christian Doctrine.* Although previous study had brought him close to the Catholic tradition, it was during his study and writing of this book that he became sure that the Catholic Church was the "One True Fold of the Redeemer." On October 9, 1845, Newman, along with two of his friends, was quietly received into the Catholic Church in his little room at Littlemore by the Passionist Father Dominic Barberi.

Shortly after Newman was received into the Catholic Church, he and a few friends moved to a house on the campus of Oscott, an old Catholic college. This residence they named Maryvale. There they remained only about a year before Newman and his friend Ambrose St. John were sent to Rome where they would do their final studies for the priesthood. On Trinity Sunday in May, 1847, Newman was ordained a Catholic priest in Rome at the age of forty-six.

320

What should Newman and his followers do now? Should they join some religious order so that they might continue to study, work and pray together as a community? These were questions they now faced. Using the model of St. Philip Neri, they decided, with the pope's blessings, to establish an Oratory in England. The Oratory was not a strictly religious order where vows were taken, but simply a band of priests living together in community, much as they had as Anglicans at Littlemore and as Catholics at Maryvale. They were held in community largely by their attraction to their leader, John Henry Newman. The Oratory soon moved from Maryvale in the country to Edgbaston, a poorer section of the large city of Birmingham. Here the Oratorians had plenty to do ministering to the poor. After a time, more priests lived at the Oratory than could be accommodated, so a new sister Oratory was started in London.

Difficulties were far from over for Newman. He experienced many trials, hurts, and disappointments as a Catholic. His conversion to Catholicism was very much like the losing of one's life to which the Gospels refer. It resulted in separating himself from his country, his church, even his family. For what? For the sake of an idea, truth, wholeness, obedience to the voice of conscience. The decision was a very difficult one for Newman, and one for which he suffered greatly. But it was a decision that had to be made because his conscience told him that it was right.

The Catholic Church in England had been underground for three centuries, and during Newman's time Catholics were still few in number and scattered in small congregations. "Papists" were still feared and despised by the British, even though, for many, religion was not taken seriously. The Church was constantly under attack. Newman felt that he had to speak up in defense of his new church. On one such occasion, he was accused of libel, tried, convicted and publicly humiliated for his efforts.

But even among Catholics, Newman often found himself mistrusted and spied upon, regarded with alarm and even envy. A persistent pattern emerged of Newman being recommended for a position for which his intelligence, talent, and leadership had prepared him, only to have it undermined by higher ecclesiastical authority. On one occasion, Cardinal Wiseman invited Newman to supervise an English translation of the Bible. The task was very appealing to Newman, so he got his translators and assistants together to begin work. However, no further word came from Wiseman; he provided no means of support for the project and even failed to answer letters. Eventually, word came that the translation was to be done in America. When Newman asked to join forces with the team in Baltimore, Wiseman did not respond. With regret, Newman abandoned the project. On another occasion, Newman worked for six months to establish an Oratory at his beloved Oxford University to serve the Catholics he hoped would enroll there. He gave up that effort when the Catholic bishops prohibited their students from attending Oxford.

Another disappointing failure occurred when Newman was invited by the Irish Archbishop Cullen to establish and then serve as Rector of a Catholic University in Dublin. He was to be responsible for everything, from raising the money to finding buildings to hiring lecturers to enrolling students. Newman was excited by the challenge since he had spent virtually all his adult life in academia. He struggled for seven years to accomplish this task while also maintaining the Oratory in Birmingham, but finally had to abandon it. He traveled up and down Ireland meeting with bishops but got virtually no support from them. Even Archbishop Cullen lost enthusiasm for the project when Newman's ideas about the university failed to conform to his own.

Not all was lost from Newman's labors to establish a Catholic University in Ireland. He did publish a collection of addresses he made both during and after this effort in *The Idea of a University*. In this classic textbook, Newman defined a university, its purpose and scope, and showed how human knowledge should be related to Christian faith. For Newman, the relationship between education and religion was intimate; one necessarily complemented the other. He never regarded religion as the censor of the university. He thought theology must be subjected to the same rigorous inquiry as every other science, even if that investigation brought it into public controversy.

In 1864, Newman came under attack in a magazine article by Charles Kingsley, who had a high literary reputation and was also chaplain to the Queen and tutor to the Prince of Wales. After several exchanges, Newman felt that the best way of answering him was "to give the true key to my whole life; I must show what I am that it may be seen what I am not. . . . I will draw out the history of my mind. . . ." Newman's *Apologia Pro Vita Sua*, a defense of his life written and published as a series, was the result of this effort. Here Newman recorded the development of his ideas on the Church in his quest for religious truth. He wrote so fairly and charitably of Anglican enemies who had snubbed and thwarted him in the past that several wrote to thank him for his kind mention. He had vindicated his reputation for honesty and advanced the process of understanding between English Protestants and Catholics immeasurably. Newman received much acclaim from Protestants and Catholics alike, and the *Apologia* was among his greatest successes.

The public response to Newman's *Apologia* also alerted his new archbishop, Manning, as well as the authorities in Rome, that Newman still had the power to arouse people and thus constituted a possible danger to the Church. He had already come under suspicion for several articles he had written, in particular, the article called "On Consulting the Faithful in Matters of Doctrine," which was published in a bishop-bashing journal called *The Rambler*. Accusations that the article's contents were heretical were actually sent to Rome, thus causing Newman's reputation to be tarnished.

For the next decade or so, Newman existed in rather chilly relationship with Catholic hierarchy. However, on a personal level, his friends had multiplied, and many of his old Anglican friends came back into his life. He continued with his writing as well as with the work of the Oratory. He led a much more peaceful existence than at any other time in his life.

In 1878, Pope Pius IX died, and his successor was Pope Leo XIII. This new pope had many ideas in common with Newman and had long admired him. On May 12, 1879, at the age of seventy-eight, John Henry Newman was appointed a Cardinal in the Catholic Church. At long last Newman's obedience and loyalty had been recognized, giving him great relief and causing him to announce: "The cloud has lifted. The cloud has lifted from me forever." The "scarlet hat" not only removed the cloud under which Newman had lived for more than three decades as a Catholic but also vindicated his life and his work, particularly his insistence upon the relationship between intellect and faith. It made him a national hero throughout all of England among Protestants and Catholics alike.

John Henry Cardinal Newman passed away quietly and peacefully on August 11, 1890, at the age of eighty-nine in his little room at the Oratory. The obituaries in the papers the next day were profuse in their praise of him. The *London Times* filled its pages with praise of this Roman Cardinal, and even went so far as to suggest: "Whether Rome canonizes him or not, he will be canonized in the thoughts of pious people of many creeds in England." During the funeral, twenty thousand people lined the streets between the Oratory and the cemetery at Rednal where Newman was buried.

— Charles Ernst

Appendix 2

Staff and Officers

YEARS	STAFF MEMBERS	FACULTY ADVISORS	NEWMAN CLUB OFFICERS
1923-1924	Rev. T. Leo Keaveny, spiritual advisor		Delia Tise, president Margaret Brennan, vice president Alice McCauley, secretary-treasurer
1924-1925	Rev. T. Leo Keaveny, spiritual advisor	Agnes H. Kerlin Marguerite McBride	Helen Stenger, president Frances Wallace, vice president Ruth Marie Whalen, secretary-treas.
1925-1926	Rev. T. Leo Keaveny, spiritual advisor	Agnes H. Kerlin	Claire Hovarka, president Henry Bettendorf, vice president Susan Mader, secretary-treasurer
1926-1927	Rev. T. Leo Keaveny, spiritual advisor	Miss C. Sheeham Mrs. A.J. Tschumperlin	Rosemary Barrett, president Lilas O'Keefe, vice president Ann Cashmore, secretary-treasurer
1927-1928	Rev. T. Leo Keaveny, spiritual advisor	Pauline Penning	Margaret Thomey, president Marion McCarthy, vice president Mary Alice Thompson, secretary Rita Vossen, treasurer
1928-1929	Rev. T. Leo Keaveny, spiritual advisor	Pauline Penning Miss Robert John Weismann	Margaret Moynihan, president Josephine Harris, vice president Luella Smith, secretary John Tribur, treasurer
1929-1930	Rev. T. Leo Keaveny, spiritual advisor	Pauline Penning John Weismann	Frances McDermott, president Marion Linneman, vice president Lois Unterecker, secretary Frank Butulla, reasurer

YEARS	STAFF MEMBERS	FACULTY ADVISORS	NEWMAN CLUB OFFICERS
1930-1931	Rev. T. Leo Keaveny, spiritual advisor	Pauline Penning	Leo Lauer, Lawrence McGovern, pres. Virginia Lahr, Charles Martin, Frank Butulla, vice pres. Kathleen Kinsella, Madeline Colletti, Irene Symons, secretary Edward Colletti, Bernadine Harpel, treas.
1931-1932	Rev. T. Leo Keaveny, spiritual advisor	Myrtle Walsh John Weismann Pauline Penning	Alex Lobas, Joseph Skudlarek, pres. Ralph Theisen, Irene Symons, vice pres. Virginia Harrington, Hildegard Schwankl, secretary Frank Kolar, Leo Fick, treasurer
1932-1933	Rev. John Denery, spiritual advisor	Pauline Penning Myrtle Walsh	Bob Hollenhorst, Ray Schrom, pres. Ray Schrom, Eugene O'Connor, v. pres. Virginia Lahr, Louis Moos, secretary Mary Berklacich, Bob Hollenhorst, treas.
1933-34	Rev. John Denery, spiritual advisor	Pauline Penning	
1934-1935	Rev. John Denery, spiritual advisor	Pauline Penning John Weismann	Douglas Ripley, Alice Nolan, Rosemary Huelskamp, pres. Alice Nolan, Douglas Ripley, Isabel Connolly, v. pres. Helene Peternel, Hortense Murphy, sec. Tore Allegrezza, Hildegarde Deutche, treasurer James Figge, program chair Douglas Ripley, pres./No. Central Fed. of Newman Clubs
1935-1936	Rev. John Denery, spiritual advisor Rev. Alphonse Kremer, spiritual advisor	Pauline Penning John Weismann	Elmer Nietfeld, Barbara Hallquist, Al Skudlarek, president Hildegard Deutsch, Betty Markson, Mary Martin, vice president Lorraine Neuwirth, Marian McCarthy, Margaret Quinn, secretary Helen Byers, Edith Martin, Irene Adams, Bette Markson, treas. Everett Barrett, program chair
1936-1937	Rev. Alphonse Kremer, spiritual advisor	Pauline Penning John Weismann	Warren Hurley, Norbert Weiss, pres. Al Skudlarek, vice president Charlotte West, Agnes Schultheis, sec. Ira Baron, treasurer Norbert Weiss, Mary Frost, prog. chair
1937-1938	Rev. Alphonse Kremer, spiritual advisor	Pauline Penning	Edith Martin, Ray Freund, president Margaret Mason, Jerome Stalberger, Donald Eveslage, vice pres. Leo Jung, Marguerite Kasner, Jeanette Gruber, secretary Ray Freund, Vernon DeZiel, treasurer

YEARS	STAFF MEMBERS	FACULTY ADVISORS	NEWMAN CLUB OFFICERS
1938-1939	Rev. Alphonse Kremer, spiritual advisor	Pauline Penning Edward Colletti	Elizebeth Roczniak, George Rukavina, president Jerome Stalberger, Doris Townsend, Clarence Denen, vice pres. Doris Townsend, Helen Kost, sec. John Schrom, Audrey Hunstiger, treas. Raymond Joyce, program chair
1939-1940	Rev. Frederick Kampsen, spiritual advisor	Pauline Penning	Raymond Joyce, Betty Nolan, Mary Ann Schoeneberger, pres. Robert Kavanagh, James Robb, LeRoy Lanners, vice pres. Bernard Broderick, Genevieve Adams, Dick Heaney, secretary Lorraine Corrigan, Earl Teas, Rita Kost, treasurer Marjorie Schelfhout, program chair
1940-1941	Rev. Frederick Kampsen, spiritual advisor	Pauline Penning Odelia Kolb George Lynch	Jean Salmon, Dorothy Yungers, pres. Francis Brennan, Jim Scherter, Kathleen Vaughn, vice pres. Bob Kavanagh, Marie Boyle, Rose Marie Tintes, secretary Anne Meuhlbauer, Kathleen Matter, Joseph Senta, treasurer Joseph Huber, Virginia Pelby, Florian Savelkaul, pro. chair
1941-1942	Rev. Frederick Kampsen, spiritual advisor	Pauline Penning Odelia Kolb George Lynch	Joe Senta, Kathleen Vaughn, pres. Don Erkenbrack, Sylvester Tomporowski, Jerome Marsolek, v.p. Rosabel LaBelle, Doris Weis, Dorothy Carlin, secretary Patricia Cashman, Marjorie Halpin, treas. Florian Savelkaul, program chair Kathleen Wasche, historian
1942-1943	Rev. Frederick Kampsen, spiritual advisor	Pauline Penning George Lynch	Myron Kennedy, president Rose Marie Tintes, vice president Gene Bayle, Theresa Renner, secretary Marjorie Halpin, treasurer Kathleen Wasche, program chair Ray Ringer, historian
1943-1944	Rev. Frederick Kampsen, spiritual advisor	Pauline Penning George Lynch	Clifford Balder, president Bernice Sauer, vice president Dorothy Swedzinski, secretary Rita Mae Hoffman, treasurer Theresa Renner, program chair
1944-1945	Rev. Leonard Gaida, spiritual advisor	Pauline Penning John Weismann	Elaine Kropp, president Rose Vasaly, vice president Constance Stelzig, secretary Irma Omann, treasurer Rose Vasaly, program chair

YEARS	STAFF MEMBERS	FACULTY ADVISORS	NEWMAN CLUB OFFICERS
1945-1946	Rev. Leonard Gaida, spiritual advisor	Pauline Penning John Weismann	Gertrude Beacon, Joan Woods, pres. Joan Woods, vice president Alice Johnson, secretary Gretchen Mamlock, treasurer Dolores Bennett, Irma Omann, pro. ch. Louise Theisen, publicity chair
1946-1947	Rev. Paul Zylla, spiritual advisor	Pauline Penning John Weismann	John Kennedy, president Mildred Revering, vice president Burt Whelan, secretary Bernard Boesen, treasurer Alice Johnson, program chair Connie Stelzig, librarian
1947-1948	Rev. Harold Kost, spiritual advisor	John Weismann Richard Meinz	Paul Porwall, president Ervin Achman, vice president Ruth Swedzinski, secretary Jim Carlin, treasurer Tina McFarlane, program chair Louis Jackson, publicity Betty Saunders, librarian
1948-1949	Rev. Harold Kost, spiritual advisor	John Weismann Richard Meinz	Helen Mayer, president Gerald Adamic, vice president Valjean Tomaseski, secretary Louis Iacarella, treasurer Clarence Grelson, Tecla Karpen, program chair Betty Saunders, historian-librarian
1949-1950	Rev. Harold Kost, spiritual advisor	John Weismann Richard Meinz	Ralph Baldrica, president Tecla Karpen, vice president Bob Mayne, secretary Bruno Zanoni, treasurer Art Pulkrabek, program chair Mary Manion, historian-librarian
1950-1951	Rev. John Laky, spiritual advisor	John Weismann Richard Meinz William Donnelly	Donald Schmidt, president Bruno Zanoni, vice president Jean Soucy, secretary Genevieve Spescha, treasurer Mary Keffle, program chair John Antognozzi, librarian Donald Hartmann, program chair
1951-1952	Rev. John Laky, spiritual advisor	John Weismann Richard Meinz	Mel Hoagland, president Donna Weis, vice president Mary Ann Sackett, secretary Ronald Koll, treasurer Joan Schmid, librarian

YEARS	STAFF MEMBERS	FACULTY ADVISORS	NEWMAN ASSOCIATION OFFICERS
1952-1953	Rev. John Laky, spiritual advisor	John Weismann Richard Meinz	George Mantzke, president Emily Bednar, vice president Jeanette Neuman, secretary Bob Jung, treasurer Helene Schmidt, program chair Virginia Olson, librarian Pat Kirscht, publications Joan Weisman, province secretary
1953-1954	Rev. Wilfred Illies, spiritual advisor	John Weismann Richard Meinz William Donnelly	Peg McIntyre, president Tom Parnell, vice president Norma Buysee, secretary Al Friedl, Vern Krier, treasurer Joan Schmid, program chair Betty Bernis, librarian Mary Jo Vashro, Pat Flynn, publications
1954-1955	Rev. Wilfred Illies, spiritual advisor		Sandy Banker, president Carol Conoryea, vice president Rosemary Simone, secretary Charles Ernst, treasurer Charlene Morse, Dennis Johnson, lib. Mary Jo Vashro, Patricia Walker, pub.
1955-1956	Rev. Wilfred Illies, spiritual advisor Rev. Harold Pavelis, choir director/organist	Arthur Erler Robert Wick	Frank Pershern, president Pat Bemis, vice president Lois Kritzeck, secretary John Anderson, treasurer Ray Lardy, Barb Bossus, publications Sandy Banker, province president
1956-1957	Rev. Wilfred Illies, spiritual advisor Ellen Winkelman, housekeeper Rev. Harold Pavelis, choir director/organist	Robert Wick	Roy Wengert, president Dee Daugherty, vice president Gen Harren, secretary Tom Hall, treasurer Skip Mahoney, program chair Lee Maus, Jim Grahm, publications
1957-1958	Rev. Wilfred Illies, chaplain Ellen Winkelman, housekeeper Rev. Harold Pavelis, choir director/organist	Robert Wick	Eugene Casey, president Robert Kantor, Tom Murray, v. pres. Margaret Fantini, secretary Robert Brinkman, treasurer Lorraine Zimmerman, librarian Bernadine Kennedy, publications
1958-1959	Rev. Wilfred Illies, chaplain Ellen Winkelman, housekeeper Rev. Harold Pavelis, choir director/organist Jeannette (Loyola) Klassen, OSB, librarian		Eugene O'Neill, president Faith Revier, vice president Zita Kennedy, secretary Pat Marcogliese, treasurer
1959-1960	Rev. Wilfred Illies, chaplain Ellen Winkelman, housekeeper Rev. Harold Pavelis, choir director/organist Jeannette (Loyola) Klassen, OSB, librarian		Bob Myers, president Dick Hess Mary Lindell Gerald Meyer Jo Yarwood

YEARS	STAFF MEMBERS	FACULTY ADVISORS	NEWMAN ASSOCIATION OFFICERS
1960-1961	Rev. Wilfred Illies, chaplain Rev. Harold Pavelis, choir director/organist Ellen Winkelman, housekeeper Jeannette (Loyola) Klassen, OSB, librarian	Robert Hall Donald Metzer	Roger Trenda, president Arthur Grachek, vice president Annette Schuette, 2nd vice president Monica Myers, secretary Jerry Kapsner, treasurer
1961-1962	Rev. Wilfred Illies, chaplain Rev. Robert Ekman, choir director Ellen Winkelman, housekeeper Jeannette (Loyola) Klassen, OSB, librarian Connie Kolbeck, secretary		Dennis John, president Bruce Perrizo, 1st vice president Rose Kelly, 2nd vice president Mary Winter, secretary Myron Umerski, treasurer
1962-1963	Rev. Wilfred Illies, chaplain Rev. Robert Ekman, choir director Connie Kolbeck, secretary Agathe Feldhege, housekeeper Jeannette (Loyola) Klassen, OSB, librarian	Mary Russell Robert Hall Charles Ernst	Jim Vonderharr, president Marty Rossini, vice president Joyce Hunt, secretary Ben Stroh, treasurer Eli Lucas, publicity chair Ron Schultz, education chair Carol Hennen, social chair Mike Boedigheimer, religious chair Barb Mack, service chair
1963-1964	Rev. Wilfred Illies, chaplain Yvonne Thielman Honer, secretary Agathe Feldhege, housekeeper Jeannette (Loyola) Klassen, OSB, librarian	Charles Ernst Mary Russell Robert Hall	Ron Schultz, president Bette Bruzek, vice president Karen Holwell, secretary Harry Larson, treasurer LuAnn Bartos Jane Lang Ed Retka
1964-1965	Rev. Wilfred Illies, chaplain Rev. Nicholas Zimmer, associate chaplain Rev. David Marthaler, choir director Yvonne Thielman Honer, secretary Agathe Feldhege, housekeeper William Jessop, custodian Jeannette (Loyola) Klassen, OSB, librarian	Charles Ernst Mary Russell Robert Hall	James Gonsior, president Sonja Anderson, vice president Jane Lang, secretary Daniel Pratt, treasurer

YEARS	STAFF MEMBERS	FACULTY ADVISORS	NEWMAN STUDENT COUNCIL OFFICERS
1965-1966	Rev. Wilfred Illies, chaplain Rev. Nicholas Zimmer, associate chaplain Rev. David Marthaler, choir director Yvonne Thielman Honer, secretary Agathe Feldhege, housekeeper William Jessop, custodian Jeannette (Loyola) Klassen, OSB, librarian		Don Teff, chair Beth Weber, assistant chair Joan Otto, secretary-treasurer Marge Fabel, education coordinator Kathy Hogan, service coordinator
1966-1967	Rev. Wilfred Illies, chaplain Rev. Nicholas Zimmer, associate chaplain Rev. David Marthaler, choir director Yvonne Thielman, secretary Agathe Feldhege, housekeeper William Jessop, custodian Jeannette (Loyola) Klassen, OSB, librarian		Don Teff, chair Pat Kuhl, assistant chair Esther Schwegler, secretary-treasurer Judy Saussen, education coordinator John Tobin, service (liturgy) coord.

YEARS	STAFF MEMBERS	FACULTY ADVISORS	NEWMAN STUDENT COUNCIL OFFICERS
1967-1968	Rev. Wilfred Illies, chaplain Rev. Nicholas Zimmer, associate chaplain Rev. David Marthaler, choir director Yvonne Thielman, secretary Agathe Feldhege, housekeeper William Jessop, custodian Jeannette (Loyola) Klassen, OSB, librarian		Jack Johannes, chair Kathy Bachul, assistant chair Joan Kolb, secretary-treasurer
1968-1969	Rev. Wilfred Illies, chaplain Rev. Nicholas Zimmer, associate chaplain Yvonne Thielman, secretary Agathe Feldhege, housekeeper Ward Trautz, custodian Jeannette (Loyola) Klassen, OSB, librarian Rev. David Marthaler, choir director Vernon Bartos, choir director		Dave Craig, chair Margaret Leibfried, assistant chair Gail Behrenbrinker, secretary Sue App, education coordinator Barb Zakrajsck, liturgy coordinator
1969-1970	Rev. William Vos, chaplain Yvonne Thielman, secretary Agathe Feldhege, housekeeper Ward Trautz, custodian Justin Zawadski, TOR, part-time assistant Veron Bartos, choir director	Ed Pluth	Margaret Leibfried, chair Fred Baches, assistant chair Sue App, secretary-treasurer Gary Loch, education coordinator Floyd Daub, Carrie Dreawves, liturgy coordinators Tom Kearney, communications
1970-1971	Rev. William Vos, chaplain Rev. Harold Pavelis, associate chaplain Katherine Kraft, OSB, pastoral minister Jan Eisenshenk, secretary Agathe Feldhege, housekeeper Ward Trautz, custodian Vernon Bartos, choir director	Ed Pluth	Gary Loch, chair Mary Jorgenson, assistant chair Arlene Frieler, secretary-treasurer Jane Martinetto, education coord. Greg Sopko, liturgy coordinator Tom Kearney, communications
1971-1972	Rev. William Vos, chaplain Rev. Adrian Ledermann, associate chaplain Katherine Kraft, OSB, pastoral minister Ethel Boyle, secretary Agathe Feldhege, housekeeper Ward Trautz, custodian Vernon Bartos, choir director	Ed Pluth	Isabel Schmidt, assistant chair Mary Heinen, secretary-treasurer Greg Sopko Carol Zachman Celeste Lucking Mary Hughes

YEARS	STAFF MEMBERS	FACULTY ADVISORS	PASTORAL COUNCIL OFFICERS
1972-1973	Rev. William Vos, pastor Rev. Adrian Ledermann, associate pastor Katherine Kraft, OSB, pastoral minister Ethel Boyle, secretary Agathe Feldhege, housekeeper Ward Trautz, custodian		Bette Bartos Patricia Ernst Arthur Grachek Dave Gruber Mary Heinen Bob Heydman Mary Hughes Barb Miller Sharon Montgomery Michael Noonan James O'Neill Greg Sopko

YEARS	STAFF MEMBERS	FACULTY ADVISORS	PASTORAL COUNCIL OFFICERS
1973-1974	Rev. William Vos, pastor Rev. Adrian Ledermann, associate pastor Katherine Kraft, OSB, pastoral minister Agathe Feldhege, housekeeper Floreine Colbert, secretary Ward Trautz, custodian		Bill Wick, president James O'Neill, vice president Bette Bartos, secretary
1974-1975	Rev. William Vos, pastor Rev. Adrian Ledermann, associate pastor Katherine Kraft, OSB, pastoral minister Katharyn Waldron, pastoral minister Delores Dufner, OSB, liturgy and music coordinator June Entwisle, OSB, liturgy and music coordinator Doreen Keable, librarian Agathe Feldhege, housekeeper Floreine Colbert, secretary Ward Trautz, custodian		Ken Johnson, president Joan Evans, vice president Mary Traynor, secretary
1975-1976	Rev. William Vos, pastor Rev. Adrian Ledermann, associate pastor Katherine Kraft, OSB, pastoral minister Katharyn Waldron, pastoral minister Arlene Ostendorf, OSF, Lynn Sander, Ken Olson, liturgy and music coordinator Agathe Feldhege, housekeeper Floreine Colbert, secretary Ward Trautz, custodian		Ken Johnson, president Paula Brixius, vice president Francis Voelker, secretary
1976-1977	Rev. William Vos, pastor Rev. Adrian Ledermann, associate pastor Paul Johnson, OP, associate pastor Katherine Kraft, OSB, pastoral minister Gale Maxwell Nelson, music coordinator Agathe Feldhege, housekeeper Floreine Colbert, secretary Marie Nunn, librarian Ward Trautz, custodian		Ed Hark, president Janese Evans, vice president Kay O'Neill, secretary
1977-1978	Rev. William Vos, pastor Rev. Adrian Ledermann, associate pastor Paul Johnson, OP, associate pastor Trudi Schomer, OSF, pastoral minister Gale Maxwell Nelson, music coordinator Agathe Feldhege, housekeeper Floreine Colbert, secretary Marie Nunn, librarian Ward Trautz, custodian		Steve Braun, president Mike Noonan, vice president Kay O'Neill, secretary
1978-1979	Rev. William Vos, pastor Rev. Adrian Ledermann, associate pastor Trudi Schomer, OSF, pastoral minister Gale Maxwell Nelson, music coordinator Jude Verley, OSC, deacon intern Agathe Feldhege, housekeeper Floreine Colbert, secretary Marie Nunn, librarian Ward Trautz, custodian		Brian Warnert, president Ginny Bisek, vice president Mary Knopik, secretary

STAFF AND OFFICERS

YEARS	STAFF MEMBERS	FACULTY ADVISORS	PASTORAL COUNCIL OFFICERS
1979-1980	Rev. Adrian Lederman, pastor Samuel Jadin, O. Praem, associate pastor Frances Nosbisch, OSF, pastoral minister Regina Mooney, pastoral minister Gale Maxwell Nelson, music coordinator Agathe Feldhege, housekeeper Floreine Colbert, secretary Marie Nunn, librarian Robert Geer, custodian		Dan Neubauer, president Mary Yoos, vice president Ed Hark, secretary
1980-1981	Rev. Adrian Ledermann, pastor Samuel Jadin, O.Praem., associate pastor Frances Nosbisch, OSF, pastoral minister Regina Mooney, pastoral minister Gale Maxwell Nelson, music coordinator Agathe Feldhege, housekeeper Floreine Colbert, secretary Marie Nunn, librarian Robert Geer, custodian		Ginny Bisek, president Lucy Huppert, vice president Jane Beste, secretary
1981-1982	Rev. Adrian Leddermann, pastor Samuel Jadin, O.Praem., associate pastor Frances Nosbisch, OSF, pastoral minister Regina Mooney, pastoral minister Gale Maxwell Nelson, music coordinator Agathe Feldhege, housekeeper Floreine Colbert, secretary Marie Nunn, librarian Robert Geer, custodian Sharon Houg, business manager		Tom Stachowski, president Janet Kilian, vice president Theresa Stepan, secretary
1982-1983	Rev. Adrian Ledermann, pastor Samuel Jadin, O.Praem., associate pastor Frances Nosbisch, OSF, pastoral minister Edith Reagan, pastoral minister Gale Maxwell Nelson, music coordinator Brenda Meemken, administrative secretary Agathe Feldhege, housekeeper Marie Nunn, librarian Robert Geer, cucoordinator		Mary Yoos, president Terry Schmelzer, vice president Lorie Pipenhagen, secretary
1983-1984	Rev. Nicholas Dressen, pastor Samuel Jadin, O.Praem., associate pastor Frances Nosbisch, OSF, pastoral minister Edith Reagan, pastoral minister Gale Maxwell Nelson, music coordinator Brenda Meemken, administrative secretary Marie Nunn, librarian Robert Geer, custodian		Tom Stachowski, president Todd Twyman, vice president Al Dehler, secretary
1984-1985	Rev. Nicholas Dressen, pastor Rev. William Dorn, associate pastor Frances Nosbisch, OSF, pastoral minister Edith Reagan, pastoral minister Gale Maxwell Nelson, music coordinator Brenda Meemken, administrative secretary Marie Nunn, librarian Robert Geer, custodian		John Miller, president Linda Weisbrich, vice president Julie Ronning, secretary

Years	Staff Members	Faculty Advisors	Pastoral Council Officers
1985-1986	Rev. Nicholas Dressen, pastor Rev. William Dorn, associate pastor Frances Nosbisch, OSF, pastoral minister Jacqueline Landry McMullan, pastoral minister Gale Maxwell Nelson, music coordinator Brenda Meemken, administrative secretary Marie Nunn, librarian Robert Geer, custodian		John Miller, president Paul Olmscheid, vice president Judy Wyne, secretary
1986-1987	Rev. Nicholas Dressen, pastor Frances Nosbisch, OSF, pastoral minister Jaqueline Landry McMullan, pastoral minister Gale Maxwell Nelson, music coordinator Brenda Meemken, administrative secretary Marie Nunn, librarian Robert Geer, custodian		Mary Jo Bot, president Lorry Goodman, vice president Judy Wyne, secretary
1987-1988	Rev. Nicholas Dressen, pastor Frances Nosbisch, OSF, pastoral minister Jacqueline Landry McMullan, pastoral minister Marlene Meierhofer, OSB, REP/pastoral minister Gale Maxwell, music coordinator Brenda Meemken, administrative secretary Marie Nunn, librarian Gary Mead, custodian		Steve Wilson, president Jenine Bertsch, vice president Judy Wyne, secretary
1988-1989	Rev. Nicholas Dressen, pastor Frances Nosbisch, OSF, pastoral minister Jacqueline Landry, pastoral minister Marlene Meierhofer, OSB, REP/pastoral minister Gale Maxwell, music coordinator Brenda Meemken, administrative secretary Marie Nunn, librarian Gary Mead, custodian		Steve Wilson, president Anne O'Neill, vice president Barb Grachek, secretary
1989-1990	Rev. Nicholas Dressen, pastor Frances Nosbisch, OSF, pastoral minister Marlene Meierhofer, OSB, REP/pastoral minister Mary Ehle, pastoral minister/music Brenda Meemken Graber, administrative secretary Kathy Woodruff, counselor Marie Nunn, librarian Gary Mead, custodian Leann Calhoun, office assistant		John Blanch, president Sonja May, vice president Ruth Braus, secretary
1990-1991	Rev. Nicholas Dressen, pastor Linda Wall, OSF, pastoral minister Marlene Meierhofer, OSB, REP/pastoral minister Mary Ehle, pastoral minister/music Brenda Meemken Graber, administrative secretary LeRoy Zabel, building maintenance engineer Kathy Woodruff, counselor Marie Nunn, librarian Chris Petters, security/maintenance Leann Calhoun, office assistant		John Blanch, president Jean Trautt, vice president Ed Pribble, secretary

Staff and Officers

Years	Staff Members	Faculty Advisors	Pastoral Council Officers
1991-1992	Rev. Nicholas Dressen, pastor Linda Wall, OSF, pastoral minister Marlene Meierhofer, OSB, REP/pastoral minister Mary Jo Bot, music director Brenda Meemken Graber, office administrator LeRoy Zabel, building maintenance engineer Kathy Woodruff, counselor Joyce Bach, youth activities coordinator Marie Nunn, librarian Chris Petters, security/maintenance Leann Calhoun, office assistant		Ludmilla Voelker, president Karen Forney, vice president Chuck Kruger, secretary
1992-1993	Rev. Nicholas Dressen, pastor Linda Wall, OSF, pastoral minister Andrew Grenier, REP/pastoral minister Mary Jo Bot, music director Brenda Meemken Graber, office administrator LeRoy Zabel, building maintenance engineer Kathy Woodruff, counselor Joyce Bach, youth activities coordinator Marie Nunn, librarian Chris Petters, security/maintenance Leann Calhoun, office assistant		Ludmilla Voelker, president Laura Krueger, vice president Rita Koll, secretary
1993-1994	Rev. Nicholas Dressen, pastor Linda Wall, OSF, pastoral minister Andrew Grenier, REP/pastoral minister Mary Jo Bot, music director Brenda Meemken Graber, office administrator LeRoy Zabel, building maintenance engineer Kathy Woodruff, counselor Joyce Bach, youth activities coordinator Marie Nunn, librarian Chris Petters, security/maintenance Leaneann Calhoun, office assistant		Charles Ernst, president Wayne Killmer, vice president Lin Holder, secretary
1994-1995	Rev. Nicholas Dressen, pastor Linda Wall, OSF, pastoral minister Michael Lopez-Kaley, REP/pastoral minister Mary Jo Bot, music director Brenda Meemken Graber, office administrator LeRoy Zabel, building maintenance engineer Kathy Woodruff, counselor Joyce Bach, youth activities coordinator Marie Nunn, librarian Chris Petters, security/maintenance		Dave Williams, president Laura Krueger, vice president Lin Holder, secretary
1995-1996	Rev. Kevin Anderson, pastor Linda Wall, OSF, pastoral minister Michael Lopez-Kaley, REP/pastoral minister Mary Jo Bot, music director Brenda Meemken Graber, office administrator LeRoy Zabel, building maintenance engineer Kathy Woodruff, counselor Marie Nunn, librarian Andy Zabel, security/maintenance Chris Petters, security/maintenance		Lin Holder, president Mike Kohler, vice president Judy Hammer, secretary

YEARS	STAFF MEMBERS	FACULTY ADVISORS	PASTORAL COUNCIL OFFICERS
1996-1997	Rev. Kevin Anderson, pastor Linda Wall, OSF, pastoral minister Michael Lopez-Kaley, REP/pastoral minister Mary Jo Bot, music director Brenda Meemken Graber, office administrator LeRoy Zabel, building maintenance engineer Kathy Woodruff, counselor Marie Nunn, librarian Laura Krueger, Walking New Ground coodinator Andy Zabel, security/maintenance Chris Petters, security/maintenance		Lin Holder, president Katie LaPlante, vice president Wendy Altobell, secretary
1997-1998	Rev. Kevin Anderson, pastor Linda Wall, OSF, pastoral minister Michael Lopez-Kaley, REP/pastoral minister Mary Jo Bot, music director Brenda Meemken Graber, office administrator LeRoy Zabel, building maintennc coordinator Kathy Woodruff, counselor Marie Nunn, librarian Andy Zabel, security/maintenance Chris Petters, security/maintenance		Lin Holder, president Emily Johnston, vice president Wendy Altobell, secretary
1998-1999	Rev. Kevin Anderson, pastor Linda Wall, OSF, pastoral minister Timothy Rowley, REP/pastoral minister Kevin Carlson, music director Brenda Meemken Graber, office administrator LeRoy Zabel, building maintennc coordinator Kathy Woodruff, counselor Marie Nunn, librarian Andy Zabel, security/maintenance Chris Petters, security/maintenance		Lin Holder, president Angela Metz, vice president Karen Van Slyke, Laura Parmenter, secretary

— Compiled by Mary Jo Bot